THE HABS

THE HABS

An Oral History of the
Montreal Canadiens,
1940–1980

Dick Irvin

Dedication

This book is dedicated to the players,
past, present, and future.

Canadian Cataloguing in Publication Data

Irvin, Dick, 1932–
The Habs

ISBN 0-7710-4356-2

1. Montreal Canadiens (Hockey team) – History.
I. Title.

GV848.M6I78 1991   796.962′64′0971428   C91-094743-0

McClelland & Stewart Inc.
The Canadian Publishers
481 University Avenue
Toronto, Ontario
M5G 2E9

Printed and bound in Canada

CONTENTS

INTRODUCTION

Early in June, 1989, I travelled to Toronto to play in a charity golf tournament in support of the Special Olympics. Several well-known hockey personalities were involved and after the tournament I shared a ride back to the city with two of them, Lanny McDonald and Jean Béliveau.

At that time Lanny McDonald was likely the most popular sports figure in Canada. Two nights before the tournament he had received a standing ovation from 45,000 baseball fans when he was introduced at a Blue Jays game at the SkyDome. Two weeks earlier Lanny had scored a key goal in the deciding game to help the Calgary Flames defeat the Montreal Canadiens and win the Stanley Cup. He then retired after sixteen NHL seasons, and there was widespread happiness that he had been able to leave the game after playing on his first Cup-winning team.

During the small talk on the ride back to our hotel Lanny asked Jean Béliveau, "How many Stanley Cups did you win?"

Big Jean, ever humble and aware that Lanny was still basking in the glory of his one and only Cup victory, quietly mumbled, "Ten."

"How many?" said McDonald.

At this point I jumped into the conversation and said, "Ten, Lanny. This guy played on a Stanley Cup winner ten times for the Montreal Canadiens."

McDonald's head, and moustache, shook in disbelief. "Ten Stanley Cups? That's amazing. Just amazing."

Amazing indeed.

7

This is a book about the Montreal Canadiens. It covers the team's greatest eras in the forty-year period beginning in 1940. From 1944 to 1979 the Canadiens won the Stanley Cup eighteen times. During that same period the only other team in sports to come close to rivalling the Canadiens' success, the New York Yankees, won the World Series twelve times.

The book didn't work out the way I had originally planned. I set out to write an informal history of the hockey team as seen through my eyes. For starters I chatted with a few players from the 1940s, principally Elmer Lach and Ken Reardon. As I listened to their memories it was obvious the story to be told wasn't mine, it was theirs. So I quickly changed course and let the players themselves tell the stories. My tape recorder and I listened and we had a wonderful time. What follows, then, is an oral history of the Montreal Canadiens, the most successful team and organization in professional sport.

I am not an historian but I have supplied a thread of history, decade by decade, to show what the team was accomplishing as the years went by. The storytelling is done by over 100 men who played for and against the Canadiens or who were associated with the team and hockey in some way.

I have been associated with the Montreal Canadiens, in some way, for the past fifty-one years. I first gained access to their dressing room as the eight-year-old son of the team's coach. My father, Dick Irvin, Sr., coached the Canadiens for fifteen years, from 1940 to 1955. Today I still have access to the dressing room as a member of the television and radio crews broadcasting Canadiens games, a job I have held for the past twenty-five years.

I conducted most of the interviews for this book during the 1990–91 NHL season. I searched out former players in Calgary, Vancouver, Toronto, Winnipeg, Los Angeles, Boston, New York, and Bloomington, Minnesota. I used the telephone to call Bob Turner in Regina, Bernie Geoffrion in Atlanta, and Howie Meeker in Parksville, B.C. I was pleased to meet Jack Portland at a Canadiens-Boston game at the Forum. At age seventy-eight Mr. Portland is one of the oldest living ex-Canadiens players.

I learned much about hockey listening to these men. I found them to have great respect for their opponents, for the game of hockey, and for themselves and what they had accomplished. Without exception they welcomed me and recounted their stories with enthusiasm, insight, and humour. As they talked and remembered, I felt that for a few moments they once again were players for the Toronto Maple Leafs, or the Boston Bruins, or the Montreal Canadiens.

To those who played against the Montreal Canadiens, my questions were usually about times in their hockey careers when they played on the losing team. Yet they all happily shared their memories, even though I'm sure the incidents under discussion were not among their personal career high-lights.

A few of the interviews were originally done for various radio or television programs. The majority were conducted by me specifically for this book, either in person or on the telephone.

Among the great things hockey has going for it are the men who played the game and how they love to talk about the goals scored, the shots stopped, and the people they met. It was a privilege to listen to them.

I

The 1940s

By today's standards the National Hockey League's "long season" wasn't very long when the 1940s began. Teams had played through a forty-eight-game schedule leading to the playoffs when the New York Rangers (that's right!) won the 1940 Stanley Cup championship. By the time the decade was ending the regular season had lengthened to seventy games.

Then, as now, the emphasis was on Cup winners in determining teams that were dominant in an era or decade. The Toronto Maple Leafs ruled the 1940s. The Maple Leafs finished in first place only once, yet in the playoffs they reached the finals six times and won the Stanley Cup five times.

During the first half of the decade hockey, like the rest of society, had to cope with World War Two. For a while there was talk of the NHL suspending play for the duration but league officials convinced both the Canadian and American governments their game would serve as a morale booster for the folks on the home front. However, the Canadian government stipulated that no player could avoid serving in the military in order to play hockey.

A steady stream of men exchanging hockey uniforms for military uniforms opened the gates for both young and old players. Stars of the time such as Doug Bentley, Bill Durnan, Bill Mosienko, and Maurice Richard were called "wartime wonders." They silenced their critics by continuing to star once hostilities were over.

But the NHL did suffer from a wartime lack of big-league talent and its product left much to be desired. To help the entertainment value the centre-ice red line was introduced for the 1943–44 season. While it decreased the need for some puck-handling skills, the red line helped open up the game by allowing passes from one zone to another. Scoring records tumbled. Until then no team had scored 200 goals in one season. That year, four of the six teams did. The Montreal Canadiens set a record with 234 goals. At the same time the New York Rangers were setting another record by allowing 310 goals against. Most fans seemed to enjoy the change.

The Montreal Canadiens finished in first place four straight seasons beginning in 1944 but won the Stanley Cup just twice. By the time the decade was ending the Canadiens were in the midst of a rebuilding program that eventually produced a record-setting dynasty. But the task then wasn't as big as the one facing those rebuilding the franchise at the start of the decade. When the 1940s began, the Montreal Canadiens were one of the worst teams in hockey history.

1

The First Hero

On March 15, 1940, an early spring had arrived in Montreal. The winter's snow was fast disappearing. The sky was sunny, the temperature mild.

There was little news from the war that day, save that Finland had finally surrendered in its valiant battle against the overwhelming force of the Russian army.

Montreal movie theatres advertised recent openings of major motion pictures. Rebecca, *an Alfred Hitchcock film featuring Laurence Olivier and Joan Fontaine, was playing at Loew's. The Capitol had* Northwest Passage, *starring Spencer Tracy in his first technicolour film. At the Palace a Canadian actor, Raymond Massey, played the title role in the movie* Abe Lincoln of Illinois.

In Hollywood, Warner Brothers announced that Ronald Reagan had been signed to play football player George Gipp in the forthcoming production of Knute Rockne - All American.

Meat rationing had just begun in England.

And the Montreal Canadiens of the National Hockey League were on the verge of going out of business.

That sounds strange today, but it was true then. The Montreal Canadiens were in deep trouble, on the ice and at the box office. Senator Donat Raymond was a kindly, white-haired gentleman who owned the team and its home, the Montreal Forum. The night before the Canadiens had played the last home game of what was the worst season in the team's long history, losing 8-4 to the Toronto Maple

Leafs. The paid attendance was, as the box office manager told the Senator, "about 1,500."

Two nights later the Canadiens' season mercifully ended, in Boston. They lost that game 7–2. Was it worth keeping the franchise in business? Did he really need the aggravation? The Senator was pondering those questions.

Two years earlier another Montreal-based NHL team, the Maroons, had folded. The Maroons were a bad team at the end, but the 1939–40 edition of the Canadiens was worse, ending the forty-eight-game season with a pitiful record of ten wins and twenty-five points.

Perhaps the lowest point in a season full of lows had come in Chicago on February 22. With five minutes to play and the Black Hawks leading the Canadiens, 5–1, Montreal goaltender Wilf Cude was hurt in a goal-crease collision and had to leave the game. In those days teams carried only one goaltender. A Canadiens' forward, Charlie Sands, volunteered to finish the game in the nets. The Black Hawks gleefully seized the opportunity and drilled the puck past Sands five times in the last five minutes. Final score, 10–1.

There were only two legitimate NHL players on the 1939–40 Canadiens. One was left-winger Hector "Toe" Blake. The year before, Blake had won both the scoring championship and the Hart Trophy as the NHL's Most Valuable Player. The other bona fide big-leaguer was Ray Getliffe, one of the league's best checking forwards. Getliffe had been traded to Montreal after helping the Boston Bruins win the Stanley Cup in 1939.

RAY GETLIFFE

I was traded from Boston to the Canadiens in the summer of 1939 after I had played on a Stanley Cup-winning team. I knew it would be quite a letdown but I didn't expect it to be as bad as it was.

There was no discipline on the team. It was every man for himself. Pit Lépine was our coach and he never seemed to worry. I remember one night Boston beat us 6–2 at the Forum. Right after the game Pit put on the big coonskin coat he always wore in the winter, gave us a big wave, and hollered, "So long, boys. See you tomorrow."

But what I remember most of all from that season is the empty brown seats. All the seats at the Forum were brown. The boxes had individual chairs and the rest of the building had benches. As the season wore on and we kept losing, all you could see when you were playing the games were brown seats. Nothing but empty brown seats.

The Montreal Canadiens plummetted from the top to the bottom during the 1930s. When the decade began they were hockey's best team. Led by their first superstar of the NHL's modern era, Howie Morenz, the Canadiens won the Stanley Cup in 1930 and 1931.

Every Montreal Canadiens' team that has dominated the NHL over an extended period of time has had one sensational player who was ahead of his teammates in the eyes and hearts of Quebec fandom. In the very early days there had been Joe Malone and Newsy Lalonde. In later years there would be Maurice Richard, Jean Béliveau, Guy Lafleur. But when Howie Morenz was at the peak of his career there had never been a Canadiens' player literally worshipped by the fans the way he was.

Howie Morenz became famous for his all-out skating style, rink-length rushes, and spectacular goals. (In later years fans who saw them both play compared Bobby Hull's style to that of Morenz.) Morenz and Boston's legendary defenceman Eddie Shore were the two most exciting players of their era. They sold tickets wherever they played.

Morenz's best-remembered teammate was Aurel Joliat. In the lore of the Canadiens their names are often linked, "Morenz and Joliat." Morenz is always first, but not by much.

Aurel Joliat was the best left-winger in hockey during the late twenties and early thirties, although he weighed a mere 135 pounds. He had been heavier and when he was twenty years old had moved from Ottawa to Regina to play football. But after suffering a broken leg along the line of scrimmage he decided to be a hockey player instead. In 1922 he was playing for the Saskatoon Shieks when they traded him to the Canadiens in exchange for one of the game's early legends, Newsy Lalonde.

Joliat played most of his career in Montreal on the same line as Morenz. He was an all-star four times and won the Hart Trophy in

1934. He played on three Stanley Cup-winning Canadiens teams.

Aurel Joliat died in 1986 at the age of eight-five. In the late 1970s I visited him in Ottawa to record a radio feature for use on the intermissions of Canadiens' broadcasts. He was always talkative, so my job was easy. I just kept the tape machine rolling.

AUREL JOLIAT

We had the best team in the early thirties. We won the Cup in '30 and '31, and should have won it again in '32. And we should have won in '29, too.

The year Morenz came in with us we opened the season in Hamilton. I remember yet Sprague Cleghorn telling Howie to be sure and stay out of the corners. Hamilton had big Leo Reise playing defence alongside big Harry Mummery. Mummery was the biggest man ever to play hockey. He weighed about 300 pounds. Those two were hard to get around. All they had to do was stand there in a small rink. You either had to crawl through their legs or jump over the boards and run down the hallways if you wanted to get around them!

Cleghorn also told Howie to look out for Kenny Randall, who played like he had a lacrosse stick in his hand. And you know how they check in lacrosse, always up around your head. And sure enough, Morenz, they forced him into the corner. They were checking him up against the boards and lifting their sticks all the time. Morenz came out of that game with his face just a mass of blood all over. He was cut all over. They were using him like a target.

When young fellows broke into the league the old fellows always tried them out. That night they tried out Morenz. He took it and never backed down. They didn't bother him much after that.

Morenz was a wonderful fellow, but he was hard to understand at times. You couldn't exactly call him a loner but I never really got close to him. He was gifted with energy. He had so much energy.

When we would get undressed in the dressing room I noticed the build he had, his shape. I never saw a man who was so barrel-chested. His chest, instead of being flat like ordinary people, it was round, like a barrel. So I said to myself, my God, I never saw a man built like that. I said, that must be where he accumulates all this speed he has, you know. He must just take two or three gulps of air and then away he goes. I think of that sometimes and I firmly believe his build had something to do with his speed and the stamina he had. It was terrific.

You're asking me what it was like to play alongside Morenz. My God, he was too fast for anybody. I told a fellow once that I played a long time with Morenz, fourteen years I played with him, and I was never even with him on the ice. I was either in front of him or behind him. I tried to keep up with him at the start but for me it was impossible. I figured I had to be in front of him or behind so I could watch the moves he was going to make.

You know, he was the most marvellous man I ever played hockey with. He was always in the right position. He was the most natural hockey player and, to me, I believe he was the greatest hockey player who ever lived.

The Canadiens eventually faced a familiar problem with Morenz, their top star. His talents began to wane. In the summer of 1934, following a season in which he scored just eight goals, he was traded to the Chicago Black Hawks. In 1934–35, Morenz scored only eight goals for Chicago, but he enjoyed one bright, shining moment at the Montreal Forum. In the final game of the season he scored a brilliant goal against the Canadiens and received a thunderous ovation. Even in a visiting team's uniform, Howie Morenz was still the all-time fan favourite in Montreal.

Fifty-four years later the ghost of that moment skated across the Forum's ice when Guy Lafleur, playing for the New York Rangers, scored a sensational goal on Patrick Roy. The two greatest cheers ever given visiting players at the Montreal Forum went to Howie Morenz in 1934 and Guy Lafleur in 1989.

Unlike "The Flower," Morenz was to play again for the Canadiens. The Hawks traded him to the Rangers. After a season there, when he scored only six times, the Rangers traded him back to Montreal. Morenz was obviously on his last legs as a hockey player and people wondered why he was still playing. There were rumours that gambling debts left him no choice but to keep going as long as someone would hire him.

The Canadiens' downward spiral to the disastrous 1939-40 season of empty brown seats at the Forum likely began in earnest on January 28, 1937. That was the night Morenz suffered a broken leg when checked into the boards by Earl Seibert of the Chicago Black Hawks. Six weeks later Howie Morenz was dead at the age of thirty-six.

There was much speculation as to the cause of his death. Depression. Pneumonia. A nervous breakdown. A heart attack. All were rumoured. Nothing was confirmed. One story still making the rounds has it that with his hospital room full of teammates and well-wishers, and with liquor flowing freely, Morenz tried to get out of bed, fell, and suffered a fatal head injury when he crashed to the floor.

Whatever the reason, hockey had lost one of its first superstars. His funeral service was held at the Forum. Every one of the building's brown seats was filled. That wouldn't happen again until six years later when a fiery French-Canadian right-winger would rocket his way into the Canadiens' lineup, creating a following greater even than that of the mighty Morenz.

When Howie Morenz died Camil DesRoches was a young sports reporter for a Montreal newspaper, Le Petit Journal. *Shortly afterwards he went to work for the Forum. Fifty-four years later he is still working for the Forum, as the director of special events. On March 11, 1937, Camil was assigned by his paper to cover the Morenz funeral.*

CAMIL DESROCHES

When I got to the Forum I was a bit late and I couldn't get in. I was covering Senior League hockey at the time and I knew the people at the building. Bert Newberry, the building manager, let me in through a side door on Closse Street. Andy O'Brien, another reporter, couldn't get in either so he came in with me.

The Forum was absolutely jammed, right up to the rafters. The ceremony had just started when we got there. To me it was the most solemn ceremony I had ever seen no matter what religion you want to name. Morenz was of Swiss descent and he was a Protestant. The minister's name was Malcolm Campbell and he was very eloquent.

The thing that really struck me was that three hockey teams were there, the Canadiens, the Maroons, and the Toronto Maple Leafs. Morenz died on the 8th of March and the Canadiens and Maroons played the next night. They didn't postpone the game and the Maroons won 4-1. The Maple Leafs were scheduled to play the Maroons two nights later, the same day as the funeral, and they didn't postpone that game either. So they played a hockey game at the Forum a few hours after the funeral. The Maroons won 3-2.

Morenz laid in rest at the Forum, right at centre ice, from about ten in the morning until two in the afternoon when the funeral started. When Frank Selke died he laid in rest in the lobby the morning of his funeral. I can't think of anyone else ever honoured that way in Montreal.

Morenz was the big man, just like Babe Ruth. After the funeral the cortege started out on Atwater Street and there were people lined two and three deep all along Atwater and all the way to the Cote des Neiges Cemetery. There must have been twenty or thirty thousand people. It was really something.

I think the best way to explain it is that to us, the French people, Morenz was French even though he wasn't. It's as simple as that.

2

A New Coach – And Two Rookies from the West

Tommy Gorman was the general manager of the pathetic Canadiens' aggregation that plodded its weary way on a treadmill to nowhere during the 1939-40 season. Gorman was a spirited, fun-loving Irishman from Ottawa who was truly one of hockey's colourful characters. In the twenties he managed the Ottawa Senators to three Stanley Cup triumphs, and he coached the Chicago Black Hawks to their first Stanley Cup win in 1934. When the Montreal Maroons won the Cup the following season, Gorman was their general manager.

Tommy Gorman was an optimistic man. He somehow convinced Senator Raymond to keep the sinking Canadiens' ship afloat and the two men proceeded to make some significant changes to their organization. The first major move in the wake of the 1939-40 disaster was to hire a new coach. It turned out to be my father, Dick Irvin, Sr., who had been coaching the Toronto Maple Leafs for nine seasons. During that time the Leafs had consistently been one of the league's top teams but had won the Stanley Cup just once.

The Maple Leafs owner, Conn Smythe, was another of the game's dominating characters. Before the end of the 1939-40 season he had decided to make a coaching change, and my father knew it. Smythe was a good hockey man. Knowing the importance of keeping a team in Montreal, he felt a coach who stressed discipline was exactly what the Canadiens needed. While the Leafs were still in the

1940 playoffs, Smythe asked my father if he would be interested in moving to Montreal.

Toronto reached the 1940 Stanley Cup finals, losing in six games to the New York Rangers. Two days later Dad was meeting with Senator Raymond and Tommy Gorman at the Senator's winter home in the Laurentian Mountains north of Montreal. The following day he signed to coach the Montreal Canadiens, the worst team in the NHL.

On October 13, 1940, the CPR Transcontinental arrived at Windsor Station in Montreal, right on time at 11 a.m. Among the disembarking passengers were two young hockey players from western Canada. One was nineteen-year-old Ken Reardon. The other was twenty-two-year-old Elmer Lach.

The next morning they skated onto the ice at the arena in St. Hyacinthe, the French-Canadian town where the Montreal Canadiens were holding their training camp. Years later, those two rookies from the West would both be inducted into the Hockey Hall of Fame.

Elmer Lach was the better known of the two. If my father had a favourite player among the hundreds he coached, it was likely the one called "Elegant Elmer."

A hard-nosed and oftentimes broken-nosed centreman with slicked-back hair parted down the middle, Lach played his entire fourteen-year NHL career with the Canadiens. Injuries would haunt Elmer – fractured arms, legs, jaw, skull, and, on several occasions, his big hooked nose. Yet he managed to earn five All-Star selections, win the scoring championship and the Hart Trophy, and help the Canadiens win three Stanley Cups. Today he is best remembered as the centre on hockey's top line of the forties, the Punch Line. His linemates were Toe Blake and Maurice Richard.

Before Elmer Lach came out of the West to join the Canadiens in 1940 he had a chance to play for the Toronto Maple Leafs. But he didn't make the Leafs because of a rare mistake in judgement of hockey talent by the team's owner, Conn Smythe.

ELMER LACH

I was playing junior in 1937. A Toronto scout, Beattie Ramsay, arranged for me and Doug Bentley to go to Toronto in the spring. We were both small. Doug weighed about 120 pounds and I was about 130. The Leafs were out of the playoffs by the time we got there, but a few of the players were asked to work out with us. There I was sitting beside big Charlie Conacher, and King Clancy was there, too. He was a great guy.

We practised in the morning. Mr. Smythe showed up to watch us and right away called us a couple of "peanuts." He didn't stay around very long.

On a Friday Mr. Selke, the manager, called us to his office and asked us if we wanted to see Niagara Falls. We didn't even know where Niagara Falls was. So he gave us $500 each to go there and told us to report back Monday morning. I hadn't seen $500 in my life.

We were on a tram going back to the hotel and I asked Doug if he was going to Niagara Falls. He said he wasn't and I said I wasn't either. We already had our train tickets, so that night we got on a train and went back home.

I got home to Moose Jaw Monday night. Tuesday morning the phone rang. It was Beattie Ramsay. He said, "What the hell are you doing out there?" I told him we knew Smythe had called us "peanuts" and had given Ramsay shit about bringing us down to Toronto. There was no way we were going to play for the Maple Leafs.

The next spring they traded Doug to Chicago and me to the Rangers. I was playing senior hockey for the Moose Jaw Millers. Art Somers was my coach. He had played for the Rangers and he told me not to go to New York because they were the cheapest bunch of bastards in hockey. I still have a letter they wrote me inviting me to their camp. They told me to bring my own skates and make sure they were sharpened.

So I didn't go and that got me off their list. I was a free agent. A Canadiens player, Paul Haynes, was hurt so they sent him scouting to the West. He saw me play and told the Canadiens he thought they should sign me. And that's how I ended up in Montreal.

A funny thing happened just before the start of my last season. I played in the All-Star game and Conn Smythe was there. I told him I was thinking of retiring and he said, "Are you crazy? You'll never earn the same money anywhere else. And besides, you still owe me $500." So he never forgot.

Elmer Lach had a reputation as a good player in Saskatchewan senior hockey. Ken Reardon was an unknown quantity.

Reardon caught the attention of Montreal scouts as a junior player in Edmonton. He wasn't much of a skater. In fact, he seemed to run rather than skate, and his puck-handling skills were rudimentary at best. But Ken Reardon made up for his lack of finesse with sheer guts and determination. It was decided he was worth at least the price of a train ticket to bring him east for a tryout.

When the Canadiens camp opened, the scouting reports as to his hockey skills seemed right on. But his determination and high spirits were very much in evidence from the time the first puck was dropped. When the Canadiens broke camp on Sunday, November 3, it was no surprise that Elmer Lach had made the team. But it was a surprise that his travelling companion from the West, Kenny Reardon, was on the same bus headed for Montreal and the season-opening game that night against the Boston Bruins.

KEN REARDON

All the old players told me to make sure to drop the minor-league clause because if they sent you to the minor leagues your salary would drop by about 50 per cent. The only negotiation I had was to ask if they would eliminate the minor-league clause, and they said yes.

I got $1,000 to sign and $4,000 for each of two years. So I got $9,000 for two years.

We trained for about a month in St. Hyacinthe. The date of my first game was November 3rd, 1940. They brought us by bus to the Queen's Hotel in Montreal. We had a meal and a rest, then they brought us to the Forum. We went in by the back door and we walked down a corridor to the dressing room. We got dressed and the coach, Dick Irvin, gave us a talk. We stood up and walked out through the corridor under the seats and skated onto the ice. That was the first time I had ever seen the ice at the Forum.

We were playing the Boston Bruins. They had Milt Schmidt, Bobby Bauer, Woody Dumart, Dit Clapper, and Frank Brimsek. Being young, I was in awe of those players. Elmer Lach was the same way as myself. That was our first experience on the Forum ice.

I was obviously quite nervous. The game ended in a 1–1 tie. You know how they got their goal? We were on a line change and I was heading for the bench. There were guys coming off our bench and I slipped and slid along the ice into the boards. I took out two or three of our guys, like a bowling ball, and they went down. That's when the Bruins scored.

Things happen when you're a rookie you don't forget.

We played a lot of home games on Saturday nights. Most Saturday mornings I would go to the barber shop on Closse Street, across from the Forum, so I would look neat for the game. One morning there was a lineup and I didn't get into the chair until about ten to eleven. We always had a team meeting in the dressing room at eleven every game day.

I told the guy to hurry up, so he gave me a quick cut. Because it was so quick he charged me thirty-five cents instead of the usual fifty cents.

I ran like crazy out of the shop and into the Forum. But when I got to the dressing room the door was locked so I had to knock. Dick opened it and I was really embarrassed at being late because all the other guys were there.

I knew there was a fine for being late, so I tried to pass it off.

"I just got a haircut for thirty-five cents," I said.

"No you didn't," Dick shot back. "You just got a haircut for twenty-five dollars and thirty-five cents."

Early in my first season we were in New York to play a Sunday night game against the Americans. We always had a team meal early in the afternoon at our hotel. This time Dick came down to the dining room to make sure everything was okay. He saw that Paul Haynes wasn't there. Haynes was a veteran centre Dick had kept on the team to help out with the rookies.

"Where's Haynes?" he asked our captain, Toe Blake.

"Don't worry about him," Blake said. "Every time we come to New York on a Sunday he spends the afternoon at the opera."

"The opera, eh?" Dick replied. He was trying to instill discipline and rules on the team and we knew from his voice that Haynes was in trouble.

That night Dick benched Haynes. The next day he cut him and he never played another game in the NHL.

3

The Punch Line

A final link with the Canadiens' tradition quietly disappeared from the scene when Georges Mantha, who had played for the team since 1929, was released six games into the 1940–41 season. That meant there wasn't a player on the roster who had previously played on a Canadiens' Stanley Cup-winning team. That held until the Stanley Cup win in 1944. Since then there has always been at least one player on the team who played on a previous Canadiens' Cup winner.

There were five players in and out of the lineup during the next four seasons who had won Stanley Cups elsewhere. Toe Blake was a seldom-used rookie on the 1935 Montreal Maroons. Ray Getliffe and Jack Portland had played on the 1939 Boston Bruins' championship team. Phil Watson was with the Rangers when they won in 1940, and Gordie Drillon had been a Maple Leaf on Toronto's 1942 Cup-winning team.

Drillon played the 1942–43 season with the Canadiens after a career in Toronto that had made him one of the Maple Leaf heroes Foster Hewitt's radio audience worshipped from coast to coast in Canada. He won the scoring championship in 1938, the last Leaf to do so, but his career in Toronto had a bad ending. The '42 Maple Leafs are famed for having come from a three-game deficit in the Stanley Cup final series to defeat the Detroit Red Wings, something that hasn't happened since in a Cup final.

Drillon was a victim of a big lineup shuffle the Leafs made when they were down by three and wasn't in uniform when they clinched the Cup. During the off-season he was dealt to the Canadiens. Drillon's lifestyle wasn't to the liking of straight-laced types Conn Smythe and Frank Selke, who were running the Toronto team. I doubt if he changed his ways all that much during his one year in Montreal but he scored twenty-eight goals, two more than he ever managed in one season in Toronto.

During that year Frank Selke said to my dad, "I don't know how you've got Drillon playing so well. I hear he didn't draw a sober breath all summer."

My dad was a teetotaller, as were Smythe and Selke, yet he always seemed to enjoy coaching free spirits like Drillon. He had coached Drillon in Toronto, so he knew what to expect.

After his one season in Montreal, Drillon joined the Air Force and didn't return to the NHL when the war ended.

Gordie Drillon was the best known of the many names that drifted in and out of the lineup in the early forties. Johnny Quilty won the rookie award in 1941 but faded fast. Joe Benoit, Tony Demers, Cliff Goupille, Tony Grabowski, Bunny Dame, Marcel Dheere, and goalies Bert Gardiner and Paul Bibeault all came on the scene and, for various reasons, left it.

There were others who were destined to stay around and play on Stanley Cup-winning teams. These included defencemen Glen Harmon, Butch Bouchard, and Leo Lameroux and forwards Buddy O'Connor, Gerry Heffernan, Bob Fillion, and Murph Chamberlain. When the Canadiens left training camp in 1942 their roster included a rookie forward, twenty-one-year-old Maurice Richard. Sixteen games into the season he suffered a broken leg. It was the latest in a series of fractures that had plagued his career in amateur hockey. "Too brittle" was the opinion of the experts.

Boy, were they ever wrong on that one.

MAURICE RICHARD

I never thought that I would be able to play professional hockey. After my junior year with Verdun Maple Leafs I signed a contract with Canadiens Seniors in the Senior Group. After a few games I had a broken ankle and I didn't play for the rest of the season.

Then in my second year with Canadiens Seniors I got a broken wrist. I only played about twenty or twenty-five games and I didn't play for the rest of the season except for the playoffs.

But in 1942 I went to Montreal Canadiens' training camp and I made the club. I was lucky, but I made the club. Then I got another injury after fifteen games. I got another broken ankle. So I never thought I was going to be a good player in the NHL.

The next season I got hurt again early, but it wasn't serious. When I got back I took the place of Charlie Sands on a line with Elmer Lach and Toe Blake. That's when my career really got going, when I started to play with Elmer and Toe.

When Maurice Richard played for the Verdun Juniors, Bob Fillion was one of his teammates. Fillion, a high scorer as a junior, likely would have made the Canadiens when Richard did but instead enlisted in the Army. He joined the Canadiens for the 1943-44 season, played for seven years as a defensive left-winger, and was on two Cup-winning teams.

BOB FILLION

In 1939 I played for the Verdun Juniors and at training camp the team was almost complete. The coach was Arthur Therrien, who was a good coach and a good teacher. He had room for one more guy on the last day of camp, so during the practice he called over me and Butch Bouchard and Paul Bibeault, our goalie. He asked us which of the players who were still left over we thought he should pick up.

We were watching this guy who had an Esso sweater on, with three stars on the front. He was skating very good and I asked Butch Bouchard what he thought of him. We didn't know his name, you see. Butch agreed with me that the guy was a good skater. So after five minutes or so we went to Arthur Therrien and asked him what he thought about the guy with the sweater with the stars. So he said okay, and he called him over and told him he would be the last guy picked to be on the team. Then we found out his name, and it was Maurice Richard.

Therrien managed a bowling alley and he told Maurice that he could play on the team under one condition, that on Monday morning he meet him at the Verdun bowling alley. Arthur told Maurice he would take him to the dentist and have all his teeth taken out, because he had very bad teeth. And Maurice agreed.

I always wondered what would have happened if we hadn't mentioned Maurice Richard to Arthur Therrien. Maybe he would have quit hockey. He was the last player picked for the team. I think that was a very important day in the career of Maurice Richard.

When I was at my first training camp with the Canadiens I got quite an initiation into one part of life in the NHL. We were all having lunch together when a woman came into the room looking for one of the players. He was a guy who had a good chance to make the team. When she saw him she threw an egg at him and was yelling and causing quite a fuss. The boys figured he owed her some money or something. Dick jumped up and got the whole story from both of them. The next day the guy was traded to the New York Rangers.

I had been a high scorer in junior but the Canadiens made me into a defensive forward, just like they did with Guy Carbonneau. I remember covering Gordie Howe the first few years he was in the league. He was very strong and always played his position well, always on his wing. I knew right away he was going to be a good player.

When Maurice Richard began his NHL career one of his teammates was a veteran defenceman, Jack Portland. Portland was on the Canadian Olympic team as a high jumper at the 1932 Games in Los Angeles. He first played for the Canadiens in 1933 when Newsy Lalonde was coaching and Howie Morenz and Aurel Joliat were starring. He was traded to the Boston Bruins in his second season. During the 1940–41 season the Bruins sent him to Chicago, and a year later he was traded back to Montreal.

In January, 1990, Jack Portland, then seventy-eight years old, attended a Canadiens-Boston game at the Forum. It was the first time he had been in the building since he was cut from the team at the 1946 training camp while attempting a comeback after serving three years in the Canadian Army.

JACK PORTLAND

I saw a lot of good young hockey players at the start of their careers in Montreal when I came back here in the early forties. There was Elmer Lach, Kenny Reardon, and Butch Bouchard. Also Leo Lameroux and Joe Benoit.

I remember when Maurice Richard first started. He used to skate with his head down. But he sort of smartened up because he got hit a lot. I was there the night he broke his leg when Crawford hit him when we were playing Boston. He could skate like the wind, right from the start. And I noticed right away that he had an excellent shot. We could see that he was going to be a great hockey player. But at the start, because he had his head down when he would carry the puck, he had to take a lot of tough body checks.

Early in the 1990–91 NHL *season, during a* Hockey Night in Canada *telecast, a graphic flashed on the screen showing the highest scoring lines, all time, on a point-per-game basis. Heading the list was the Punch Line of the Montreal Canadiens during the 1940s.*

Elmer Lach was the centre on the line, Toe Blake played left wing, and Maurice Richard was on right wing. During the 1944–45 season, when Richard scored his fabled 50 goals in 50 games, the line averaged 4.4 points per game, still a league record. Lach won the scoring championship with 80 points. Richard was second with 73, Blake third with 67. The line played together four full seasons. During that time the Canadiens finished in first place four times and won two Stanley Cups.

Individually they dominated the league. Lach won the scoring championship and the Hart Trophy as the MVP *the same year. Two years later Richard won the Hart. Blake, who at one time drew a lot of penalties, reformed and won the Lady Byng Trophy as the most gentlemanly player in 1946.*

At the end of the 1944–45 season the Canadiens took five of the six spots on the first All-Star team. The Punch Line was voted en masse, along with goalie Bill Durnan and defenceman Butch Bouchard. Richard made the first team three times during the four years.

Blake's winning of the Lady Byng Trophy was quite a surprise. A few years ago I was doing some research into trophy winners and called him to ask how many penalties he had the year he won the Byng. There was a long pause at the other end of the line and I was afraid he had drawn a blank. Then came his terse answer.

"One. And I didn't deserve it!" End of conversation.

Later I learned that Blake had been penalized for clobbering Chicago's great left-winger Doug Bentley, who suffered a knee injury on the play and was out of the lineup for a lengthy period.

Blake was a tough competitor, a trait he displayed not just in games but in practice as well. It played a big part in the success of the Punch Line.

ELMER LACH

Every player on the team knew what his responsibility was. I knew mine, Toe knew his, Rocket knew his. We were taught that if I did this, Rocket did that, and vice versa. A lot of times when I passed the puck I didn't have to really look all that much because I knew Rocket would be there. I knew by feel. It was very clear in my mind. If I went into the corner I knew exactly where I would throw the pass because I knew Rocket would be there. It was a great combination.

They don't play lines together these days like we used to. I don't think they are getting the proper direction. I don't think the coaches know the fundamentals. Dick always used to say that the right wing plays right wing, defence plays defence, and the goalie plays goal.

A guy who really helped me and spent a lot of time with me when I first broke in was Paul Haynes. Unfortunately, I took Paul's job.

And of course there was Toe Blake, who was there long before I was. He was good for me and Rocket. We called him the Old Man. He was in his thirties. One thing about Toe was the way he practised. Boy, how he would work. He always said the way you practised was the way you played. He never fooled around in a practice. That's what made us successful.

We used to scrimmage a lot, reds against whites. Some of our practices were better than the games. Dick used to go to Rocket and tell him that Butch Bouchard, our best defenceman, was betting he wouldn't get a goal in practice. Then he would go to Butch and tell him Rocket said he was going to get a hat full against Butch's pairing. Jeez, how they used to work against each other.

Toe and Bill Durnan, our goalie, were the toughest rivals. They were the best of buddies but I don't think Blake ever scored a goal on him in practice. It's amazing when you think about it.

There was a good senior player in Valleyfield named Kitoutte Joanette. He came to practice one day for a tryout. Our toughest forward was Murph Chamberlain. We called him "Hardrock."

Before practice Murph said to me, "They've got another cen-treman coming in here. You leave him to me. I'll look after him." And Murph beat the shit out of him.

Joanette never made the Canadiens. A few years ago I was playing in a golf tournament in Valleyfield and he was there. I asked him if he remembered coming to the Canadiens for a tryout and playing against Chamberlain. And he said, "That son of a bitch." He never forgot it.

The Canadiens took advantage of a wartime technicality to add a very important player to their roster for the 1943-44 season. Phil Watson was a good centreman for the New York Rangers and had played on the Rangers' 1940 Cup-winning team.

Watson was a loquacious, fun-loving French Canadian from Montreal. In the summer of 1943 he ran into passport problems with American authorities who told him he would not be allowed to cross the border into the States. Tommy Gorman heard of this and made a trade with the Rangers, sending Charlie Sands and Dutch Hiller to New York. The plan was for Watson to play in all the Canadiens' home games, plus on the road in Toronto. But by the time the season began, Gorman had pulled a few strings with some of his political cronies in Ottawa, and Watson was cleared to cross the border. He played the entire season, adding a great deal of zest to the team both on and off the ice. The Canadiens won the Stanley Cup, and the following year he was back with the Rangers.

Phil Watson retired to Vancouver. I interviewed him there in late

December, 1990. One month after our conversation he passed away, the victim of a heart attack.

PHIL WATSON

The first thing I want to talk to you about is your dad's pigeons. We were coming home from a game in Chicago and he had a basket of those damn pigeons and he put it in the washroom. Maurice Richard wanted to let the pigeons out of the basket but the guys stopped him. Afterwards, we were likely sorry we did. We figured that with the pigeons being smuggled across the border it was like travelling with Al Capone! But we had such a good team that year we could afford to laugh and fool around.

There were some characters, let me tell you. Ray Getliffe and Murph Chamberlain, they were cards. They used to do anything. They were on my line and we used to get together and talk about guys like Doug Bentley and Billy Mosienko. I remember a couple of nights against those guys the game had hardly started and they were already on the bench because we'd clobbered them.

That was the first year of the Punch Line. I didn't know if Richard was going to be a big star or not but one thing I remember is that all those French people in Montreal, they all thought he was the greatest right from the start. To give you an example, if Elmer Lach scored a goal the guy would announce, "Goal by Elmer Lach." Then Toe Blake would get one and the guy would say, "Goal by Toe Blake." But when it came to Maurice Richard, they guy would start yelling, "Goal scored by MAUU-REEEEECE REEEECHAAAARD!!"

I still remember the money they paid us after we won the Cup. In 1940 when the Rangers won the Stanley Cup the league gave us $1,200 and the Rangers came along and gave us another $500. So there we were with big, big money – $1,700. The Canadiens gave us a little more. Tommy Gorman had a big heart and he gave us each $1,300, just from the team.

There were only ninety or so players in the league then. I remember playing for the Rangers for $3,500 for the season. I went in to see Lester Patrick for a raise and he told me, "Get the hell out of here. I'll trade you to the New York Americans."

The good part for Maurice Richard and Butch Bouchard and all those guys is that they could stay in Montreal. Butch opened a restaurant and all that. But a lot of us had to go and play somewhere else. I didn't mind. They gave me a good break in New York. But being from Montreal, it was nice to play there for that one year with my friends and family there, too.

Today, I don't mind all the players getting the big money. I just hope the income tax takes it all!

In the 1940s three forward lines in the NHL had distinctive nicknames. The Canadiens had the Punch Line of Lach, Blake, and Richard. Boston featured the Kraut Line of Milt Schmidt, Bobby Bauer, and Woody Dumart. In Chicago there was the high-scoring Pony Line with Max Bentley at centre, his brother Doug on left wing, and Billy Mosienko on the right side.

The Bentley brothers made the town of Delisle, Saskatchewan, famous from a hockey standpoint. Mosienko was from Winnipeg. None weighed as much as 150 pounds, yet no line could put on a show of skating, passing, and puck-handling the way the Pony Line could in its prime. It was Doug Bentley who, along with Elmer Lach, had been too small for Conn Smythe's liking when they tried out with the Maple Leafs in the late thirties. Ten years later Max was just what Smythe wanted, despite his Bentley-like size, and a multiplayer deal was made that broke up the Pony Line in Chicago.

While they were together Max won two scoring championships, Doug one. Max won the Hart and Lady Byng trophies. Mosienko was also a Lady Byng winner, and Doug Bentley was the first-team All-Star left wing three times.

Following the 1947 playoffs the Canadiens played a series of exhibition games in western Canada against a team of NHL all-stars that included the Pony Line. The games were of the "put on a show for the fans" variety. Given the circumstances, the Bentleys and Mosienko were able to fly. When the series was over my father said he had never truly realized just how good they were. He thought they were three of the most talented players he had ever seen.

Billy Mosienko was recognized as the fastest skater in hockey. During the forties special speed-skating contests were held in both Montreal and Toronto with each NHL team sending a representative.

Mosienko won both times. He earned his most lasting claim to fame on March 23, 1952, when he scored three goals in twenty-one seconds in a game against the New York Rangers.

BILLY MOSIENKO

IN 1943–44 Max was in the service. Clint Smith was the centre for me and Doug and we set the record for a line with 219 points. Wouldn't you know it, the next year the Punch Line broke it. They got 220.

But I always enjoyed the games we had against Montreal in those days. Bill Durnan was just a great goaltender. He was the one who could switch his stick from one hand to the other. When you'd come down on him you always had to take a good look to find out which side was the stick side. He was a stand-up goaltender and I always thought he was just super.

Elmer was a hard worker. He plugged away and never stopped, always digging. I remember an incident when we were in the playoffs against Montreal. I think it was in the finals in 1944. We were in Montreal and tickets were real hard to get. Elmer came up to me and asked me to get him some tickets because he knew the visiting team always got tickets. So I got him some. I think I got him four. The game starts and we get on the ice together and he spears me in the back. I get him the tickets and then he gives me the spear job. I thought, holy smokes! But we turned out to be good friends.

They had a better team than we did and they won the first three games easy. In the fourth game, somehow, we had them down 4–1 after the second period. Then in the third the Punch Line really got going and there just wasn't anything we could do about it. They beat us in overtime. Toe Blake got the winning goal.

I remember incidents with Richard. He was a good, clean player as far as I was concerned. The only reason he got rough was because so many guys would try to antagonize him. I never saw him hit a guy with his stick or anything like that. I remember him when he would cut in on the net and big defencemen would be draped all over him. Earl Seibert was one, but he would still score. Oh, he was strong.

Hockey was fun in Chicago in those days. We played in Boston and Jack Shewchuk gave me a knee and put me out of commission. They really played that up and when Boston came back to Chicago they had 20,008 people at the game. That was the record until they built that big rink in Detroit. But we didn't have a very good team because management wouldn't gamble and hang on to good, young players. A guy like Bill Gadsby, for example – they let him get away. The Canadiens did and that was a big reason for their success over so many years.

Anyone in the media business who has interviewed Maurice Richard has learned that he isn't all that interested in recalling highlights of his career. But when the Rocket is asked about his most memorable game he always mentions the one played at the Forum against the Detroit Red Wings, December 28, 1944. That was the night he set the NHL record of eight points in a single game when teenaged Harry Lumley was in goal for Detroit.

MAURICE RICHARD

It's the night that I score five goals and three assists because the night before I had moved my family to another house. I think I slept about two or three hours during the night.

I went to Dick and told him that I didn't feel very good and that if he wanted to put somebody in my place I would be glad to rest.

He said, "Oh no. You get dressed and see how it's gonna go." And that night I got five goals and three assists. So that's why I remember that night more than anything else.

4

Yes, There Was a War

"He's just a wartime hockey player."

A few critics said that about Maurice Richard, who was the game's dominant goal-scorer in the mid-forties and whose spectacular style of play earned him the nickname "the Rocket." In his case, the nickname became an identity. In post-war years, with Richard still rocketing, my father used to remind the one-time critics that, "Yes, there was a war, and it must still be going on if what you guys said was true."

But there is no doubt the NHL's product was watered down when the Punch Line enjoyed its most productive years. Several top players joined the services. The Boston Bruins lost their top three forwards, the Kraut Line of Milt Schmidt, Woody Dumart, and Bobby Bauer. The New York Rangers also lost a complete line to the Army, the Colville brothers, Mac and Neil, and Alex Shibicky, plus their goaltender, "Sugar" Jim Henry. Syl Apps and Turk Broda, two fine Toronto players, also saw service. Boston goalie Frank Brimsek joined the U.S. Coast Guard.

The Canadiens were criticized because so few of their players joined up. The team claimed most of them were workers in essential services, and to a degree this was true. One of the directors of the team, Len Peto, was an executive with a firm that manufactured equipment for the Army. He arranged to have many of the Canadiens work at his plant, and practices were often held in the late *afternoon or early evening instead of in the morning because the players were working at their so-called wartime jobs.*

One Canadien who did leave the team and join the Army was Ken Reardon, who played in just two seasons before he enlisted.

KEN REARDON

A couple of years after the war started a team from Toronto made up of Air Force guys had won the Allan Cup in Canadian senior hockey. They had the Kraut Line of Schmidt, Dumart, and Bauer from Boston.

So the Army got interested and put together a team in Ottawa, the Commandos, and I was on it. We had some good players – the Colville brothers and Shibicky. They were a line that had played for the Rangers. We were lucky enough to win the Allan Cup the year after the Air Force team had won it.

When I went overseas I still managed to play some hockey. We played a game in Brighton for the Canadian Army championship. Conn Smythe was there and he brought along Field Marshal Montgomery. Smythe was really glad to see us. He was a real military man. I think he felt every player from the NHL should have joined up.

When the game was over the teams lined up along the blue lines and Smythe and Montgomery came on the ice to shake our hands. My brother Terry was playing on the other team and he was the first man Montgomery met.

I was at the end of the line on our team so I was the last guy he met. When I gave him my name and rank Montgomery said, "There's a Reardon playing for the other team."

I said, "He's my brother, sir."

Monty then said, "Well, good luck to both of you."

I was very impressed that he could have remembered the name after shaking hands with so many strangers.

I received a Certificate of Gallantry signed by Montgomery. I was awarded that after a couple of nights of excursions with the 6th Airborne. Actually, I was put in for a medal but I didn't get it. Montgomery was the type who always liked to give a consolation prize. That's how I got my Certificate of Gallantry.

One NHL player, Dudley "Red" Garrett, who played twenty-three games for the New York Rangers in 1942–43, lost his life in World War Two. And several promising young hockey players never came back.

Jack Fox was all set to play for the Maple Leafs when he enlisted. He lost his life. Ab Tilson, a star player for the Oshawa Generals junior team, was killed overseas. The Ontario Hockey League's MVP still receives the Tilson Trophy, named in his memory.

I was growing up in Regina during the war. The local Naval Command entered a team in the Saskatchewan junior league. Its star was a centreman named Clayton White. I thought he was the greatest junior player I had ever seen and the New York Rangers had him on their list. White lost his life when his ship went down in the North Atlantic.

Charles Bell was a good defenceman for the Regina Abbott Juniors and he, too, was on the Rangers' list. He joined the Air Force and was killed when his plane was shot down in Holland.

The war took its toll.

In a 1943 Warner Brothers movie, Thank Your Lucky Stars, *film great Bette Davis sang a song titled "They're Either Too Young or Too Old." Her lament had to do with the poor calibre of men who were on the home front while the cream of the crop was off to war. It could have applied to the National Hockey League as well.*

Drastic times led to drastic measures, and there were more than a few strange happenings on the personnel front in hockey during World War Two. Too young or too old applied there as well.

The Toronto Maple Leafs used Benny Grant, a thirty-five-year-old goaltender, who hadn't played in the NHL in ten years. The New York Rangers uncovered a true character in goaltender Steve Buzinski, who had been playing intermediate hockey in Swift Current, Saskatchewan. Buzinski started the 1942–43 season with the Rangers, played nine games, and allowed fifty-five goals-against. One of them was scored by Maurice Richard on October 8, 1942. It was his first in the NHL, one of ten the Canadiens scored that night.

The best-remembered tale about Buzinski has him getting clobbered one night in Toronto. After a half-dozen or so goals had gone by him he made a great glove save, sprawling on the ice to rob the Leafs of what looked like another sure goal. Buzinski hopped onto his feet, casually tossed the puck to the referee, and told his team-mates, "Nothing to it. Just like pickin' cherries."

Another goalie, Harry Lumley, was just seventeen when he played three games one wartime season, and eighteen when he played almost the full season a year later. During that season Lumley was in goal for the Detroit Red Wings when Richard, by now very much the Rocket, scored five goals on him in a game in Montreal.

The Boston Bruins started the 1942–43 season with Armand "Bep" Guidolin in their lineup. Guidolin was sixteen years old, and still holds the distinction of being the youngest player in the history of the NHL. Guidolin turned seventeen two months after the season began. He played in forty-two of the Bruins fifty games, scored seven goals, and had fifteen assists.

During that time the Canadiens had a "youngest" in their history as well. Floyd Curry was a solid right-winger for the team for many seasons in the late forties through to the late fifties and was on four Stanley Cup winners. Today, over forty years after he first played for the team, Curry still works for the organization as a front-office employee. But when he first showed up at the Canadiens' training camp he was just fifteen years old. And nobody knew he was coming.

FLOYD "BUSHER" CURRY

I was playing minor hockey in Kirkland Lake in 1940, when I was only fifteen years old. Somebody told Paul Haynes about me. He was scouting for the Canadiens, and he scouted me. He told me they were going to invite me to their camp.

We waited but we didn't hear anything. So my mother told me, "Your dad and I will pay your way to Montreal. You go ahead."

So that was how I got to Montreal, and I wasn't supposed to be there. The camp was in St. Hyacinthe, and when I got there I didn't think they would let me stay around. But they did and they told me to practise.

I put on the equipment but I still didn't think I should be there. The funny thing is, the guy who told me to go on the ice was Toe Blake. I didn't even know who he was, and he was their best player. He told me, "You go out there. We're all the same as you.

We all have two arms and two legs." I remember him sayin' that.

Your father was running the camp and he let me stay. I thought for sure he was going to let me go right away, but he kept me a week. Then he came to me and said, "We're going to have to let you go. You're a little too young for this league. We can't play you. But we'll arrange to pay your way home so you'll get some money."

So I said thanks, and I went home. The next year I got a call right away to go to camp, and from there I went to the Oshawa juniors. There was a big rumpus one year when I was in Oshawa because the Canadiens were in Toronto and they were short of players and wanted me to play against the Leafs. I had gone home for Christmas and then I got a telegram telling me to report to the Canadiens in Toronto. It was quite a thrill for the family, that's for sure.

Charlie Conacher was coaching Oshawa then and he heard about it. So when I got to Toronto he was waiting for me at Maple Leaf Gardens. I told him that Mr. Irvin wanted me to play for him. In those days the odd kid would be called up for a game and get a hundred dollars and then go back to his junior team. I told him I thought that would be the case with me. Conacher said that was okay with him as long as the Canadiens signed me to a pro contract. I just looked at him. I was just a kid and I wasn't going to fight with that big guy. And I knew the Canadiens weren't going to sign me to a contract. So I didn't play. I was dying to get the opportunity, but I never did. Not as a junior anyway.

When I turned pro it was tough to make the NHL. They sent me first to Buffalo and I played part of the year there and part in Montreal. The next year I was in Buffalo all the way. The year after that they sent for me and I played quite a bit and was with them for the playoffs against Detroit. I thought I had a good playoff but the following year, don't they send me to Buffalo again.

After just a few weeks the team got a call to send me back again. The trainer, Frankie Christie, told me about it but I wasn't supposed to know because they were playing that night and the manager, Art Chapman, wanted to use me. All through the game Christie kept whispering in my ear, "Busher, you're going to Montreal."

The next day Chapman called me in and told me and asked me how much money I had with me. I said about a hundred dollars and he said that was enough to get me there. He wouldn't pay my train fare. So they sure kept you guessing all the time. But when I got to Montreal that time, I never went back to the minors.

I got the nickname "Busher" because I was such a kid when I first went to the camp. But it sure took a long time after that for me to finally become a player with the Montreal Canadiens.

5

Frank Selke Takes Over

Despite the total domination of the Punch Line in the NHL's scoring summaries, the Canadiens didn't win the Stanley Cup in 1945. The Toronto Maple Leafs did. The Leafs had finished in third place, twenty-eight points back of Montreal. Yet they upset the Canadiens, Punch Line and all, in the semifinals. Toronto then defeated Detroit to win the Cup.

The Canadiens got back on top the following year, finishing in first place by five points over Boston and winning the Stanley Cup in just one game more than the playoff minimum of eight games.

They played Chicago in the first round and swept the Hawks, scoring twenty-six goals in the four games. They lost once to Boston in the finals, and Toe Blake scored his second Cup-winning goal in three years. In those nine playoff games the Punch Line amassed forty-one scoring points. Elmer Lach led the way with seventeen. Blake had thirteen, while Maurice Richard, who had followed up his fifty-goal season with twenty-seven goals, had eleven.

Ken Reardon had returned from the Army to join Butch Bouchard, Leo Lameroux, and Glen Harmon on defence in front of Bill Durnan, who won his third straight Vezina Trophy. Jimmy Peters, Ken Mosdell, and Frankie Eddolls were others who had their names engraved on the Stanley Cup for the first time. The Canadiens were definitely on top of the hockey world. But deep within the ranks an "old age" problem was slowly building. There would be another first-place finish the following year, but no Stanley Cup. Another

*rebuilding job would soon be needed, but Tommy Gorman wouldn't
be around to do it.*

*Shortly after the 1946 Cup victory, Gorman and Canadiens'
owner Senator Donat Raymond parted company. Gorman had
been the right man for the job that had been done up to that point in
the 1940s. The Canadiens had needed someone who was willing to
keep a staggering franchise in business by wheeling and dealing,
and Gorman did just that. But by 1946 the team required a steadier
hand to overhaul the franchise at the NHL level and elsewhere.
Frank Selke was the right man for that situation.*

*Selke had worked for Conn Smythe in Toronto since the 1920s, be-
fore Maple Leaf Gardens was built. After their surprise Stanley Cup
win in 1945 the Maple Leafs finished out of the playoffs the following season. In Toronto, as in Montreal, there was a falling out between the owner and his manager. Tommy Gorman went back to his
native Ottawa. Frank Selke, like my father had done six years before,
left the Toronto Maple Leafs to join the Montreal Canadiens.*

*Shortly after the Selke family moved to Montreal, Frank Selke, Jr.,
also became an employee at the Forum. He stayed there for over
twenty years.*

FRANK SELKE, JR.

When my dad resigned from the Gardens in April of '46 his plan
was to put together a group of people to invest in a rink in
Cincinnati. He had already started that even before he left the
Gardens. When the job opportunity came up in Montreal I
remember him, quite distinctly, telling us that he had told Senator
Raymond that he was going to move to Cincinnati as soon as the
arena was built. He told the Senator that he would come to work
for him at the Forum for the one or two years it took to get the
building built down there, and then leave.

One of the most prophetic quotes that I have ever run across
was when Senator Raymond then told him, "Mr. Selke, no one
who has ever worked for me has left my employ voluntarily. You
won't leave here for Cincinnati. I'm sure of that." What could
have been closer to the truth?

My first impression of walking into the Forum came when I

went there, with my mum and dad, during an afternoon when there was no event taking place. I don't remember any colour in the place other than the advertising billboards and the MacDonald Tobacco score clocks. Any colour that was in there was a shade of brown. There wasn't any red, any white, any blue or green, or anything. It was like walking into a huge cave. When I think back to my first year in Montreal that's what strikes me. That building had absolutely no character whatsoever.

There were no individual box seats. They were all loose chairs. I think that other than the first tier above the boxes, all the seats were benches. They had faint numbers painted in white on the backs, and that was your seat. It was an old and ugly looking place.

One of the first things my dad did when he got there was take out that famous Millionaires section in the north end. There were some 4,000 seats that were priced at fifty cents. The Forum had only 9,600 seats, so roughly 40 per cent of the seats were priced at under one dollar. I quite clearly remember seeing a box office statement from the previous year when a sell-out of the building, in the playoffs, grossed $11,500. You wonder how they could have survived. Then again, great players like the Rocket and Bill Durnan were likely being paid about $4,500 to play.

The first major job my dad undertook was painting the place to get some colour in there. You and I could have retired on the money they spent that year on paint. I started to work there as kind of a grunt, a mechanic's helper and a plumber's helper, and cleaning the ice and that sort of thing. As you know I ended up spending most of my career in the publicity end of things. I started October 10th, 1946, and was there until the 2nd of May, 1967. I don't know why I still remember those dates, but I do.

With the Selke-Irvin tandem running the show at the Forum, it was natural there would be a big Montreal-Toronto rivalry. In Frank Selke's first year in Montreal it was not only big, it was bitter. Very bitter.

The Maple Leafs rebounded from their poor season the year before to finish a strong second behind the Canadiens, six points back of Montreal's leading total of seventy-eight. Toronto was the only team in the league to score over 200 goals. The Canadiens were by far the best team defensively. Goaltender Bill Durnan played in all sixty games and allowed only 138 goals-against, thirty-four fewer than his nearest opposing goaltender, Toronto's Turk Broda.

Goaltenders were ironmen in those days. Early that season Durnan was hit square on his maskless face by a puck in a game at the Forum. The game was held up for over twenty minutes while he received a dozen or so stitches. Then he came back and continued to play.

Members of the Montreal Royals baseball team, the Brooklyn Dodgers Triple A farm club, attended the game on the eve of the opening of the Little World Series against St. Paul. The Royals' first baseman, Chuck Connors, later famous as TV's Rifleman, *was sitting with his general manager, Buzzy Bavasi. Connors had been complaining about a sore thumb and was saying he didn't feel he could play the next day.*

Bavasi loved to tell how, when Durnan returned to the ice with his battered face full of stitches, he turned to Connors and quietly asked, "How's your thumb?" Connors played the next day.

Maurice Richard had a great season. The Rocket scored forty-five goals in an NHL where all players who had served in the war were back in hockey action. He finished one point behind the scoring champion, Chicago's Max Bentley. But Richard and Toe Blake played half the season without Elmer Lach centring them on the Punch Line.

Lach had an injury-plagued season. First he suffered a broken cheekbone in a collision with Chicago defenceman Johnny Mariucci. He returned to action in early February and scored twice in a 3-2 win in Boston.

The next night the Maple Leafs, trailing the Canadiens by three points, played at the Forum. The Canadiens won the game, 8-2, but in the process lost Lach for the balance of the season. Lach was dealt a heavy bodycheck by Don Metz, struck his head on the ice when he fell, and suffered a fractured skull.

My father screamed blue murder, accusing Metz of deliberately injuring Lach. He demanded that the league suspend the Toronto player, who received a two-minute penalty on the play.

Conn Smythe returned the fire, citing a vicious check Ken Rear-

don levelled on Metz after the Lach injury as his version of a deliberate attempt to injure. No further penalties were handed out, but the battle lines were drawn.

The next time they met, in Toronto, there was a major brawl. Toronto's "Wild Bill" Ezinicki and the Canadiens' "Hardrock" Murph Chamberlain were front and centre.

In the first round of the playoffs the Canadiens eliminated Boston and Toronto defeated Detroit. The fans were going to get what they wanted, a Montreal-Toronto final.

My father wasted no time proclaiming to the press that the Canadiens would "win the Cup for Elmer." His boast looked pretty good when his team whipped the Leafs 6–0 in the opener at the Forum.

Following the game Bill Durnan asked, "How did the Leafs ever get this far?" The quote would come back to haunt him.

In the Toronto lineup that year was the eventual winner of the Calder Trophy as rookie of the year, a kid from Kitchener with a brushcut, Howie Meeker, who played on a line with Ted Kennedy and Vic Lynn. Trying to revive the days of the Leafs' famed 1930s Kid Line of Busher Jackson, Joe Primeau, and Charlie Conacher, the Toronto press dubbed the Kennedy, Meeker, and Lynn trio as the new "Kid Line."

HOWIE MEEKER

Our line started the second game and it turned out we had a good night. We got two goals in the first period and when the Apps line got another in the second period we were home free. We won that game 4–0. I think the fact that we won that game got us thinking, hey, what the hell, we're as good as they are. We weren't supposed to be.

But it all really started with Conn Smythe. That day he held a meeting and really gave it to us. I remember that when he came in and he was going to give it to you there were sparks coming out of his eyes, and his cheeks were as red as Mackintosh apples. He came walking in the door and circled around the room and got in the middle of the floor. Our coach, Hap Day, faded out of the picture.

Smythe started with Apps, and then went to Broda. The senior guys first. He even went after Nick Metz. Geez, when he gave Nick Metz shit we knew he was serious. Then there was Kennedy, Mortson, Thomson, all of us. I don't think there was a guy in the room that escaped his anger.

I think it was by far the toughest series I ever played in. The Rocket cut Lynn and Ezinicki with his stick in the second game and Campbell suspended him for the next game. Later, when I was in management in Toronto, Hap Day told me that he drove to the first game we played in Toronto with Smythe. Day told Smythe he was afraid that the way the guys were playing there could be a really big riot. It was rough all right, but generally, I think we all played within the rules. The games in the regular season were a lot dirtier than the series was. More high-sticking, slashing, and retaliation.

I think that when it's all over and you have won the Stanley Cup your goaltender has to be the best guy on your team. That year Broda was. I thought he was head and shoulders above Durnan, and Durnan was good. We were outplayed and outchanced in scoring chances, I would think, by about three to two. Turk Broda was the guy who won that series.

KEN REARDON

We had a lot of injuries. Mosdell had a broken arm and I couldn't play in the first two games. I severed the tendon in my big toe and it hung down, like a guy with a broken finger. When I went to put my foot in the skate boot it wouldn't go in because the toe was buckled underneath. They used to freeze it and put a piece of tape under my stocking. It was like a string and I'd pull the tape to hold the toe up. Then I'd take out the laces so I could get my foot in the boot without doubling the toe underneath.

Bouchard was badly hurt, too. He had about eighteen stitches in the calf of his leg, or some place. Buddy O'Connor took over from Elmer with Rocket and Toe and he was okay. But we really missed Elmer. We couldn't beat them without Elmer.

The Maple Leafs won the 1947 final series in six games. While there was no way anyone could know it at the time, the era of the Punch

Line was over. Officially, it ended the next season, on January 11, during a game against the New York Rangers. Toe Blake, then thirty-five years old, suffered a broken leg when body-checked solidly by defenceman Bill Juzda. Blake never played another game.

The four full seasons of the Punch Line established Maurice Richard as hockey's number-one goal-scorer. During his line's four seasons at the top the Rocket scored 185 times, including thirty-one goals in the playoffs.

He was, without question, the game's most exciting personality. My father used to say that Richard not only scored his way to the top, he fought his way to the top as well. Every tough-checking left-winger in the league was assigned to check and antagonize him, which meant that the Rocket's road to superstardom included many a battle. Most of the time he used his fists, but there were times when he used his stick as well.

Twice while playing on the Punch Line, Richard scored five goals in one game. The first time was in the 1944 semifinal playoffs against Toronto. The final score was 5–1. After the game they announced the three stars as "Richard, Richard, and Richard."

His other five-goal performance came the next season, December 28, 1944, against the Detroit Red Wings. I had an ice-level view of that game because the Canadiens' coach let his twelve-year-old son, visiting Montreal from Regina during the Christmas holidays, sit on the players' bench. I was thrilled, but another youngster at the Forum that night, eighteen-year-old Harry Lumley, wasn't. Harry was in goal for the Red Wings.

HARRY LUMLEY

I had played Junior B hockey in Barrie and then went to Indianapolis when I was seventeen. The Red Wings brought me up for two games. I played one in New York and one in Chicago. Then there I was sitting in the stands watching the next game. I was going to catch a train back to Indianapolis later that night. The New York goalie, Ken McCauley, got injured so they called me out of the stands. I played the third period for the Rangers.

The next season I played most of the games for Detroit. That's when Richard scored the five goals against me and I'll never forget it because he set a record, eight points in one game. Apparently I wasn't ready yet but I was there, of course, because of the war. Nobody was mad at me or said anything to me after the game. The damage had been done. He owned me that year. I think he scored eighteen or so on Detroit that season. But the next year he didn't get too many.

There was one game against Montreal a few years later, in Detroit, and I think they only had six shots on me that night. We had about thirty on Durnan and we won the game 1–0. I was a nervous wreck. I think we went through the first period and a half and I never had a shot. I guess it was part of a plan Dick had because they'd just shoot the puck into our end and turn around and backcheck.

Then we had a real tough series against them in 1949. Went seven games, and we were supposed to be a much better team. In one game, it was tied in the third period and Joe Carveth had a breakaway on me and I stopped him. We went up to the other end of the rink and scored. Joe was so mad he went to hit his stick over the boards and he hit a fellow named Scotty Carmichael, a photographer. Cut him for a few stitches.

One of the phrases heard in stories about Maurice Richard in his prime is how he "carried players on his back" on the way to scoring goals.

Earl Seibert, a big defenceman for Chicago and then the Red Wings, was trying to defend against the Rocket one night in Detroit and found himself riding on the back of a Number 9 Montreal sweater on the way to the net and another Richard goal. When he returned to the players' bench Seibert was blasted by his coach, Jack Adams.

"Mr. Adams," Seibert replied when his coach had finally finished, "I weigh over 200 pounds. Any guy who can carry me on his back from the blue line to the net deserves to score a goal."

A similar Richard play is well remembered by Emile Francis, once a goalie in the NHL and for many years an executive with the Rangers, Blues, and Whalers.

Nicknamed "The Cat," Francis is a feisty little guy who played amateur hockey in his native Saskatchewan. As a teenager in Reg-

ina I watched Emile play for the Regina Caps in the old Western Senior League. He left the Caps and signed with the Chicago Black Hawks midway through the 1946–47 season. I recall my chagrin when some of my buddies taunted me over the story that in his first game against the mighty Rocket Richard, Francis stopped him cold on a breakaway and finished the play by tripping Richard and sending him sprawling into the boards.

EMILE FRANCIS

I was playing junior hockey for the Moose Jaw Canucks and we had a good club. Bert Olmstead was on the team. One day they got a call from Regina. They had a senior team there, the Caps, and they needed a goalie for the game the next night. They had lost twenty-three straight. Eddie Wiseman was our coach and he asked me to go and asked me how much money I would want to play. I didn't have a winter coat and I had seen one in a store for thirty-five dollars. So I told him I wanted thirty-five dollars and the Caps said okay.

They put me on a bus and when I got to Regina I was taken for lunch with some of the players and then to the Ehrle Hotel. Cliff Ehrle owned the hockey team and the hotel. I kept asking for my thirty-five dollars and they told me to wait. The trainer, Doc Hughes, took me to my room and when he left I heard a "click," and sure enough the door was locked. I called downstairs and they told me they had orders not to let me out of my room until they came to get me for the game at six o'clock.

At six Doc Hughes came again and drove me to the rink. When we got there I asked for my money and they said I'd get it once the people started to come to the game. They didn't have any money at all. So I put on my equipment and sure enough, just before the game, a guy came in and gave me all kinds of money, dollar bills, quarters, nickels, and dimes. I figured it must add up to thirty-five dollars so I didn't count it. We won the game 3–2 and I went back to Moose Jaw on the bus and bought my winter coat.

A couple of years later I was playing for the Regina Caps and we had a pretty good team. The Chicago Black Hawks owned my rights and they called me up during the season of '46–'47.

I think the Rocket was the most exciting player I have ever seen. You know there was always the argument as to who was the better player, him or Gordie Howe. They were both in my era and that would be a tough decision to make.

From the blue line in I have never seen a player as exciting as Rocket Richard. The thing that I didn't like about him when I played against him, although you had to admire him for it, was that when he scored he didn't just put it in the net, he tried to put it right through the net. That's where a lot of players today make a mistake. They think they've got the goalkeeper beat and they don't really bear down on the shot, and the goalkeeper recovers.

But Richard, when he came in on you his eyes would just light up and I can still see him coming in off that right wing.

The best play I think I've ever seen in hockey was made by him. Bill Gadsby was a big defenceman in those days, and Ralph Nattrass was another big defenceman. They were a year out of junior and I had just been brought in to Chicago.

Rocket came in from the blue line and he carried both those guys on his back and then he beat me. So he beat three of us on the play. The two guys were tugging on him and hanging on to him all the way from the blue line in. He was on his knees by the time he got to the net and so help me he got the shot away and put it past me into the top corner. Like I said, that was maybe the greatest play I ever saw, certainly as a goalie.

And incidentally, when the play was over I took a look over to the Canadiens' bench and who was sitting there, with that familiar hat of his pulled over his eyes, but your dad. And I was mad at him, too. I wondered how one westerner could do that to another westerner.

"I don't watch hockey anymore."

That's a phrase often directed at people like me who are in the hockey broadcasting business. Two popular reasons are given by those who say it. Too many teams. Too much violence.

There are more teams, for sure. But is there more violence? Old-timers will tell you there isn't.

Television makes it seem like fighting and goonery are on the rise. Fights and ugly incidents are replayed over and over again, espe-

cially on local sportscasts. The pictures are usually augmented by commentaries of gloom and doom by announcers who often haven't been at a hockey practice or game in years.

In the "old days" the only people who saw the violence were the fans at the games. Long-time referee Red Storey always claims the rough stuff isn't as prevalent now as it once was.

"I'd do a game in Chicago on a Sunday and there might be a real pier-sixer," Red said once on a TV show with me. "I'd go to Detroit for a game two nights later and nobody there even knew about the fight in Chicago."

I saw a picture taken of a brawl in New York in the late thirties between the Toronto Maple Leafs and the New York Americans. Every player in uniform was on the ice, and so were members of the New York Police Department, who had been called to help stop the hockey riot. If the cops were ever called out in that way today they'd have the case brought up in the House of Commons.

One player who was in the middle of more than a few battles in the forties and fifties was a Winnipegger, Bill Juzda. Built like a fire-plug and nicknamed "the Beast" (most players seemed to have nicknames then), Juzda never backed down when a fight beckoned. He played for the New York Rangers and Toronto and was a main participant in one particular wild brawl in New York during a Rangers-Canadiens game.

BILL JUZDA

We had a game against Montreal in a home-and-home double-header and I've never seen stick swinging, even in this day, like we had that night in New York.

All you saw was a Montreal sweater and if it was there I guess what you thought about was taking a swing at the guy who was wearing it. I hit Buddy O'Connor with a left hand. Buddy was one of the sweetest guys you could ever meet and wasn't really involved in the fight. My punch broke his jaw. That was one I didn't feel too good about when I realized who I had hit.

Funny thing was, a year or so later he got traded to our team. The first time he walked into our dressing room he wanted to know where the guy was who broke his jaw.

I had to do a lot of fancy talking to get around it, but he never held it against me. He almost won the scoring championship the first year he played with us but he lost by one point to Elmer Lach.

In the old days you used to get fined $25 if you got into a fight at the end of a game. One night some guy was harassing our goalie, Charlie Rayner, so when the game ended I got into a fight with him. The next pay day I got my cheque and they had taken $25 off it. In those days that was almost the whole amount of my pay cheque!

I don't think Rocket Richard ever liked playing against me. In fact, we played an old-timers' game in Vancouver a few years ago and I had him pinned up against the boards. He said to me, "Goddamn you, Juzda. You're still as strong as ever."

Once in Toronto, when we had won the Stanley Cup and were playing against the All-Stars in the All-Star game the next fall, I saw him getting off the elevator at the hotel. I said hello to him and he answered right back, "You're not a good hockey player. You should have been a wrestler."

One of the most talked-about incidents of hockey violence in that era concerned an ongoing feud between Ken Reardon and Cal Gardner. It began when Gardner was playing for the New York Rangers and continued a couple of years later after Gardner had been traded to the Toronto Maple Leafs.

KEN REARDON

We were playing in New York and we were ahead by a goal in the last minute. Dick put me on and told me not to do what I had done the last time in a situation like that. In the previous game I had iced the puck in the last minute and after the face-off in our end the Rangers had scored.

This game meant that if we won we finished in first place. With about thirty seconds to go a fellow named Cal Gardner cross-checked me. He knocked out a couple of teeth in the front and I think I had about twenty stitches to sew up my lip. I resented that. He wasn't usually a dirty player but I thought that was a dirty trick.

A little later I gave a magazine an interview and I said that before I quit hockey I was going to get Cal Gardner. And then one night I did. I accidentally ran into him and broke his jaw awful on both sides. I didn't even see him.

So when that happened, Clarence Campbell made me post a $1,000 good behaviour bond. That was about 10 per cent of my salary. But I got it back when I quit playing.

Ken Reardon told me the story of his "accidental" hit on Cal Gardner when he was a guest on my TV show in Montreal, Hockey Magazine. *And he told the story with an absolutely straight face.*

Cal Gardner is a native of Winnipeg who played twelve seasons in the NHL. His two sons, Dave and Paul, also played in the league. Cal broke in with the New York Rangers in 1946, at the age of twenty-one.

CAL GARDNER

When I played in New York a bunch of us lived in what was called "Hell's Kitchen," which was just down from the old Madison Square Garden. I came out one day to go to practice and across the street there was a guy sitting down against a door in a concert hall building. The police had arrived so I went over to see what was happening and the police were shaking him. He fell over and there was a knife in his back. That was a great thing for me to see.

I went on to the practice and I was so shaken I couldn't even tie my skates. Bryan Hextall told me to go see the coach, Frank Boucher, and he told me to go see Dr. Nardiello, who was the team doctor. He gave me a couple of pills to calm me down. But boy, that shook me for the rest of my career in New York.

With Reardon, the first incident was in New York and I don't think he knew at the time who hit him. You know how he used to galavant around on his skates. We were trying to tie the game and I was on the point and I let a shot go and he was coming at me. I just pulled away and my stick caught him on his lip.

That's when we had the big brawl in New York. Bouchard hit Hextall twice over the head with his hockey stick. Hextall grabbed Bouchard and I don't know how many times he hit him and down he went. Reardon swore, or something, and some sixty-year-old guy, who was sitting behind the bench with a girl who was about twenty-five, yelled, "You can't swear like that in front of my fiancée." So Rocket Richard hit him over the head with a hockey stick. The guy was cut and there was blood all over the place. It was unbelievable.

Reardon broke my jaw in Montreal. After that he had to post his $1,000 bond. Then I think we had another set-to in Toronto, so it kept on going.

In the last half-century the Montreal Canadiens have failed to qualify for the Stanley Cup playoffs only twice. The first time was in 1948, a sad ending to a season when nothing went right.

In the summer of 1947 centre Buddy O'Connor and defenceman Frankie Eddolls were traded to the New York Rangers for defence-man Hal Laycoe and two so-called promising forwards, Joe Bell and George Robertson. Laycoe suffered through an injury-plagued season, while neither Robertson nor Bell were NHLers. To make matters worse, O'Connor had a career year. He won both the Hart and Lady Byng trophies and battled with Elmer Lach down to the final game to decide the scoring championship. Lach won by scoring twice in the last game in Boston to edge O'Connor by one point. It was the only bright spot in an otherwise dismal season.

Toe Blake's career ended when he broke his leg. Bill Durnan didn't win the Vezina Trophy, the only time that happened in his seven-year career. Lach and Maurice Richard were the only Mont-real players who posted more than twenty-five points in the sixty-game schedule.

When the season ended seven players who had been on the Cana-diens' first-place team the previous season were either retired or playing elsewhere. Most of their replacements came up very short. It was rebuilding time, again, at the Forum.

FRANK SELKE, JR.

When my father came to Montreal, junior hockey was almost non-existent. My recollection is that the junior teams played late at night, very often at the Forum after the NHL game. There was nobody in the building to watch, and nobody seemed to care.

As unimportant as junior hockey was in the scheme of things, the senior Royals in the Quebec League were almost as popular as the NHL Canadiens. Many times the Royals' Sunday afternoon games would outdraw what the Canadiens had had the night before.

They played in a league that was very wide open. There was almost no backchecking and there were several ex-NHL players who were very stylish and who could put on a good show for the fans.

My dad worked very hard to develop a junior system, not only in Quebec but across the country. It wasn't very long before they had junior farm teams in just about every major hockey area in Canada. It wasn't too long after he got there that the Montreal junior teams, the Royals and the Junior Canadiens, were winning Memorial Cups.

The senior Royals won the Allan Cup in 1947. Oddly enough, the fellows who came out of that team and who were supposed to make the Canadiens were not capable of doing it. With the exception of Doug Harvey and Floyd Curry, and Gerry McNeil who came along a year or two later and was a classy goaltender, none of them were able to stick in the NHL. They came from the number-one farm team but just weren't good enough. That's what my dad and your dad were faced with at the time.

6

A Team in Transition

Shortly after joining the Canadiens, Frank Selke, Sr., made an astute move when he hired Sam Pollock to work at the amateur and minor pro level. Pollock was only twenty-one but already was well known in Montreal for his work in minor hockey. What most impressed Selke was the way young Pollock managed a softball team made up mainly of Canadiens' players.

A dour type known as "Sad Sam," Pollock did everything for the Canadiens at all levels of their minor-league operation. He put together teams that won Memorial Cups, Senior League champion-ships, and Central League championships. Out of those teams came many of the players who were on Stanley Cup-winning teams in Montreal in the fifties, sixties, and seventies. Ironically, when Selke was forced to step down in 1964, Pollock took his place as the Canadiens' general manager. By the time he retired in 1978 the Canadiens had won nine more Stanley Cups.

SAM POLLOCK

When I joined the Canadiens there was only one office in the Forum - Mr. Selke's. Your dad had a desk in the hallway. He was coaching in the NHL, for God's sake, and he had a desk in the hallway.

They gave me a desk at the other end of the hall. Dick was

really good to me right from the start. I don't know if I would have made it without him.

The NHL statistics used to come out every Tuesday morning. In those days not many guys paid much attention to them. I think he was the first to study them. He'd call me over. "Mr. Pollock," he'd say. He always called me Mr. Pollock even though I was only twenty-one. "Mr. Pollock, take a look at this. Here's (so-and-so) of the Maple Leafs. One goal. Here's (so-and-so) of the Bruins. One goal. Do you know who they scored these goals against?" Things like that. Usually, they had scored them against us.

One day he came in after the team just got back from a road trip and yelled at me down the hall. "Ask your friend Billy Reay how he slept last night!" Then he went into Mr. Selke's office. When he came out he sat down and I went over to him and asked him, "What's the matter, coach?" He was steaming over something. "Go ask him, ask your friend Billy Reay if he slept last night."

So finally, a while later, I went to him and said, "Okay, what happened?"

Dick said, "How would you like to be trying to go to sleep and some guy is saying, 'Bid four hearts, bid four diamonds.' All bloody night. So you know what I did? I told the porter to take all the goddamn sheets and everything else out of Reay's berth. I'd have liked to have seen his face when he got there. There was nothing but a slab of wood for him to sleep on."

You used to have all those things. You never had fun like that later. But those guys were loyal, I remember that. You ask Floyd Curry. I remember one night they had played a terrible game. Afterwards Dick said, "I can't talk to you guys. I don't even want to see you."

So the next day he calls them into a room, one by one, and I guess he really gave it to them. You had guys like Curry and others coming out with tears in their eyes. They had begged him to give them another chance. I mean, these guys were tough, tough hockey players. They played hurt. Oh, did they ever. They were tough, and they played hurt and I always thought they were afraid of their coach. Can you imagine that today?

*Defenceman Hal Laycoe was the main man the Canadiens received
in the controversial trade that sent Buddy O'Connor and Frankie
Eddolls to the New York Rangers. Laycoe was unique in that he
wore glasses when he played. He spent three years with the Canadiens plus part of a fourth before being traded to the Boston Bruins
for another defenceman, Ross Lowe, during the 1950-51 season.*

HAL LAYCOE

The thing I noticed right away when I joined the Canadiens was
the discipline. There was no fooling around. I remember my first
training camp, at St. Hyacinthe. When we started to scrimmage I
couldn't believe the intensity. It was tougher than a lot of games I
had played in.

Dick was always after you about your weight. I always thought
I was thin but early one season he really gave it to me in front of
all the players at a team meeting. He told me I had played very
well the year before but that I wasn't playing as well then because
I was three or four pounds heavier. To show how thin I had been
the year before he took a hockey stick and ran it across a radiator,
making a hell of a noise. He said that was how thin I should be,
like the pipes. I think he was using me as an example for everyone
else. After that the boys nicknamed me "Radiator."

One year I played a lot with Ken Reardon and they told me not
to rush with the puck at all. I was supposed to stay back because
Reardon was always charging up the ice. I was very frustrated but
that was the season I learned how to play defence, block shots and
all that.

Frank Selke told me once there would be a bonus for me if we
won the Vezina Trophy. I think it was $750. I told him I didn't
agree with that kind of thinking. I thought there were too many
times when we fell back to protect a lead in close games and it
cost us. I said I didn't want that kind of a bonus and he didn't like
that. But I was always outspoken.

Dick was always thinking up ways to keep us on our toes. I
remember he used to give us written tests, and one day he walked
into the room wearing a cap and gown, like a professor. He used

to test us on the rules. One time he had the defencemen write down six things that made a good defenceman. It was interesting because usually players don't think that way.

The discipline rubbed off. One morning I whistled into the Forum around 10:30 for practice and saw that everyone was on the ice. The practice was at ten and I thought it was eleven. I don't think I ever felt as bad about anything in my hockey life as I did that day because I was late for practice.

You know how the market for old hockey cards is today. One time a guy came to us and offered every player on the team fifty dollars to have his picture on a hockey card. Rocket said nobody was going to get his picture for just fifty dollars. The guy said it was everybody or nobody. So none of us got the fifty.

We made a road trip just before I got traded. Dick had everyone put some money into a pot and then told us that he would use units of five for every game on the road. The unit with the best goals for and against rating would win the money. I was paired with Doug Harvey and Billy Reay was the centre on our forward line. We didn't think we had a chance and we forgot all about it.

When we got back to Montreal they told me I had been traded to Boston. I went into the dressing room to shake hands and Billy Reay stopped me. He reached into his wallet and gave me some money because we had won the pot. I think he gave me sixty dollars. So I always said I left Montreal a winner, in one way anyway.

In the two seasons following their fifth-place finish in 1948, the Canadiens were indeed a team in transition. Sixteen new players arrived with a shot at becoming regulars. Only a few made it for more than a little while.

Doug Harvey was there to stay. Others appeared briefly who later would return to the lineup of teams that would win the Stanley Cup six times in eight years, beginning in 1953: Floyd Curry, Tom Johnson, Gerry McNeil, Bud McPherson, Paul Meger, and Calum "Baldy" McKay.

In 1948-49 the Canadiens finished third with sixty-five points, a fourteen-point improvement. They were only ten points back of league champion Detroit. The Red Wings eliminated them in the first playoff round, but not before the underdogs had battled them through a tough seven-game series.

While there were players coming and going, one very imposing presence remained on defence in the person of big Emile "Butch" Bouchard, the Canadiens' captain from 1948 until he retired in 1956.

BUTCH BOUCHARD

I started skating in high school. I never had a pair of skates until I was sixteen. I always borrowed skates or rented skates. In those days you could rent a pair of skates for a night for five cents and play a game of hockey. Otherwise I would play in the park and I would be the goalie, without skates. We were quite poor around 1935 and '36. My father was working for the CPR but he only worked in the winter.

I went to a school called Le Plateau and I borrowed thirty-five dollars from my brother, Marcel. He was older than me and he was working. For the thirty-five dollars I bought skates, a pair of pads, a pair of pants, shoulder pads, and gloves. All that for thirty-five dollars in those days.

I played for our team at Le Plateau and the second year I was there Arthur Therrien came to me and asked if I could play junior for him with the Verdun team. So I played one year junior and two years senior. The year that I played junior I was playing for them, also for Le Plateau, and also for an intermediate team. I guess because I was such a big kid they thought I was strong enough to do all that. And all three teams won the championship of their league.

After my second year in senior hockey I was with the Canadiens. So I made the NHL just four years after I had my first pair of skates and three years after that I was on my first Stanley Cup winner. That was in 1944 and we beat Chicago. I assisted Toe Blake on the winning goal in overtime. We had a breakaway and I had the puck. I passed it to Toe because he was paid to score goals and I wasn't, and he scored. They gave us a big parade and everything because it had been a long time since the Canadiens had won the Stanley Cup.

The best life for me was when we had Toe Blake, Bill Durnan, Ken Mosdell, and Elmer Lach and Rocket and Ken Reardon. They were a great bunch and we had a good team and a lot of fun, too.

I remember one time coming home from Toronto on the train. Your father had been showing some of his chickens at the big Winter Fair and he had them with him in a cage in his compartment. He went to the dining car and Fernand Majeau went into the compartment and let the chickens out of their cage. When Dick got back his chickens were walking up and down the train car.

Bill Durnan was our goalie and he was the best there was and he was a fabulous fellow. He was a goalie who would never blame his defencemen because they blocked his view or something. He always took the blame whenever a goal went in. He was a real team player. He had those good hands and in the last year he played he hurt his hand badly. He quit in the playoffs because of his nerves, but I think he was really worried that he couldn't help the team because of his hand. He couldn't handle the puck properly at all.

The best player I ever faced? I remember Syl Apps was a great skater with the Maple Leafs. But I think the best was Milt Schmidt. He was tough, a big guy, and he was one of the best skaters I ever saw. He gave me a cold one night, the "breeze" I called it, the first year I played. He gave me a big shift and went around me and when I went to the bench Dick asked me if I had caught a cold because of the breeze that Schmidt made when he went by me.

In 1949 the Canadiens weren't good enough to beat the Detroit Red Wings in the playoffs even if they did take the Wings the full seven-game distance. In 1950 it was thought they were good enough to beat the New York Rangers in the first round, but they didn't.

The 1949–50 season had been a pretty good one. Bill Durnan won the Vezina Trophy again and Maurice Richard led the league with forty-three goals. On defence, Doug Harvey was showing signs of becoming Doug Harvey.

The Canadiens finished in second place, eleven points back of the league champion Red Wings. Detroit's Production Line of Ted Lindsay, Sid Abel, and Gordie Howe finished in that order in the top three spots in the scoring race. Richard was fourth.

In the six-team NHL, first played third and second played fourth in the opening round of the playoffs. The Canadiens had finished ten points ahead of the fourth-place Rangers. Because of their annual collision with the circus at Madison Square Garden, the best the Rangers could hope for was two home games in the Montreal series. But against the Canadiens that year it didn't matter.

New York won the two games played in New York plus one at the Forum to take a three-game lead. The Canadiens won game four in Montreal on an overtime goal by Elmer Lach. The Rangers then clinched the series with a 3–0 win in game five.

Two Canadiens greats played their final games in the series. In the second game Ken Reardon was hit by Ranger defenceman Gus Kyle. Reardon suffered a badly separated shoulder and never played again, retiring at the age of thirty.

After game three, a 4–1 loss in New York, Bill Durnan retired. Simply, his nerves were shot. Durnan had played until he was thirty-five, longer than most goaltenders in that era. He bowed to the pressure, and his age, and was replaced by Gerry McNeil. In his seven seasons in the NHL Bill Durnan had won the Vezina Trophy six times and was the first All-Star goaltender six times. Again, the end of an era at the Forum.

A big stumbling block for the Canadiens in the series was New York's goaltender, Charlie "Chuck" Rayner. A native of Winnipeg, Rayner's career was interrupted by three years of service in the Canadian Navy. Rayner was good enough to get elected to the Hall of Fame, yet he never played on a Stanley Cup-winning team.

CHARLIE RAYNER

I turned pro when I was nineteen and was playing for Eddie Shore's team in Springfield. He had an agreement with the New

York Americans and we were in Pittsburgh when they told me I was being called up. My first game was against Toronto and they beat us 2-1. I played twelve games that season, '40-'41, and most of the next season. Then I joined the Navy.

The Americans had a lot of tough old pros then. Charlie Conacher and Busher Jackson were there and so was Murph Chamberlain. Then there were the kids like me, Ken Mosdell, and Harry Watson. We heard a lot of pretty rough stories about the older guys but all I can tell you is that they took good care of us. Chamberlain was really good to me. It was like two teams there, the young and the old.

The team was run by Red Dutton and he was a real character. In my second year we were called the Brooklyn Americans. We were losing a lot and Dutton said it was because we were getting "too much Broadway." He kept harping on "too much Broadway." All us young guys were living in the Piccadilly Hotel and the rooms were three dollars a day. We shared rooms so it cost us a buck and a half a day. Dutton told us to move out and sent us to a hotel in Brooklyn. When we got there we saw it was the worst flea-bag you could imagine. So we got back on the subway and went back to New York.

We won our next two games and all the papers played it up how Dutton had found the answer and moved us out of New York. Heck, we were still living in New York, right back on Broadway. I think he thought we were still at that hotel in Brooklyn.

One night we were playing Toronto and it was tied late in the game. I was about to clear a rebound from in front of the net when one of our defencemen, Pat Egan, yelled at me that he'd do it. He cleared it all right. He shot it into our net as clean as a whistle. Dutton used to wear a white fedora and the next thing I see the fedora is flying onto the ice.

We lost the game and as soon as it was over Dutton raced into the dressing room and kicked at a bunch of sticks lined up against the wall. He lost his balance and fell down and the blade of one of the sticks sliced his pants and he had quite a cut on his leg. The New York sports doctor in those days was Dr. Vincent Nardiello. When we all got into the room there was Dutton sprawled out on the rubbing table with his pants down around his ankles and the blood all over his leg, and the doctor trying to fix him up. We all started to laugh and he could have killed us, he was so mad.

I guess my best memory about the Canadiens was the series we won from them in 1950. I remember in those days going into Montreal just praying to get a win and we hardly ever did. Then all of a sudden our team caught fire in the last part of the season and things turned a little bit. We won the first game of the series in New York, and things just kept going for us. It was guys like Pentti Lund and Buddy O'Connor who did it for us, and Tony Leswick, who was always checking the Rocket. Tony used to try to talk French to Maurice, if you can believe it, and he used to drive him nuts.

But you know, I'm often asked about the players from that time and just who was who. You can't do anything but pick the Rocket right off the top. You know, he was a son of a gun. A lot of guys would seem to go for two miles to get up the speed he used to get in two steps. He was just terrible for the goalies to handle around the net, and he worked so hard.

I can still remember very, very well one time in Montreal when they had us about 4–1 or something in the third period. That team was a great team at that time. I remember Maurice coming in and, damn it, I stopped him. But the puck went in behind me a little bit and there was nothing between the puck and the net. He just reached over and he drilled that thing into the net like it was the last goal he'd ever score. I said to him, "What the hell are you trying to do, Maurice?" And he said, "All I want to do, Charlie, is score the goal." But that was his determination.

I was in goal for the Rangers the night Jean Béliveau got his first hat trick in the NHL. He was brought up for a tryout and he scored three times on me. Wasn't he a great hockey player?

In our day we seemed to have a better rapport with the other players. It was a great pleasure to talk with guys like Richard, and Howe, and Schmidt. I don't think the players have that sort of thing today.

Goalies like me had to learn about the other guys on our own. I remember asking our coach, Frank Boucher, how to play certain players and that's what he told me. "You're on your own." It must help them today with the videos and everything. Of course, there were some players you could study for a hundred years and not know what they were going to do. Rocket was in that category, for sure.

One more thing about 1950. After we beat Montreal we lost in the finals to Detroit, in overtime, in the seventh game. I kind of blame myself for that one. Edgar Laprade was one of our best centres and he had been on the ice for a long time. There was a face-off in our end and I thought he looked tired. So I told Frankie Eddolls that maybe they should take him off the ice. Eddolls went to Lynn Patrick, our coach, and the next thing I saw Laprade was going off and Buddy O'Connor was coming on. Poor Buddy. He lost the face-off and they scored. Pete Babando. Maybe if I'd kept my mouth shut I might have won a Stanley Cup.

II

The Early 1950s

As the National Hockey League moved through the first half of the 1950s the Montreal Canadiens were always chasing the Detroit Red Wings. They never caught them, at least not during the regular season. Beginning in 1948–49 Detroit ended the regular season in first place seven straight years. The Canadiens were second five times.

Detroit had a great hockey club, led by the Production Line of Sid Abel, Ted Lindsay, and Gordie Howe. Howe ran off four straight scoring championships and it wasn't even close. The nearest anyone came to him was in 1953–54 when the runner-up, Maurice Richard, was fourteen points off big Gordie's pace. But in three of those seven league championship seasons, the Red Wings didn't win the Stanley Cup.

As in any era there were great careers starting and great careers ending. Detroit goaltender Terry Sawchuk was voted the NHL's outstanding rookie in 1951, an award won the next two years by Bernie Geoffrion of the Canadiens and Gump Worsley of the New York Rangers. All three have been elected to the Hockey Hall of Fame, a unique triple that has happened only once since, when Tony Esposito, Ken Dryden, and Gilbert Perreault were consecutive rookie award winners in the early 1970s.

Before the fifties were half over several other future Hall of Fame players had retired. This list included Milt Schmidt, Elmer Lach, Sid Abel, Turk Broda, Bill Durnan, and the Bentley brothers, Doug and Max.

The Toronto Maple Leafs won the Stanley Cup the last three years of the 1940s and again in 1951. That string of four in five years was the end of a championship era at Maple Leaf Gardens. The Leafs didn't win the Cup again until 1962 and missed the playoffs three times in the intervening eleven years.

While the Toronto Maple Leafs were sliding through the early 1950s the Montreal Canadiens were heading the other way. Frank Selke's rebuilding project was under a full head of steam. The Canadiens now owned successful junior teams in Montreal, Hull-Ottawa, Winnipeg, and Regina, and their graduates began filtering into the lineups of the organization's professional farm clubs in Buffalo and Cincinnati and to the Montreal Royals senior team. Over the next few years organization-bred players would work their way through the ranks to the Canadiens' dressing room: Plante, Moore, St. Laurent, Marshall, Goyette, Provost, Turner, Talbot, and a Richard they were calling "the Pocket Rocket."

Also on the way up was a young sensation named Jean Béliveau, who would leave Montreal fans waiting and wondering for a couple of years before finally arriving to stay at the Forum. Béliveau's NHL rights were owned by the Canadiens but he opted to play senior hockey in Quebec City where he was making at least as much money as the Canadiens were willing to pay him, maybe even more.

Selke's master plan started paying off in 1951 when the Canadiens made their first of a record ten straight appearances in the Stanley Cup finals. They were beaten that year by the Maple Leafs in a series that was ended by one of the most famous goals in Stanley Cup history.

7

The Barilko Goal

When the New York Rangers eliminated the Montreal Canadiens in the first round of the 1950 Stanley Cup playoffs it marked the last time any team would do that until 1961. In each of the first four of those years a well-remembered goal was scored in a series involving the Canadiens. Two for, two against. Gerry McNeil, who replaced Bill Durnan, was in goal every time.

GERRY MCNEIL

I never played junior hockey at all. I only played kids' hockey, I guess you'd call it, in Quebec City. Somehow the Canadiens knew about me and I went to their camp when I was seventeen. That was in 1943.

The first exhibition game that year was in Quebec City against Boston. Their goalie, Frank Brimsek, was my idol and they put me in to play that game. Brimsek was playing for them and it ended up 3–3. I was really happy about that.

It was funny that first year, because that was Durnan's first year. Up to a couple of hours before the opening game he wasn't sure of playing. He hadn't signed a contract. Dick came to me and told me to be ready because if Durnan didn't play he was going to use me. I can tell you, I was a little nervous. But Durnan signed at the very last minute.

I stayed in Montreal and played for the Royals, the senior team. I never played for the Canadiens until '47–'48 when Bill was hurt for a couple of games. I never felt frustrated that they kept me in senior hockey. I was quite happy about that. From '43 on I was always practising with Canadiens.

When Bill decided to quit, well, there was quite a session with him, me, and Dick. I guess he just had some kind of a breakdown. There was always pressure but he was the type who kept it inside. It never showed with him on the outside.

The thing I remember best about the two games I played against the Rangers in that playoff was that the first game went into overtime and I stopped Buddy O'Connor on a breakaway. That would have put us out four straight if he had scored.

I was the regular goalie after that and didn't miss a game the next two years.

Gerry McNeil wasn't the only newcomer in the Canadiens lineup during the 1950–51 season. When the season was over the team had used a total of thirty-nine players, an all-time high for the franchise. Six different players wore the number twelve.

On December 16 of that season the Canadiens played at the Forum against the New York Rangers with two top Quebec Junior League stars in their lineup for the first time, Jean Béliveau and Bernie "Boom Boom" Geoffrion. The game ended in a 1–1 tie. Geoffrion scored the Canadiens' goal. Historically, it was a night similar to November 3, 1940, when Elmer Lach and Ken Reardon made their debuts. Lach and Reardon eventually made the Hockey Hall of Fame, and so did Béliveau and Geoffrion.

The two junior stars were called upon again on January 27 to play against Chicago. The Canadiens won 4–3 with Geoffrion scoring again and Béliveau getting his first NHL goal. Harry Lumley was the Chicago goaltender. Two weeks later Geoffrion signed a pro contract and joined the team permanently. Two more seasons would pass before Béliveau would do the same.

Detroit and Toronto were the class of the league. The Red Wings finished first with a record 101 points, six ahead of the Maple Leafs. The Canadiens battled all season just to make the playoffs, finally finishing in third place with sixty-five points, three ahead of Boston.

The Rangers were only four points back of the Canadiens but didn't make the playoffs.

Through all of the player juggling during the 1950–51 season, the most significant move was made just before Christmas when the Canadiens acquired Bert Olmstead from Detroit. The team had been lacking a solid two-way left-winger since the night Toe Blake broke his leg. They got one in Olmstead. He definitely fit the term "hard-nosed competitor." In many ways he was a Toe Blake clone.

BERT OLMSTEAD

I played the year before in Chicago but the next year they sent me to Milwaukee in the United States Hockey League. I stayed there two weeks. That was the rule. Red Hamill was our coach and I bugged him every day about trading me and he was on the phone every day to Chicago. They finally traded me to Detroit but I never played there. I ended up with Montreal in a three-way deal and I can tell you I was really, really happy.

The team had played in Chicago and I joined them the next morning. I think they got beaten. We took the train back to Montreal. Dick always had the custom of talking with players in his compartment, especially if they were in a slump and they would talk about the reasons why.

He had me in there for a long time on that trip and when I finally came out the guys were asking, "What'd he say? What'd he say?" and I told them all we did was talk baseball.

He was a great baseball fan and I often thought that he went to bat for me because I had played some very good baseball the summer before, in Moose Jaw. He was watching and we won the tournament and I think he held that pretty high. So I was happy the way that baseball tournament turned out.

I pretty well stayed with Elmer and the Rocket right from the start, except the first couple of weeks when I wasn't really in all that good condition. But after a lot of hard practices I was ready to keep up with them.

I am not alone when I say that one of my favourite people in Canadian sports is "the Old Redhead," Red Storey.

Red burst onto the scene in 1938 when he came off the Toronto Argonauts' bench to score three touchdowns in the final thirteen minutes of the Grey Cup, one of them on a 102-yard run. He's been running, skating, and talking ever since.

Red played hockey and lacrosse as well as football. He began refereeing when injuries ended his playing days and worked in the NHL *from 1951 to 1959. He's in his seventies now yet still referees close to 100 hockey games a year, winter and summer, most of them charity affairs. Red has become one of Canada's wittiest and busiest after-dinner speakers, and a story he tells of Olmstead from this period is odd, to say the least.*

RED STOREY

When you had the Rocket and Bert Olmstead on the same team, let me tell you, you had guys who were two of the toughest competitors you could imagine. Off the ice, too.

I was working a series between the Canadiens and the Bruins in the fifties and on the off day between games a bunch of us went to the race track in Providence.

After the races we went to a spot called Freddy's Bar and Grill, which was a bit of a sports hangout. I didn't know the Canadiens were going to be there but they showed up and were having a party in a private room. Boom Boom was singing and there was a lot of noise.

I was sitting at the bar when Olmstead came out of the party room and asked if he could sit with me. He said he didn't like parties like that. So we sat there for about a half-hour talking about families, and pensions, and hockey. The usual stuff.

Then all of a sudden he says to me, "What would you do if I told you I think you're a yellow son of a bitch?" Just like that, out of the blue.

I said, "I'd beat the shit out of you."

Olmstead said, "Okay. That's all I wanted to know," and then we started talking again about families, and pensions, and hockey. But it really bothered me. I've never forgotten that.

The Canadiens played their final game of the 1950–51 season in Detroit and were clobbered 5–0 by the high-flying Red Wings. That,

plus the fact that they had finished the season thirty-six points be-
hind the league champions, meant that even the staunchest Habs
supporters had little hope for their team in the first round of the
playoffs, which opened two nights later at the Olympia in Detroit.
Two weeks later, the Canadiens were playing in the Stanley Cup
finals against Toronto after having dumped Detroit in six games.

The first two games are the most memorable part of the Big Upset
of '51. Both were played in Detroit, and both were long overtime
games. And Rocket Richard scored the winning goal both times.

In the opener the teams played into a fourth overtime period be-
fore Richard scored on Terry Sawchuk at 1:09 for a 3–2 Montreal
victory.

The second game was scoreless through to the 2:20 mark of the
third overtime period when Richard whipped a backhand shot past
Sawchuk, and Richard's co-hero, Gerry McNeil, had a dramatic
shutout victory.

The Canadiens' rookie goaltender was magnificent. A newspaper
action photo taken during one of the overtime periods shows
Detroit's Ted Lindsay skating in front of the Canadiens' net with his
stick raised in the air signalling what he thought was the game-
winning goal. McNeil is sprawled on the ice, his catching glove
barely outside the goal line, clutching the puck. Those who followed
the series claim that picture pretty well tells the story. As usually
happens in a playoff upset, a hot goaltender was the difference
between winning and losing.

GERRY MCNEIL

Until this day those two games are, for me, more of a thrill than
when we won the Stanley Cup. It's funny for a goaltender when
games go that long but the pressure is over by then. The game is
just happening, that's all. I don't think I really felt any extra
pressure at that stage when the games went that long.

The first game went into four overtimes and then came the
second game and that turned out to be almost the same thing.
Only in that game I got a shutout. . . . You have to be lucky, of
course. And don't forget, I had the Rocket on my side. That made
it really lucky for me.

It's nice to remember winning games. Then we had the Toronto series and every game went into overtime. Every one, and there were five. But we lost four of those.

The Red Wings evened the series with two wins in Montreal, but the Canadiens won again in Detroit and completed the upset with a 3-2 victory in the sixth game at the Forum. The referee that night, Bill Chadwick, didn't call a single penalty and still claims it was one of the greatest games ever played.

The Maple Leafs had no trouble eliminating Boston in the other semifinal. That series included a 1-1 final score. Sunday curfew laws in Toronto prevented the teams from playing past the first overtime period.

The Montreal-Toronto final series featured those five overtime games. Sid Smith scored the winner for the Leafs in the first game. Maurice Richard scored his third sudden-death goal of the year in the second. In Montreal the overtime winning goals were both scored by Maple Leafs, Ted Kennedy and Harry Watson.

That set the stage for the Leafs to be able to win the Stanley Cup on home ice in the fifth game, and that's what happened when Bill Barilko scored one of the most famous overtime goals in the long history of the Toronto team. The Canadiens were leading 2-1 in the final minute of the third period. Toronto coach Joe Primeau pulled goalie Al Rollins with thirty-two seconds remaining and a face-off set for the Montreal zone. Max Bentley's shot from the point was deflected into the net by Tod Sloan, sending the teams into overtime for the fifth straight game.

Toronto defenceman Bill Barilko was an unlikely scoring hero. Barilko was a tough guy and one of the best bodycheckers in a league that had a lot of good bodycheckers. My father used to complain loudly to the press about Barilko's rough play against his Canadiens. Privately, he felt that half the players in the NHL were frightened of Barilko and wished he had him on his team.

Playing for Toronto that year was Fleming Mackell, who had been a high school hockey star while growing up in Montreal. But the Canadiens let him get away and he became a Maple Leaf after playing on the Toronto St. Mikes Memorial Cup-winning junior team in 1947.

FLEMING MACKELL

The first time I played in the NHL I was in one of the most famous games ever played, the first All-Star game. In those days the Stanley Cup champions played an All-Star team just before the season began. The Leafs were the champions. I seemed to have made the team at their training camp and they used me in the All-Star game. I was eighteen years and five months old. A few years ago they said Dale Hawerchuk was the youngest ever to play in an All-Star game. But I was about four months younger than he was, so I think I have that record.

They had all the players at a luncheon the day of the game. I walked in and couldn't believe the guys who were in the room. There was Milt Schmidt and Rocket Richard and Ted Lindsay, Doug Bentley, Bill Durnan. You name it, they were there. I was scared to death.

Hap Day was the Toronto coach. I told him I didn't belong. He said I had to stay. I did, for a little while. But I felt so out of place I sneaked out and took a streetcar home. I ate my lunch at home. Then I got back on the streetcar and went to the Gardens for the game. I thought Day would be mad at me, but he didn't say anything. Maybe he didn't miss me at the lunch.

I played quite a bit in the game and got two penalties. One was for tripping Kenny Reardon. I started the season but they sent me down to Pittsburgh after a few games.

In that game when Barilko scored, a funny thing happened in the last minute of the third period. They had us down by one and they shot the puck into our end. For some reason the Canadiens started to change their players on the fly. The centremen changed. I don't know if it was the players themselves who did it or what. They might have been tired. Instead of forechecking us and trying to keep us in our end, they gave us a lot of room to move the puck out. I think it was Harry Watson who carried it up the ice. We ended up getting a face-off in their end and that's when we tied the game. But if they had been forechecking us we might not have got the chance to do that.

There were no television cameras in Maple Leaf Gardens when the

*Stanley Cup was won in 1951. But there was a photograph taken
the instant Bill Barilko's shot went into the net behind Gerry McNeil,
freezing the moment for all time.*

*In the photo Barilko is falling to the ice. McNeil is in a sitting
position with the puck going over him into the net. Canadiens'
defenceman Tom Johnson has Howie Meeker pinned against the
boards behind the net. Maurice Richard and Butch Bouchard are
other Canadiens in the picture. Harry Watson and Cal Gardner are
the other Maple Leaf players seen. Gardner was in his third season
in Toronto after being traded there from New York. He was the
closest player to Barilko when the Cup-winning goal went into the
net.*

CAL GARDNER

This is hard to believe, but Conn Smythe was going to fine me
$1,000 because I didn't score the goal. Honest to God. The day
after we had won the Cup he called me in and said he wanted me
to see a film he had of the game. He showed me the film and said,
"Now why didn't you put the puck in the net?"

I said that my main thought was that Rocket was just about
eight feet away from me and I thought I had better watch him
rather than go for the puck. When I started to go toward the
Rocket, then Barilko came in and "Boom," it was in the net.

Before we looked at the film he said that he was thinking of
fining me. Then after we looked at it two or three times he
realized my thoughts were right. But there's no doubt about it, he
was upset with me because I hadn't jumped on the opportunity to
score.

But that was Smythe. No nonsense with him. I recall the first
day I was with the Leafs and had to go to his office. When we met
I called him "Conny," like a cocky kid, I guess. Ten minutes later
I was leaving the office and it was, "Yes, Mr. Smythe, no, Mr.
Smythe, that's right, Mr. Smythe." I learned my lesson fast.

I thought that the 1951 final was just an outstanding series. We
were more dedicated then and I guess they had us over a barrel in
those days. If you didn't play well they sent you down to the
minors. They can't do that today. The series was so close and so

competitive and it was line against line. It didn't matter if we were playing in Toronto or Montreal it was the same way, you played against the same line in both places. It was great hockey, every game.

Few if any big-league goaltenders can match Gerry McNeil's initiation to the Stanley Cup playoffs. In his first thirteen post-season games McNeil found himself in overtime eight times. Five of the eight overtimes were in the Montreal-Toronto final in 1951. The last shot in that series eluded little Gerry to become known as the "Barilko goal," one of the most famous in Stanley Cup history. When Bill Barilko lost his life in an airplane crash four months later, the goal became truly legendary.

GERRY MCNEIL

I'm afraid I can't help you much with the Barilko goal. To this day I'm not really sure what happened. I remember him coming in from the blue line and whacking it, but what happened to the puck, I still don't know.

Either I was screened or it touched something. Something went wrong, but I don't know. The picture of the goal shows that I'm down on the ice, sitting down it looks like, but I have no idea how I got there. I seemed to go for it and then it wasn't there. That's why I really couldn't tell you what happened.

Howie Meeker knows whereof he speaks when he analyses hockey games in his colourful and sometimes controversial television style. Howie played on four Cup-winning teams in seven years with the Toronto Maple Leafs. His fourth was in 1951 when he assisted on the Barilko goal.

HOWIE MEEKER

I took part in two of the winning goals in that series. In the second game, in Toronto, we got into overtime and on my first shift I came out over our blue line and the centre opened up and then I got to their blue line and I ran into the Rocket. He took the puck off me and took off. He went around Thomson like you wouldn't believe, cut in front of Mortson, took Broda out, and drilled one home, high into the top corner. Game over, series tied 1–1, and I had to be out there watching him do it.

Then there was the Barilko goal, and I should have scored it. I remember it was our first shift in overtime and we faced off somewhere near centre ice. I made a turn and Gardner gave me the puck and I went in and saw that there was about eighteen inches open at the net, along the ice at the far side. I shot it for there and missed the net, as usual!

I went around behind the net and got the puck and Tom Johnson was following me. I just threw the puck back out in front and as I did Johnson pinned me face first up against the glass. Just as I was trying to get away from him I see the red light go on and hear the big cheer. I never saw the goal go in.

I pulled away from Johnson and said to him, "How do you like that, you big son of a bitch?"

8

The Rocket's Goal

On April 8, 1952, Maurice Richard scored the greatest goal of his career. That's what Richard fans will tell you because it's the one they remember best out of the 626 their hero scored, regular season and playoffs. As for Richard himself, he isn't sure because he doesn't remember too much about it.

If ever Maurice Richard had a season of highs and lows, it was the 1951–52 campaign. It began well enough for him and at the halfway point the Rocket had nineteen goals. A week or two later he began to struggle because of a persistent groin injury. On January 12 he scored three times against Chicago but right after the game the Canadiens announced that Richard would be given some time off because of his injury. The rest of his season turned out to be mainly that – time off.

Early in February Richard tried to play but couldn't. The team sent him to Florida, hoping some sunshine would provide a cure. He didn't play again until March 19, in the final week of the regular season.

Richard may have been an early victim of an injury now fairly common in hockey. In the mid-1980s Al Secord missed most of a season because of the same kind of injury. A few years ago Richard told me he now feels his problem began when he tried out a new pair of skates that weren't right for him. Whatever, in 1951–52 he missed twenty-two games. Even so, he finished with twenty-seven goals. Only four players scored more, including Gordie Howe, who led the league with forty-seven.

Dickie Moore, a future star, made his debut with the Canadiens on December 15 that season. He played thirty-three games and had thirty-three points. Another newcomer who would be a regular for many years was defenceman Dollard St. Laurent, who replaced the retired Glen Harmon.

Those were the days when popular players were given "nights." On March 8 Elmer Lach was honoured before a game at the Forum. Among the gifts wheeled out to centre ice were a car, a rowboat, a dining-room suite, and something not too many people had in 1952, a television set.

The Detroit Red Wings again ran away with the league championship. The Wings total of 100 points left them twenty-two ahead of the second-place Canadiens. Detroit played Toronto in the opening playoff series and swept the Maple Leafs four straight. The other semifinal, between Montreal and Boston, was a different story.

The Canadiens were favoured but needed a come-from-behind overtime win in Boston in the sixth game to stay alive. A journeyman forward, Paul Masnick, jammed the winning goal past Boston goalie Sugar Jim Henry off a Doug Harvey rebound.

Game seven was played at the Forum on April 8. Early in the second period Richard was knocked out in a collision with Bruins forward Leo Labine. He was helped to his feet and steered to the Forum clinic. He was in bad shape and needed stitches to close an ugly cut over his left eye. The medical men felt he was finished for the night.

On the play, Richard had tried to jump between the two Boston defencemen and was off his feet when Labine hit him. One of the defencemen the Rocket was trying to beat on the play was a former teammate, Hal Laycoe.

HAL LAYCOE

I had a bird's eye view of that one. I could have touched the two of them when that collision took place. Rocket was cutting around me and Leo come across and went right behind me. Rocket didn't see him and it was a vicious upending and he hit his head on the ice. I don't think he had ever been upended that violently and it was amazing that he could come back after something like that and score the kind of a goal he did. He was gone after that for most of the game but came back and scored the damn goal that beat us.

I didn't even see the goal because I had got into a scrap with Billy Reay. It was right near the end of the game and Billy hit me over the head, so I hit him over the head. Just clips, you know. So we both had to go to be stitched up, and the dirty buggers, they fixed him first, of course. So he went out, and then I heard the roar, and that was it.

The roar that Hal Laycoe heard as he was being slowly stitched up by the Canadiens' medics came from the collective throats of 15,100 fans in the Forum, fans who would remember the moment for years to come.

Richard, still groggy, had returned to the Canadiens' bench late in the third period when the game was tied 1–1. But when my father asked him, perhaps tentatively, if he was able to play the Rocket nodded that he was okay.

Four minutes remained in the third period when Richard returned to the ice alongside Elmer Lach and Bert Olmstead. He took a pass from Butch Bouchard deep in his own zone, skated the length of the ice, wheeled around defenceman Bill Quackenbush, charged to the front of the Boston goal crease, and shot the puck past Bruins goaltender Sugar Jim Henry. It was at that precise moment Hal Laycoe heard what was surely the loudest cheer ever in the then twenty-eight-year history of the Montreal Forum.

Jim Henry was first called "Sugar" when he was still a toddler in his native Brandon, Manitoba. He was always looking for anything that was sweet to eat. One of the neighbours started calling him "Sugar" and the nickname stuck.

Sugar Jim was a sensation as a nineteen-year-old when he back-stopped the Regina Rangers to the senior championship of Canada in 1941. He turned pro with the New York Rangers the next season. He then spent three years in the Canadian Army and played on another Allan Cup-winning team, the Ottawa Army Commandos. After his wartime service, Henry played eight more NHL seasons with New York, Chicago, and Boston.

Sugar Jim Henry

I have a few memories of things that happened in the Forum. I recall when I first played there with the Rangers, there would only be about 6,000 people in the building. The seats were all dark-coloured. Of course, when I went back there after the war they were all painted different colours and it looked very nice.

I was playing for the Rangers the night Toe Blake broke his leg. Bill Juzda bodychecked him, a good, fair, honest check. Toe even said himself after there was nothing dirty about it. Toe went down on the ice and we all went to him. Toe was saying, "Don't move me. Don't move me." He knew it was broken right then.

Then there were a couple of goals I guess a lot of people remember. I know the Rocket got a big one against me in the seventh game in the 1952 series. Of course, as everyone knows he was one great hockey player. He was a real fiery competitor. He had such a wide shift. When he'd come in on you it would seem he'd have a shift maybe half as wide again as the other players. Them legs of his would go apart. He just seemed to hop from one leg to the other when he made the shift, always so wide. A normal guy, you had half a chance to stop him. With Rocket, you really had to move to try and stop him. He had a pretty good shot, too. He was always shooting, and you know, he never telegraphed it too much. He was a hard guy to figure out, which I guess is why he was the leading goal-scorer at that time. They score more goals today, but the game is much different than it was then.

About that goal he scored that knocked us out that year, he come down the wing and I don't know who it was, I think it was Porky Dumart, he shook him off and someone else and ended up in the corner of the rink. He pulled out in front and cut across the goal and, I don't know, I guess it was just a bang-bang shot right at the crease.

There was a picture taken after that game of me and Rocket shaking hands – him with the blood streaming down his face and me with a black eye. I had got hit in the eye by the puck the game before. . . .

When you ask me about it now, I don't feel too bad about the Rocket scoring like that because he scored on a lot of guys.

The late Terry Sawchuk, one of hockey's greatest goaltenders, was once asked what he remembered most about playing against Maurice Richard. Sawchuk answered, "His eyes. There was always fire in his eyes."

When I interviewed men who played against the Rocket they seemed to have the same memory of how he played the game. They all talked about his competitive spirit and emotion much more than about his physical skills as a player. Hal Laycoe played with and against Richard and saw him at his best more often as an opponent than as a teammate.

HAL LAYCOE

Rocket played with so much emotion. Nobody ever played the game with as much emotion as he had. I think he was the most emotional hockey player who ever played, and he used it as a strength. Bossy finally passed him for the record for playoff goals. But when you consider the number of games Rocket played [133], his record [82 goals] was one of the most unbelievable records in hockey. He could rise to the occasion, and he did it so often.

I never had the good fortune to play with Rocket when he was really going. One of the years I played with him, he only got about twenty goals, and three of those were empty-net goals. Then I went to Boston, it was like he was reborn. Seems I was always playing against players at their greatest and big teams who were dynasties. First there was Toronto. Then Detroit. Then Montreal. Guys like Howe, and Rocket. They were all on top when I played against them.

Hal Laycoe's comments today about Rocket Richard's emotional style of play, which helped him work wonders like that winning goal in 1952, are interesting in light of what eventually happened three years later. That's when Richard and Laycoe would be the main participants in one of the fiercest and most controversial fights in the history of hockey.

The Canadiens were no match for the Detroit Red Wings in the 1952 Stanley Cup finals. The Wings, coming off their sweep of Toronto, also swept Montreal, becoming the first team to win the

Cup in the minimum eight games under that particular playoff format.

The Production Line of Gordie Howe, Ted Lindsay, and Sid Abel was awesome, and so was Detroit goaltender Terry Sawchuk. The Canadiens scored only two goals in the four games. In Detroit's eight playoff games, Sawchuk had four shutouts.

The Canadiens were a battered team. Ken Mosdell had broken his leg in the Boston series. Dollard St. Laurent spent the time between games in hospital because of a skin condition. Defensive specialist Johnny McCormack had a broken arm. And Maurice Richard lacked the emotion he usually displayed in the playoffs. He had spent it all against the Bruins.

In later years Canadiens fans would recall only Richard's big goal when remembering 1952. A few minutes after he had scored it Richard's nerves cracked and he broke into uncontrollable sobs in the Canadiens' dressing room.

Among those witnessing the strange scene was veteran newspaperman Elmer Ferguson. Fergy, who had covered the meeting when the NHL was formed in 1917, looked at the Rocket and said, "That beautiful bastard scored semi-conscious."

When the individual trophies were handed out following the 1952 playoffs the Canadiens had a winner, which was unusual in those days. Between 1947, when Maurice Richard won the Hart Trophy, and 1955, when Doug Harvey won the Norris Trophy, the only time a Montreal player was voted tops in his category was when Bernie Geoffrion was the NHL's rookie of the year, in 1952.

Geoffrion had joined the Canadiens the previous season straight out of the Quebec Junior League where he had been starring for the Montreal Nationales. He would become one of the most colourful, controversial, and best players in the history of the Canadiens. By the time he arrived in the NHL, eighteen-year-old Bernie Geoffrion was already sporting his famous nickname, "Boom Boom."

BERNIE GEOFFRION

When I was young, I'd say about ten or eleven years old, I start to develop a slap shot in the back yard of my school. Just as a joke I start slapping the puck and I saw that thing go pretty hard. I started to use it as a junior. My coach was Sylvio Mantha. He was not too keen about it because he always liked his players to have a wrist shot. So I said to him, "Hey, look, I honestly believe if I practise it I can correct a lot of mistakes with it." So he finally said to me, "If you think you can score goals with it I don't care which way you shoot as long as the puck goes in."

So I kept practising and practising. One day I was practising at the Forum and shooting the puck hard against the boards and it was making a pretty big noise. A newspaper guy, Charlie Boire, asked me if it would be okay if he started calling me "Boom Boom." So I said if nicknames are good for a lot of other guys, why not? Since that day the name stayed.

They brought me up from junior for one game and I got my first goal, against Chuck Rayner. They brought me up for two more games and I scored against Chicago and another one in New York. Then they decided to bring me up to stay. But Mr. Selke and Dick told me that I was only allowed to play eighteen games. If I were to play more than eighteen games I wouldn't be eligible the following year for rookie of the year. That was very, very smart for me. So I played in eighteen games and the following year scored thirty goals and won the rookie award.

After my first eighteen games it didn't matter if you played in the playoffs. That was the year we beat Detroit (1951) and I guess you could say I scored my first important goal in that series. The series was tied 2–2 and we were in Detroit and the game was tied. I shot one from just inside their blue line. I had faked Bob Gold-ham, who went down before I shot the puck. I went around him and didn't hesitate one second and shot the puck past Terry Saw-chuk. I really ripped it. Terry didn't move. We won that game and then the series. That was my first big goal.

9

Elmer's Goal

Some history was made off the ice when the Canadiens opened their 1952–53 season. Television cameras were in the Forum for the first time as Radio Canada beamed the game into the few households that had television sets. Legendary broadcaster René Lecavalier called the play-by-play.

At the other end of the broadcast booth another first took place. Danny Gallivan was making his debut, on radio, as the English voice of the Canadiens, a role he would admirably fill for the next thirty-two years.

So from a broadcasting standpoint October 9, 1952, represented two significant steps forward for viewers and listeners in the Montreal area. The only negative note was the final score. The Chicago Black Hawks defeated the Canadiens 3–2.

Maurice Richard began the season needing six goals to break Nels Stewart's record of 324 in a career. So, picking up right where he left off the previous spring, Richard was again the centre of attention in Montreal.

On October 27 he scored twice in Toronto to equal the record, but the Canadiens lost the game, 7–5, because my father was too stubborn to change goaltenders when he should have.

GERRY MCNEIL

In the first five minutes of the game Ted Kennedy took a shot and the puck hit me right on the cheekbone. I didn't know it at the time, but it was busted.

In those days you didn't have a spare goalie and the home team had to supply one. I think the one in Toronto that night was from a Junior B team. Dick didn't want to use him. We were in the medical room and he asked me if I could see. I told him that I could because I didn't want to be the one to say no.

At the time it was okay, but then the swelling started and my eye kept closing. So we lost the game by a pretty big score. By the time it was over my eye was completely shut.

After the game Dick asked me why I didn't tell him that I couldn't see. Rocket got pretty mad at him then and told him he was the coach and should have been able to tell that I couldn't see. They went at it pretty good. But those things happened once in a while.

By the time the Canadiens played their next game their crusty old coach had finally admitted that McNeil did indeed have a broken cheekbone. Twenty-three-year-old Jacques Plante, the goaltender for the Montreal Royals senior team, replaced McNeil for the next three games and allowed only four goals. Obviously it was an omen of things to come.

If Plante played a fourth game in the NHL he would have had to sign a contract with the Canadiens. Frank Selke didn't want that to happen. That is why another rookie, Hal Murphy, was in goal against Chicago on November 8, which turned out to be another historic night at the Forum.

Richard hadn't scored since the game in Toronto. So the Rocket was still one goal short of a milestone, and so was Elmer Lach, whose career total stood at 199 goals. Early in the second period Lach reached his target with the first of two goals he would get that night. A minute or so later Richard shot the puck toward Chicago goalie Al Rollins. Bert Olmstead was down in front of the crease. The puck disappeared under Olmstead, then under Rollins, and suddenly there it was, rolling over the goal line and into the net.

Olmstead appeared to have touched the puck, which would have made him the goal-scorer. But with referee Red Storey signalling that Richard had scored, and the Forum fans cheering madly because their hero had set an all-time record, there was no way Bert Olmstead, from Sceptre, Saskatchewan, was going to argue that he should get credit for the goal.

BERT OLMSTEAD

I couldn't take that goal. I was afraid to take it because Red Storey had pointed at Rocket so he already had declared who scored the goal. Jimmy McFadden was on the ice for Chicago and when we lined up for the face-off he said to me, "Why didn't you own up to that goal?" I said, "I'd get shot if I did." So that was the end of that.

But I'll tell you a story about that game. I scored three goals that night and only got credit for one. One went in off Dewsbury and they gave it to Lach. I scored that 325th, and I scored another one.

Nobody knows this, but I was first into the dressing room. They had wastebaskets around on the floor, about six of them. They were metal baskets, and I whacked the shit out of every one of them. Then I threw my stick at the clock at the end of the room, and I missed.

Andy O'Brien, the newspaperman, was standing there at the door coming from the medical room. He looked at me and said, "You seem a little upset." I caught myself. I don't know what I said, something like, "Yeah, a little."

I scored three that night and only got credit for one, so I was really upset.

While Bert Olmstead was not pleased with what had transpired that night, everyone else in the Canadiens' dressing room was. After Bert did his number on the wastebaskets, the room turned into a mob scene of well-wishers congratulating Richard and Lach. One was Jean Béliveau, who had been a spectator at the game. Béliveau was asked to pose for pictures with the two heroes, a fact that upset some of the players who weren't asked to pose for pictures.

A month later the Canadiens were missing several players, including Lach, because of injuries. Béliveau was called up from the Quebec Senior League team for three games. In the first he scored three goals against the New York Rangers, and in the third he scored twice in Boston. Fans were clamouring for him to leave Quebec and join the Canadiens. But that wouldn't happen until the following season.

In this day of NHL *teams playing against teams from the Soviet Union the name Aggie Kukulowicz is very familiar. Aggie is a former pro hockey player who is fluent in Russian. For many years he has served as an interpreter, mainly during the games themselves. He is usually stationed in the penalty box, ready to help out should there be a problem between players and officials.*

Aggie was very much involved in a hassle at the Philadelphia Spectrum on a Sunday afternoon in January, 1976, when the Soviet Red Army team left the ice and threatened to go home because of a dispute with the referee. Aggie and Alan Eagleson were the negotiators, although the prospect of losing a fair amount of U.S. dollars likely was the major reason the Soviets agreed to finish the game.

Aggie's NHL *career amounted to only four games with the New York Rangers in the early 1950s. He had been a good junior out of Winnipeg and it was quite a thrill for him to play one of his* NHL *games in the Montreal Forum. It was a night when old pro Elmer Lach took advantage of the inexperienced rookie from the West.*

AGGIE KUKULOWICZ

The Rangers had a bad team and they brought me up from Quebec City because they had a lot of players hurt. It was early in 1953 and I was only nineteen years old.

We played at the Forum on a Saturday night. Two nights before I had scored my first NHL goal in New York. We were playing Chicago and the goalie was Al Rollins. I was so excited I forgot to get the puck but Billy Mosienko got it for me. He was a star with Chicago and was one of our neighbours in Winnipeg. The Hawks beat us 6–4.

In Montreal I had a pretty good night. I hit Rocket Richard a good bodycheck. Camille Henry was on my team in Quebec City and he was listening to the game on the radio. He said the announcer talked about the young rookie standing over the fallen superstar, or something like that.

Late in the game we were leading 4–3, which was a surprise

because in those days the Rangers didn't lead too many games late in the third period. There was a face-off in our end and our coach, Frank Boucher, figured I was having a good game so he sent me out to take it.

I'll never forget looking up at the Canadiens as I got ready. Elmer Lach was the centre, Richard and Bert Olmstead on the wings. On defence there was Tom Johnson and Butch Bouchard. Red Storey was the referee.

Storey was all set to drop the puck when Lach said to me, "Hey kid, your skate lace is undone." I lifted up my stick and looked down at my feet, and that's when Storey dropped the puck. Lach took it, passed to Richard, and it was in our net before you could blink.

Gump Worsley was our goalie and he started yelling at me, "What's the matter with you, you big Polack! Go back to Winnipeg, you dumb son of a bitch!" He was steaming.

Boucher took me off right away. He always wore a fedora tilted back on his head and he had taken it and slammed it on the floor. The guys said they had never seen him do that before. When I got to the bench he yelled, "What the hell were you doing out there!" I told him the truth. He couldn't believe I'd fallen for such an old trick. The game ended 4–4.

You know, I used to wonder if Lach ever pulled that stunt with anyone else when Storey was the referee. Their timing was perfect. Storey dropped the puck right when I looked down at my feet. I know that kind of thing wouldn't happen, but I did wonder about it at the time.

The 1952–53 season followed a predictable pattern. Even though Sid Abel had left Detroit to become playing coach in Chicago, the Red Wings were still the class of the league. They finished first again, fifteen points ahead of the second-place Canadiens.

The Canadiens played in Detroit on the final night of the season. The game meant nothing in the standings, yet there was as much tension in the Olympia as there would have been for a deciding Stanley Cup game. Again, enter the Rocket.

Gordie Howe had by this time become Richard's arch rival. The biggest argument among fans was, "Who's the best? Richard or Howe?" Gordie had the stats on his side and won another scoring championship going away. But the tension was there because of the forty-nine goals he had scored going into the final night of the season. Richard was still the only player to have scored fifty in a single season and he was passionately proud of his record. The press had a field day, especially in Detroit, where they were blatantly hoping Howe would first tie, then break the record, on a night when Richard would be forced to watch him do it.

Now, enter Bert Olmstead and Gerry McNeil.

GERRY MCNEIL

One of the games I remember best of all was the night we went into Detroit on the final night of the season and Howe was going for fifty goals.

He didn't get it and it was quite a thrill for me, one of my biggest. He had a couple of good chances and one of them was kind of a breakaway. He certainly had a good chance at it a couple of times, that's for sure. But I was able to stop him.

It was very important for him to get that fiftieth goal. Bert Olmstead did quite a job on him, checking him all night. But there was a lot of pressure and I felt it. Every time Howe's line would come on it would get very tense. Then every time I saw him go back to the bench I breathed a sigh of relief.

BERT OLMSTEAD

I usually covered Howe and I knew I would get the job that night. So I asked Dick what he wanted me to do. All he told me was, "Go where he goes."

So that's what I did, all night. I think Howe was a little bit disappointed when he saw what I was doing. He'd go back to talk to Sawchuk, so I'd go back with him and there'd be the three of us standing there. They would yell at me, "What are you doing back here?" I wouldn't talk to them. I'd just stand there and I knew I was getting their goat.

Gerry was good that night and made a couple of big saves off him. So we stopped him and I remember when we got back into the dressing room after the game Gerry said, "Well, Rock, he's got to start at one again."

The first major story of the 1953 Stanley Cup playoffs was provided by the Boston Bruins. The Bruins were given no chance to defeat the league champion Red Wings, who had finished twenty-one points ahead of them in the standings. But just as happened in 1951, a third-place team defeated the first-place Red Wings. Detroit lost in six games. Veteran left-winger Woody Dumart was given a big share of the credit for the upset for the job he did shadowing Gordie Howe in the last part of the series.

In Montreal, my father chortled to the press that Howe's failure to reach the fifty-goal mark in the final regular season game had upset the Wings and was one of the reasons they lost to Boston. But he didn't say it until after his team had gone through a very harrowing experience in their semifinal against Chicago.

The Black Hawks led the series three games to two and the sixth game was in Chicago. Dad made several lineup changes, principally in goal with Jacques Plante replacing Gerry McNeil. Eddie Mazur and Lorne Davis were other rookies added to the lineup. My father was sure he would be fired if the Canadiens lost the game, but his team saved his job. Plante shut out the Hawks 3–0 in an impressive Stanley Cup debut, and the Canadiens won the series in game seven in Montreal. They went on to defeat Boston and win the Stanley Cup when Elmer Lach beat Sugar Jim Henry to score his most famous goal, in overtime, in the Cup-clinching game.

One of the strangest career stories during the early fifties was that of Eddie Mazur, a gangling forward out of Winnipeg who was nicknamed "Spider."

Mazur was in the Canadiens' lineup for the Stanley Cup-winning game three straight years, beginning in 1951. In 1953 he started the play leading to Elmer Lach's winning goal in overtime. In those three years Mazur appeared in fourteen playoff games, had four goals and two assists, posed happily in a Canadiens' Stanley Cup team picture, and played in the 1953 All-Star game. Yet up to then, Eddie Mazur had never played in a regular season game in the NHL.

EDDIE MAZUR

I signed a C form with the Canadiens when I was seventeen years old. [That gave Montreal the rights to his professional services.] When I was nineteen I still had a year of junior left but Mr. Selke signed me to a pro contract and I went to Dallas. I played there one year on defence. I had never played defence before. The next year I went to Victoria as a forward and got forty-three goals. That's when they started bringing me up for the playoffs. My first series was the Toronto series. I played in the game when Barilko scored his goal.

The next year I went back to Victoria and then they brought me up again for the playoffs. That was when we were down three games to two against Boston and they had us down 2–1 going into the third period. I had scored our goal and it was my first goal in the NHL.

I remember the speech Dick made in the dressing room. He went around the room from player to player and he talked so long we were late going onto the ice for the third period. Rocket scored to tie it up and we won in overtime when Paul Masnick scored. Then we went back to Montreal and that was the game Rocket scored the goal after he was knocked out. I got another goal in that game.

The next year it was the same thing and I was back again for the playoffs. That's when Elmer scored the winning goal. I remember the play because I carried the puck down the left wing and backhanded it on the net. It went in behind and then Milt Schmidt tried to shoot it out and it went to Elmer and he scored. I didn't get an assist on it but I remember Dick thought I should have. That's when Rocket jumped on Elmer and broke his nose. I was standing right there.

I played fairly regularly the next two seasons until I hurt my knee. One of the things I remember best was the way we would practise. Dick had a system where he wanted us to headman the puck, always keep it moving. He had a horn and if anyone took more than two strides and didn't pass the puck he'd blow the horn and everybody had to stop. And that's how you learned. He'd start that kind of practice at training camp and then do it once or twice a week during the year. He'd just browbeat the system into your head. It was incredible.

And the practices would get rough. If a guy was in a slump the other guys would lean on him to try and motivate him, and when we'd scrimmage, geez, it would get so rough. I remember many times Dick would have to call off the scrimmage because it was almost getting out of hand.

When we'd be in a slump there would be a lot of skating drills. We'd do figure eights at top speed, around and around, and you know who was always leading? The Rocket. He never liked to be trailing the other guys in skating drills.

I learned a lot of things early. In those days we had to take cabs everywhere we went in the cities on the road and there would be one guy who was the cab captain. Everybody belonged to a group with a captain and in my first year Elmer Lach was mine. We had to be ready when he was or else you could get left behind. He left me behind twice, once at a train station and once at a rink. If you weren't there when Elmer was ready, he would just leave without you.

When I was in junior high school I was the sports editor of our school paper. I was a Canadiens fan and I wrote once how great it would be to play on a line with Elmer Lach and Maurice Richard. And four or five years later, I did. And I was on the ice with the two of them when we scored a Stanley Cup-winning goal. Imagine that. Incredible.

The 1953 Stanley Cup final brought the Montreal Canadiens and the Boston Bruins together in the playoffs for the second straight year. By 1958 the teams had been playoff opponents six times in seven years. The Canadiens won every time.

Boston sports writer Leo Monohan began covering the Bruins during that period. A feisty, popular little Irishman, Monohan has some vivid memories of his first road trip to Montreal.

LEO MONOHAN

1953 was the first year I travelled with the Bruins in the playoffs. In the first round, Boston put out Detroit in a big upset. Detroit won the first game 7–0 but the Bruins won the series. Woody Dumart and Joe Klukay did a great job checking Howe and Lindsay.

Sugar Jim Henry was the Boston goalie and they brought up Gordon "Red" Henry, from Hershey, as the backup. The first two games were in Montreal. Those were my drinkin' years and the night before a game I was out on the town with Hammie Moore, the trainer of the Bruins. We were in a joint called the Scandinavian Club, no doubt well the worse for wear, and it's about three o'clock in the mornin' and who do we see but Gordon "Red" Henry. So we had a few drinks with him. That same night Sugar Jim gets hurt. So they had to bring in Red Henry. I said to myself, "Not long ago this guy was in bad shape, so it doesn't look too good for us."

I can remember the warmup. They let goalies warm up when they came into a game then, and as they were warmin' him up he went out to stop a shot and he slid right on his ass. I said, "That's it." And it was.

Another thing I remember was that at the end of the Detroit series Milt Schmidt sat on his skate. That was before they had the little plastic protector thing on the back end of the skates, and he had a very deep cut on his backside. It was so bad he couldn't play against the Canadiens in the first game of the series. Milt said it was the worst injury he ever had in hockey because he had to take treatment for it pretty well all the next summer.

Anyway, Milt was tryin' to practise at the Forum before the first game and he pulled the stitches out. The blood was all over his hockey pants and his stockings, and of course he was the key player for the Bruins. So he went to the dressing room and he was lyin' face down on the trainer's table gettin' sewn up again, and there are about twenty of us standin' there lookin' at Milt Schmidt's bare ass.

A couple of players had been stitched up for cuts in their face. They were there and one of them was Hal Laycoe. Laycoe and Fleming Mackell never got along. Mackell came by and said, "Take a look at that, you guys. The doctor did a better job on Milt's ass than he did on your faces."

Sugar Jim Henry was back in goal for Boston for what turned out to be the Cup-clinching fifth game of the 1953 finals. Henry was hurting that night – for the second straight year he was the victim of a dramatic playoff goal scored by a legendary Canadiens player in a game at the Montreal Forum.

SUGAR JIM HENRY

I twisted an ankle in that series and they had to put Red Henry in goal. I was still on the bench in the clinic getting attention and the first thing you know the door opened and they brought Red in. He'd got a cut on his arm. So I had to get off the bench so they could stitch him up and let him play. My ankle was too bad and I couldn't play.

I played when we went back to Montreal for the fifth game. Hal Laycoe arranged for some fellow that he knew in Montreal to bandage up my ankle so that I could play that night.

That's when Elmer scored. It was a 1-0 game. I remember the goal. The puck went in behind the net and Schmidt was intending to throw it up to Dumart. Elmer intercepted it and shot it and it went in on the right-hand side. It hit the post, bang, and it went in.

When you're a goaltender at a time like that you feel terrible. The game is in overtime, and it's all over, and you realize it right away.

I had my share of highs and lows. That was a low. The biggest thrill I ever had in hockey was when we won the Allan Cup with the Regina Rangers in 1941. There's nothing that can touch it when something happens like that. And I still think it's the best game in the world.

When the overtime began in the fifth game Elmer Lach and Milt Schmidt were the starting centremen, poised head-to-head for the drop of the puck, as they had done for so many years. In an era of outstanding centre-ice players, Lach and Schmidt were among the best, but in 1953 their great careers were winding down. Each would play just one more complete season. Between them they accounted for nine All-Star team selections. They both were Hart Trophy winners and scoring champions.

During their playing days when they were bitter rivals on the ice, Elmer Lach and Milt Schmidt were the best of friends and often shared off-season holidays with their families. As I talked with them about Elmer's Cup-winning overtime goal, thirty-seven years after the fact, I found Milt still happy for his friend Elmer, and Elmer still feeling sorry for his friend Milt.

ELMER LACH

I guess I've seen that goal a lot of times, as they say.

That was a hell of a game that night . . . a hell of a game. I think I still have the film of it. The winning goal was kind of simple, I guess. It was one of those plays that happens so fast you just do it, without thinking too much about it. You don't take the time to think.

Poor old Milt. I always see him sitting on the ice when I look at the film. Rocket and him chased the puck around behind their net. Milt got it and dumped it out and it hit my stick. I just turned around and let it go. I was as surprised as anyone in the place when it went in the net.

Rocket jumped on me right away. He broke my nose when he jumped on me. But I can tell you that was a great series . . . a hell of a series.

MILT SCHMIDT

I remember it like it happened yesterday.

I was trying to get the puck out of our zone. I passed to Woody Dumart, just out of his reach. It landed right on Elmer's stick. He spun around to shoot the puck and I sprawled in front of him to block it. It found its way underneath me and under a few others and ended up in the net behind our goalie, Sugar Jim Henry.

I watched Elmer and the Rocket jump up and start hugging each other. There was me with a forlorn look on my face, like I'd just lost my house, my family, everything. But at that moment, losing the Stanley Cup seemed just as bad.

The next year I was in Montreal having a few beers in the Press Club at the Mount Royal Hotel. There was a big picture of the play hanging behind the bar. Elmer and the Rocket were jumping up in the air and I was sitting on the ice. I told the bartender, "If that thing is still there next year I'll throw a bottle of beer at it."

I never went back there so it likely hung in the same place for a few more years.

Then a few years later someone made a jigsaw puzzle out of the picture and sent one to me. I threw it in the fireplace as soon as I opened it. Maybe I should have kept it. Might be worth a lot of money today!

Elmer got that goal and I always had a lot of respect for him as a player. We became good friends even though we didn't play against each other that way. Maurice got most of the credit for the Punch Line but Elmer was the top guy as far as I was concerned. He knew when to pass to Rocket and when not to pass to him.

He was chippy. But if you minded your own business it was usually a case of ability against ability. But if you gave him a shot, you knew you would get one back.

And he was always needling you. Always yapping. There was a big fat guy who used to sit along the boards by the Canadiens' bench and he was always yelling at me and giving me a bad time. I was bitching about him to Elmer one night on a face-off and Elmer told me to go over to him and tell him to "mange le merde." I had no idea what that meant, but I went over and said it. The guy jumped up and took a swing at me and almost hit me. I went back to face off and Elmer was laughing. When I asked him what that was all about he told me I had just told the guy to "Go eat shit" or something like that. I was all upset and not concentrating when they dropped the puck and the next thing I knew Elmer nailed me with an elbow right on the kisser.

Today, players aren't educated how to take a good hit or a good bodycheck. They always want to retaliate right away. In our day, when you got hit, you'd wait to get even, sometime. I probably got even with Elmer for that one, somewhere down the road.

10

Leswick's Goal

During their training camp in the fall of 1953 the Canadiens played an exhibition game in Valleyfield against the Quebec Senior League team coached by Toe Blake. Maurice Richard was nursing a slight injury and left the game halfway through the second period. He changed into civvies and, with all the seats filled, started watching what was left of the game from the standing-room section.

A few fans started giving the Rocket a rough time, accusing him of bailing out of the game. Naturally, he had been the big attraction for ticket buyers. The hassling got quite intense. Words led to push, then to shove, then to punch, and Richard was in the middle of a brawl.

The Rocket was never shy about taking care of himself, and before the gendarmes arrived he had belted his main tormentor in the eye, knocking him down the stairs and into dream street.

A few days later I was with my father at a Montreal Royals baseball game. Toe Blake was there and he sat with us. Dad asked Toe if the guy the Rocket had punched out was thinking of suing him.

"Suing?" replied Blake. "He's walking around showing off his shiner and telling everyone, 'Look what the Rocket did to me.' He's the most popular guy in town and loving every minute of it."

The Canadiens were Stanley Cup champions, yet the news out of their camp was dominated by a player who had not been on the team the previous season. Jean Béliveau had attended training camps in the past, but this time there seemed to be a pretty good chance he would finally agree to play with Montreal.

To give the situation a modern-day perspective, think of Wayne Gretzky or Mario Lemieux not joining an NHL team when eligible but instead playing for a senior hockey team in a league that played its games in the building that housed the NHL team holding the rights to his professional services. That's where Béliveau was after he graduated out of junior hockey in Quebec City. He stayed there, playing for the Aces in the Quebec Senior League, likely making more money than the Canadiens were first prepared to offer him.

When the Quebec team would play the Montreal Royals at the Forum, especially on a Sunday afternoon, hundreds of fans would be turned away at the door. Camil DesRoches would get on a loudspeaker and announce that "No more tickets are available. Please go home."

Béliveau had shared stardom in junior hockey with other high-profile Quebec-based youngsters such as Dickie Moore and Bernie Geoffrion. They had become regulars on a Stanley Cup championship team while Béliveau was still playing senior hockey and keeping Habs fans in suspense as to when, or if, he would finally join their team. After all, things couldn't have been much better for him in Montreal than they were in Quebec City. When he was a nineteen-year-old junior star the fans had given him a new Nash automobile. The publicity in Quebec City surrounding his marriage to Elise Couture on June 27, 1953, was a forerunner to the Gretzky-Jones wedding in Edmonton in 1988. Well, sort of.

While the Canadiens were winning the Stanley Cup in 1953 the Quebec Aces, coached by Punch Imlach and starring the best player outside the NHL, had won the senior championship of Canada. Béliveau was the scoring champion in each of his two years in the Senior League. But by the time he had to make his decision, again, about where he would play hockey there was some speculation that perhaps he didn't want to play in the NHL. Maybe the big guy didn't think he was up to the challenge that had been successfully met by his former junior rivals Moore and Geoffrion.

When Béliveau finally signed with the Canadiens, on the morning of the 1953 All-Star game that was to be played at the Forum, Frank Selke told the press that he "just opened up the vault and told

Jean to take what he liked." The rumour at the time was that Jean liked about $25,000 per year, which made him the highest-paid player on the Canadiens. Certainly it was the most money ever paid a rookie in the NHL. But even Mr. Selke had expressed a few doubts along the way as the negotiations had continued.

By this time Ken Reardon was firmly ensconced in the Canadiens' front office. He had taken a job there after his retirement in 1950.

KEN REARDON

An interesting thing about Jean Béliveau coming to the Canadiens was Frank Selke's juggling of the situation. When we were trying to sign him Selke said to me, "You know, Kenny, I think the big guy wants to play but he thinks in his own mind he's not good enough. He's a star in Quebec and I think he's afraid to try it with us."

That's when we could bring up players from the Senior Group for a three-game trial. So Selke picked three games on a weekend with two pretty weak teams and Béliveau got five goals in the three games. That made up Béliveau's mind that he was good enough to play.

We finally signed him for the next season. It was on a Saturday morning in Selke's office and I was there. Selke had an adviser with him, Brigadier Jimmy DeLalanne, because Béliveau brought his brother-in-law as an adviser. We played against the All-Stars that night and he was in uniform.

Béliveau had been at the training camp but because of all the negotiations that were going on, Dick had taken it easy on him. He had been married in the off-season and he showed up at camp a lot overweight. But once he signed he went through quite a routine to get in shape as quick as possible. Dick was pretty tough on him but Béliveau never complained and I know Dick was impressed, the way he worked to lose the weight.

JEAN BÉLIVEAU

See that picture on the wall? That's the junior team I played with in Victoriaville when I was seventeen. I had been playing hockey in school before that. They had the junior team there only one year so I had the chance to play in Montreal and Quebec City, where people could see me. I often wonder what would have happened if the team had been in Victoriaville for just one year before then, when I was under-age, or later when maybe I would have been too old. Maybe by then I might have lost interest. I think about that often when I see that picture.

When I signed my contract with Canadiens my brother-in-law came with me and he was involved strictly on account of taxes. The amount was negotiated by me and Mr. Selke.

I was very happy to finally sign because it had been going on for about three years. I could have joined the Canadiens, I believe, in my last year as a junior. But the circumstances were a little special. I used to come to training camp with the Canadiens because they were starting earlier. Every time I was leaving Quebec City they used to tell me, "Whatever they are offering in Montreal, same here."

You know me, I'm a very loyal person to those who are right with me, straight with me. People are very important in my life. I ended up playing four years in Quebec City, and I have no regrets.

Big Jean's rookie season was far from memorable. He opened the season centring Maurice Richard and Bert Olmstead and scored two goals in his third game, against the New York Rangers. In his sixth game, in Chicago, Béliveau cracked a bone in his ankle and didn't play again until December 10. In his second game back after the ankle injury, he suffered a broken cheekbone. In all, he missed twenty-six games.

The injuries, added to the problems trying to break into the NHL with some of the league's toughest checkers going out of their way to give a rough welcome to the high-priced rookie, made for a miserable season. Along the way my father got into a small dispute with Jean's former coach in Quebec, Punch Imlach. Imlach was at a game in Toronto when Béliveau had a bad night. Afterwards he told a newspaperman that Irvin wasn't coaching him the right way.

Dickie Moore played only thirteen games because of a knee injury and scored just one goal. Then in the playoffs Moore led all scorers with five goals and eight assists.

The youngsters weren't the only ones getting hurt. Elmer Lach, in what would be the last of his fourteen seasons with the Canadiens, missed twenty-two games because of a broken ankle.

The final standings had a familiar look as the Detroit Red Wings again finished in first place. Yet despite the long absences of a couple of key young players, the Canadiens finished a strong second with eighty-one points, seven back of Detroit. Maurice Richard had a fine season and led the league with thirty-seven goals. He finished second in the scoring race to his Detroit nemesis, Gordie Howe.

Béliveau arrived on the scene at the height of the intense Montreal-Detroit rivalry. The two teams were the class of the league and they proved it every time they played each other. While my father wouldn't dare publicly praise anything to do with the Detroit organization, privately he admired many of their players. One was defenceman Marcel Pronovost, a Quebecer who played in the NHL for twenty seasons. Pronovost was on three Stanley Cup winners in Detroit and another in Toronto as a member of Punch Imlach's "Over the Hill Gang" that defeated the Canadiens in the finals in 1967.

My father once told me that one of the greatest goals he ever saw was scored by Pronovost, against the Canadiens, in a game at the Detroit Olympia.

MARCEL PRONOVOST

I know the one he meant. I got two that night in Detroit. We beat them 3–2. I carried the puck out of our end and when I got to their blue line I went inside-outside on Doug Harvey. He went for the deke. That put me in alone and I shot it upstairs, under the crossbar. It was the winning goal. You ask if I remember it. There are a few like that you can't ever forget.

The Canadiens were our biggest rivals. We'd play them twice on a weekend and it was a 120-minute game for four points. In the second game you'd pick up right where you left off in the first. The intensity was unbelievable.

You'd walk into the Forum or the Olympia those nights and there was electricity in the air. Imagine me, a French Canadian, playing at the Forum against Rocket, Béliveau, and Geoffrion. For me, it was really something.

The games were tough but they weren't all that dirty. If you got hit it was mostly with a clean check. Both teams had great power plays and you couldn't afford to take too many penalties, and the guys knew that. If you did get a dirty one you waited to pay it back. Don't forget, we played each other fourteen times.

To me, the greatest competitors were Ted Lindsay and the Rocket. People today don't realize the intensity with which those guys played the game. They wanted to win. That's all it was to them, all they thought about. You don't see that today.

Gordie didn't play the game the way Rocket did. The Rocket had the ability to lift 16,000 people out of their seats. I had pretty good luck against him. Whenever we played Montreal they always put me on left defence so I would be on the same side of the ice Richard was on. I had good speed so he didn't go around me too often to the outside. But he never stopped trying. He would try everything to get by me. Under me. Over me. Right through me. He just never stopped trying.

I used to frustrate him, I guess. If we ever were on the street near the rink at the same time he would cross to the other side so he wouldn't have to talk to me. He took a lot of punishment. He had five guys after his skin every time he was on the ice. They had a lot of good players, but you always thought of the Rocket before anyone else.

If there is a player today who comes close to the old style of intensity and competitiveness, it's Gretzky. Consistency proves greatness. I give him credit for being the best, year after year. He would have been a big star in our day.

The height of the Montreal-Detroit rivalry in the 1950s coincided with the height of the rivalry between the game's premiere right-wingers, Gordie Howe and Maurice Richard. Theirs were usually the only names mentioned when fans argued about who was hockey's best player. Today it's Wayne and Mario. Then it was Gordie and the Rocket.

At the same time there was no argument as to who was the best left-winger in hockey. Beginning in 1948 Detroit's Ted Lindsay was the first-team All-Star left-wing selection eight times in ten years.

Every bit as intense a competitor as Richard, "Terrible Ted" was just that, terrible in the eyes of non-Red Wing fans. They hated his cocky, aggressive, combative style of play. To make things worse for the Lindsay-haters, Ted was also a very skilled player who once won the scoring championship. Opposing players weren't too thrilled with him either, including the Rocket.

GORDIE HOWE

When we used to face the Canadiens the first name that always came to mind was Richard.

I respected him but I didn't like him.

When I broke Rocket's record for all-time points in a career it wasn't a big deal. It should have been.

He was the man who led the way for the rest of us. Without a pacemaker there's nothing to shoot for. He was my pacemaker, first for career points, then for career goals.

Like I tell all of the kids, if you really want to learn the game of hockey, pick somebody you admire and emulate him.

I picked the Rocket and he showed me a lot.

MAURICE RICHARD

I was never the best player in the league. I knew that.

I was a bad skater, but I worked hard. I think there were a lot of guys who played in the NHL who could have played better than me. But I had more drive from the blue line in. That's what gave me the chance to score more goals than they did.

Detroit was our big rival, there's no doubt about that. I remember I used to meet their players in the aisleway of the train. We'd pass by each other and I wouldn't say hello to anybody.

I didn't hate too many players, except the guy who played with Gordie Howe. Number 7. Ted Lindsay.

TED LINDSAY

I hated 'em all.

I respected Maurice Richard's ability. From the blue line in he's

107

still the greatest hockey player I've ever seen in my life. There never has been anybody like him from the blue line in.

It was always close when we played in the playoffs. Toronto was good then, too. You had three very good hockey teams. But we had good defensive players, especially the line of Glen Skov, Marty Pavelich, and Tony Leswick. Pavelich was great. Maybe Bob Gainey has been the only player lately that I've seen who was like him. They were worth a half a goal a game to us. They took on the best lines, and when they held them scoreless that was like scoring a goal. Pavelich could play defensive hockey as good as anybody.

And we had the goaltending from Terry Sawchuk. When he weighed 205 and first came up you could say he was the best. Maybe the best ever. But then he lost weight and went down to 160 or something and never was as good after that. At least I didn't think he was.

Doug Harvey was the greatest defenceman I've ever seen, and that includes Bobby Orr or anybody else. The only place Orr beat him was on his skating. When you look at the talent he had, how he could control the speed of a game, any way he wanted, he was a real general out there.

It's tough to pick out a game or an incident now. So many years have gone by. I recall that all you ever worried about was the next goal. We always knew that whenever we came into Montreal we had to play well. Start off half asleep and you'd get blown out. You had to be on your mark and ready to go as soon as that puck was dropped.

I guess any of us who played then remember the train trips when both teams would travel from Montreal to Detroit and get there at 2:30 in the afternoon. Even on the train the rivalry was there. No fights, but there were times it wasn't too far away from that.

Nobody remembers, but after we beat them in the finals the second straight year Jack Adams traded seven players away from that championship team. That's when Montreal started their streak of five in a row.

Now I see Rocket at old-timers' games and charity things. It's amazing how our temperaments and personalities have changed.

Who'd ever have thought that Howe and Lindsay would be on the ice with Rocket under those beautiful and friendly circumstances. But it's wonderful.

I try not to live in the past. I still see a lot of games at the Joe Louis Arena. But when you ask me about the games we had with the Canadiens back then, I say there was never hockey like that before, and there hasn't been since. There'll never be hockey like that again.

The only thing remembered about the 1954 playoffs is the final shot on goal, the one taken by Tony Leswick of the Detroit Red Wings that won the Stanley Cup for his team – the "fluke" Stanley Cup win, as Montreal fans called it.

Montreal and Detroit disposed of their first-round opponents quickly. While the Red Wings eliminated Toronto in five games, the Canadiens swept the Boston Bruins.

In the finals the first two games, in Detroit, were split. The Wings then won the next two in Montreal and it appeared only the formalities would be needed for them to win the Cup in the fifth game at the Olympia. But the Canadiens made some changes, principally in goal with Gerry McNeil taking over from Jacques Plante. McNeil was brilliant and the Canadiens won 1–0 on an overtime goal by Ken Mosdell.

Back in Montreal the Canadiens won again, 4–1. So it was show-down time at the Olympia three nights later, Good Friday. It couldn't have been any closer, with the game tied 1–1 at the end of regulation time. The Canadiens had been the better team on the night, but Sawchuk had been magnificent. The two best teams in hockey were down to deciding the Stanley Cup in overtime.

Tony Leswick was a thirty-one-year-old defensive forward who played six seasons for the New York Rangers before being traded to Detroit in 1951. In 1953–54 he scored only six goals in seventy regular-season games and had scored twice in the playoffs when the teams faced off in the most dramatic overtime situation in hockey. Leswick was an unlikely hero.

Tony Leswick

When I played against Rocket Richard I wasn't crazy about him, but I respected him. He was probably one of the greatest hockey players of all time then. At least that's my opinion, and I was forced to check him and Gordie Howe. I checked Howe when I played for the Rangers.

One thing I could do was skate and I was pretty strong on my feet. Make sure you say in your book that I came second once in a fast-skating contest. We went to Montreal and all the teams had a guy in it. You had to carry the puck around the rink and they timed you. I finished second to Billy Mosienko. He beat me by about a minute and a half. (laughs) No, not really, it was a couple of seconds.

Anyway, when it came to checking the Rocket I could keep up with him and I guess I did needle him a lot. I remember one night in a Stanley Cup playoff game I thought I was checking him pretty good, but he got a goal on me. We used to use what you might call coarse language, but I said something like, "You're lucky you got that goal." And he said to me, and I've always remembered it, he said, "Tony, I'd rather be lucky than good."

I used to say things to him in French, like "comment ça va" and "tres bien" and I'd say to him, "Why don't you learn to speak English." Stuff like that. . . .

The overtime goal? Well, there was a line change and I came over the boards and the puck came right to me. Apparently, so they say, because at times like that you don't always realize what happened, the puck went off Harvey's shoulder, or arm, into the net. I just let it go toward the net. Of course, nobody says anything about my bullet shot. (laughs) Harvey told me after he could read the label on the puck as it was coming at him.

Eddie Mazur

The crazy thing about it was that Leswick was calling him "Richard" all night, using the English way to say it. He'd be saying, "Hey, Richard, you're not going to score tonight." Then in the overtime Leswick was off his wing, on my side, and Rocket was coming across the ice to hit him, so Leswick flipped the puck into our end. Doug Harvey, God rest his soul, who played Double A baseball and likely could have played in the majors, Doug went to catch it and he missed it. He didn't get it right in the palm of his glove and it hit the side of his glove. Gerry McNeil could have had the shot. Gerry had it all lined up. It would have been a simple catch for him. He'll tell you that.

GERRY MCNEIL

Detroit was our big rival, no doubt about that. After a game with them in Montreal you'd go to the Westmount Station because both teams would be catching the same train and, God, you could hardly look at one another. I've seen the police there. And on the train, the conductor would tell you what time you could go to the club car so both teams wouldn't be there together.

There were always good games, especially in the playoffs. It seemed that no matter what happened in the final standings, we'd always be on an even keel with them in the playoffs.

You call that overtime goal the Leswick goal. I call it the Harvey goal. It was a real bad one. It was just a flip. He was near centre ice, over by the boards, and he just flipped it to go and change lines. Doug thought he'd grab it and go with it. He tried to play it with his hand, just kind of push it in front of his stick or something. Sometimes those pucks, they'll drop, just like in base-ball. He seemed very sure, and I was sure, too. But it hit some-where on the side of his hand and he hit it right into the corner of the net.

I saw it all the way. So it was a real simple goal, I'll tell you. Especially for the seventh game, in overtime. Boy, it was a long skate back to the other end of the rink because our dressing room was there. There's no way you can express how you feel at a time like that when you're a goalie. It's like the end of the world. I'll always remember that long skate to the other end. That was the last playoff game I was in.

After I retired I would be interviewed on the "Hot Stove

League" or somewhere and, especially at playoff time, every year they'd bring up the Barilko goal and the Leswick goal. And it seemed every person on the street would ask, when the playoffs would come. I can't get away from it.

11

The Rocket's Riot

The Leswick goal came in the final game in the career of Elmer Lach, one of the rookies from the West who had arrived on the Canadiens scene in 1940 to play a major role in lifting the franchise from the bottom to the top. Lach retired at the age of thirty-six. Another era had ended at the Forum.

ELMER LACH

I thought of quitting after I played in the All-Star game that year but Conn Smythe talked me out of it. When I told him he said, "Christ, what do you want to quit for. You can't make any money any easier than you're doing now." That's when he reminded me I still owed him $500 from when I tried out for the Leafs.

So I played that year and Selke wanted me to play the following year on a part-time basis. But I said no because I didn't think I could do that.

I broke my leg my last season. I broke it in Chicago and then played the next game in Toronto. They couldn't find anything then but the break finally showed up. Funny thing when you look at it. Rocket broke his leg. Toe broke his leg his last season. Henri Richard broke his leg the year he quit.

I was prepared to quit. Don't forget, I was working then, too, and I was making more money working than I was playing hockey.

I liked hockey. It was good to me and I think I was good to it, too. I tried to put as much back as I could. I coached a bit after but I didn't stay with it too long because the people changed.

You know, after I quit I finally found out what it was Dick was trying to do with me and for me all those years he coached me. I didn't understand it at the time but I learned a lot about myself after I quit playing.

You only get out of hockey what you put into it. I watch today and see all the mistakes. If we had played that way, we'd have been on the ice the next morning doing things over and over and over, until we got it right. I turn the games on and can watch about ten or fifteen minutes. That's all.

In the first season that Elmer Lach wasn't alongside him, Maurice Richard knew the best of times, and the worst. It is one of the most memorable in the Rocket's career, for all the wrong reasons.

Richard had never won a scoring championship. In those days that title was the personal possession of his hated rival, Gordie Howe. But with three games remaining in the season Richard was in first place, fifteen points ahead of Howe. His nearest pursuer was teammate Bernie Geoffrion. Richard's pursuit of an important personal accomplishment sparked as much attention as did the race to the wire for first place in the standings, which, naturally, involved the Canadiens and the Detroit Red Wings.

Richard's season had not been without incident. Just after Christmas the Canadiens played in Toronto and Richard received quite an ovation from the fans at Maple Leaf Gardens when he scored career goal 401 early in the game. But with a few minutes remaining in the third period he became embroiled in a violent fight with Toronto forward Bob Bailey. When it was over Richard had received a major and two misconduct penalties. The incident would come back to haunt the Rocket before the season was over.

The referee that night in Toronto was Red Storey.

RED STOREY

You might not like hearing this but your dad, Dick, he was responsible for that one. Every time we'd get the Rocket straightened out he'd go over to the bench and Dick would give him another stick. When we saw the replay he'd had five different sticks before it was over.

What Rocket was mad about was not the fact that anybody hit him. He was mad because Bailey tried to gouge his eyes out. That's what it was all about because that's what Bailey was trying to do instead of fighting. Rocket just went berserk. That's when he took his glove off and slapped my linesman, George Hayes, with his glove. Fortunately it was George and me. Somebody else likely would have turned him in with a lot stiffer report.

That was a terrible evening but when I found out what happened, that Bailey had kept going after his eyes, I likely would have tried to kill him, too.

You know, people talk to me about the Rocket and how hard he must have been to handle. For me, he was the easiest on the team to handle. All he wanted to do was score goals. He wasn't hunting for trouble any night. But I'll tell you, when trouble started, he finished it.

With four games remaining in their season the Canadiens led the Red Wings by two points, but Detroit was on a roll. Since losing in Montreal on February 17 the Wings were unbeaten in nine games, with seven wins and two ties.

The Canadiens played their sixty-seventh game in Boston, Sunday, March 13. Late in the third period, with the Bruins leading 4–2, Richard and Boston defenceman Hal Laycoe got into a fight that would become one of the most famous in hockey history.

Fleming Mackell, the Montrealer who started his NHL career in Toronto, was playing for the Bruins. Mackell was on the ice when the fight broke out.

FLEMING MACKELL

Rocket was in pain because he had hurt his back the night before in Montreal. He came down the ice and he high-sticked Laycoe at the blue line. In fact, he cut Laycoe.

Laycoe hit him back. He dropped his stick on Richard's head. In fact, he gave him a good cuff with his stick. To my mind he must have hit what we call a "bleeder" because blood started on the side of Rocket's head. They were just scuffling around. Then the blood proceeded to come right into his eyes. Then the Rocket, when he saw the blood, I thought went a little bit loco.

They started swinging sticks at this point, and they were swinging sticks at each other . . . at the head . . . off the shoulder . . . two-handers, which was frightening.

The linesmen jumped in. One linesman grabbed the Rocket and held him down. It was Cliff Thompson. He had the Rocket down and I thought the incident was pretty much over. It was a severe incident but nothing too grave at that time.

Then, to my recollection, Doug Harvey appeared and he was scuffling with somebody, I think it was Fernie Flaman. Then he grabbed the linesman and pulled him away from Rocket. The Rocket got free again. He had no stick then, but he grabbed another stick. Then he went at Laycoe again with the stick.

Laycoe didn't have a stick. He was trying to protect himself with his gloves and his arms. I tried to give him my stick but he wouldn't take it. That probably was the smartest thing because either one of them might have been maimed for life. . . . That could have happened.

Rocket got suspended for hitting the linesman, although from where I was I never saw that happen. But Rocket had lost control.

Here's the strangest thing. There were 13,900 people in the Boston Garden. You couldn't hear a sound. You could have heard a pin drop, everything was so quiet. In fact, when the incident was completely finished a lot of people, over half the crowd probably, got up and left the building. It was very frightening. The fans were scared when Rocket went after Laycoe with the stick. That's the only time I ever saw fans act like that.

HAL LAYCOE

It was unfortunate, really, what happened. There were no ill feelings between Rocket and me. Hell, we used to play tennis together in the summertime.

He hit me in the face and I clipped him over the head, and then all hell broke loose. We were leading 4-2 and they had pulled the goalie. I took the face-off and I won the draw from Béliveau. It was outside our blue line and I was just going to throw a backhand down the ice. Then Rocket barged in on the right of me and pitchforked me in the face. I let the puck go and I dinged him as he went by. Then it went beyond all reason. There's never been an incident like it. Fortunately I didn't get hurt, but I don't know why. He broke numerous sticks over me.

I think that what the people don't realize, even to this day, is that the guy who really caused it to be what it was was my buddy Doug Harvey. [Linesman] Cliff Thompson had pinned Rocket, he was sitting right on him. Then Doug knocked Thompson off Rocket. Rocket got up off the ice quicker than Thompson and he nailed him, nailed him with a couple of dandies.

Another real sad thing in that incident was that Jacques Beauchamp [of *Montréal Matin*] was at the game, and another writer there was Vince Lunny [*Montreal Star*]. They went back together to Montreal and agreed on their story. Then Jacques didn't write the true story of what happened in Boston, but Vince Lunny did. Jacques was a real contributor to the problems that followed. He riled the French-speaking people with what he wrote. If he had written what Vince Lunny did, I don't think there would have been a problem. They wouldn't have had the riot or the aftermath. There wasn't a thing on film. If any of that had been shown there wouldn't have been a thing to follow up.

Richard was headed for trouble because he had slugged linesman Cliff Thompson, a fact he has never denied. He was mad because Thompson kept grabbing him from behind, "jumping" on him as Richard would describe it. He called Thompson a "homer," figuring he was trying to help Laycoe win the fight.

A hearing was held in the Montreal office of NHL president Clarence Campbell on March 16, three days following the fight. But on the day after the events in Boston, another meeting took place that had a lot to do with Campbell's shocking decision to suspend Richard for the final three games of the season, plus the playoffs. That meeting, held in New York, involved the owners and governors of the NHL.

When Campbell convened the Richard hearing the Rocket was

*accompanied by my father and Ken Reardon, Laycoe was present,
as were Boston general manager Lynn Patrick and the game officials.*

KEN REARDON

That Richard hearing, that's a long story, my friend. There was
Dick and me and Rocket there. Laycoe from Boston and other
people from that team. The officials, and Carl Voss, the referee-
in-chief. That was in the days before there was very much TV
coverage, but the hallways were jammed with guys when we got
there. We had to shoulder our way into Campbell's office, and it
was the same thing when we left.

I can remember two and a half hours when I never moved in my
chair. I got to talk for about an hour, trying to defend Rocket.
When I came out of there my shirt was soaking wet through. My
suit coat was wet, too.

I can tell you this. I knew before we went in that he was gone.
Selke phoned me and told me to go. He thought there was no use
for him to go. There had been an owners' meeting the day before
in New York. It was decided there that Rocket was gone. The
owners said he was getting too big for hockey and he was gone.

I'll give you a scoop and here's what I mean. Earlier in that
season Rocket had hit an official in Toronto. It was linesman
George Hayes and he cuffed him with his glove. But Rocket didn't
get much, and then Lindsay got it, and that's very important.
People have forgotten about that. You look it up and you'll see that
Lindsay got it earlier that same year.

[Detroit's Ted Lindsay got involved in a tussle with a fan in
Toronto. He was suspended for ten days, which meant he missed
four games.]

So here's Rocket up again and these guys are asking Campbell,
"Who the hell does this guy think he is?" And Jack Adams and
Norris of Detroit are saying, "Look, here's what you gave Lind-
say. Now what are you going to give Richard?" That's why
Rocket was suspended like he was and nobody ever seems to
remember that.

I wouldn't swear on a stack of Bibles, but I think the decision was really made in that meeting of the owners, and Selke knew it, too. He said to me, "Kenny, they won't put up with him anymore. It was his second time, and with Adams and Norris yelling and screaming, I didn't have a chance."

I can't honestly say that Selke knew Rocket was gone for the playoffs, but I'm inclined to think he did know. I knew before I went into the meeting that he was gone. Selke was very discouraged. He didn't even come home from the meeting to go to the hearing.

You know the way the Detroit and Montreal rivalry was in those days. Those guys really put the pressure on. You can imagine what Adams would have been like, or Norris, with Lindsay getting what he got if Campbell had given Rocket less. They really leaned on the fact that it was Rocket's second time involved with an official.

Rocket said very little at the meeting. I told Campbell that he had backed down once. When Campbell was a referee someone hit him and he never did anything about it. I reminded him of that. But it didn't help. I still say I defended Rocket very well.

And then there was Hal Laycoe. He said how he felt a "terrific impact" on his glasses. He testified against Richard, Laycoe did, in that meeting. A few years later Laycoe was coaching in Portland and I drafted the best player he had. I think his name was Jones. Everyone asked me why and I said, "That one was for the Rocket."

HAL LAYCOE

I remember the hearing very, very well. One of the most outspoken people about the incident was Frank Selke, Sr. He was not in Boston for the game and he did not go to the hearing. He let Dick and Ken Reardon go. Nobody who could speak French was at that hearing and I never forgot that. I thought, what in the hell are they trying to do? They could have given Rocket better representation than that. He certainly should have had somebody there who was bilingual.

Frank Udvari had that game and he had it absolutely letter perfect at the hearing. He was the referee and he described everything that happened. Years later I read an article quoting Udvari about it and it wasn't even the same incident. It didn't happen the way he said it did in the article, but he was absolutely letter perfect in the hearing.

Was I surprised at the suspension Campbell gave him? No. It was beyond all belief.

MAURICE RICHARD

First of all, I didn't deserve that much, that kind of a suspension. The linesman was the problem. After that he was out of the league and never worked there again. He was the one that was to blame.

The linesman was holding me from behind and I warned him. I warned him three times to leave me alone. Laycoe was in front of me and he was throwing punches at me and he hit me a few times. The linesman kept grabbing me from behind and that's when I told him to leave me alone. I never said I was going to hit him, but when I pushed him against the boards he couldn't go anywhere else. So that's when I hit him.

When it was over I thought I would get a suspension for the last three games that season and for a few games the following season. I never thought I would get suspended for the playoffs.

In the hearing the referee, Frank Udvari, talked about things I know he didn't see that night in Boston. And Laycoe, too. I don't think he said the right things. That's why I didn't like him.

Some people said I played differently after that, had a different approach to the game. They said I mellowed quite a bit, but I don't think so. I played the same way except that I was overweight at that time, especially the last three or four years. I was too heavy and my reflexes weren't the same. I remember a few times I would get a hit and I couldn't retaliate. By then it wasn't the same for me. Not the same at all.

With an incident as emotional as that one was, it is no surprise that different people remember things in different ways. Both Hal Laycoe and Fleming Mackell recall today that Richard struck the first blow. Yet the official report of the incident states, "Richard skates past Laycoe who high-sticked him on the head. Referee Udvari signalled a penalty to Laycoe."

I was interested to hear Laycoe say that the referee, Frank Udvari, described exactly what happened when he testified at the meeting. Until his dying day my father insisted that the game officials had, as he put it, "lied through their teeth" when telling their version of the incident to Clarence Campbell.

Clarence Campbell said he would announce his ruling on the Richard case the following morning. The Canadiens and the Detroit Red Wings were scheduled to play at the Forum that night, March 17, in a showdown for first place.

Richard was at the Forum that morning when he learned he had been suspended for the remaining three games of the season and, what really was the shocker, all of the 1955 playoffs. Campbell's decision contained a detailed reconstruction of the Richard-Laycoe fight, and stated that Laycoe had struck the first blow. As Red Storey said, Richard didn't start trouble too often, but when he got involved he usually finished it. This time it was the Rocket who was finished.

Within minutes of the announcement, "Kill Campbell" became the slogan of the day in Montreal. The NHL offices in the Sun Life Building received bomb threats. Placards were quickly manufactured portraying the NHL president as a "pig" and other phrases and drawings to that effect. The main gathering point was the Forum, where crowds, hatred, and trouble grew to huge proportions all during the day and through to game time, which in those days was 8:30 in the evening.

When the hockey game started a rookie reporter for the Montreal Star, Red Fisher, was covering the scene inside the Forum. It was his first NHL assignment. Thirty-five years later Red Fisher is still following the Montreal Canadiens, home and away. He has covered the Canadiens longer than any reporter has covered any team, anywhere, in professional sports.

RED FISHER

My first night covering an NHL game was what you might call fairly memorable – March 17, 1955, the night of the Richard Riot.

I was assigned to do colour on the game because everybody in Montreal knew something was going to happen that night. Clarence Campbell had been told not to go to the game because something serious might happen. Campbell said there was no way he was going to be bulldozed, or intimidated, to stay away.

You could feel the tension building all day long throughout the city, particularly around the Forum. My boss told me to get a seat in the stands and write a mood piece, how the fans feel, and so on and so forth.

I got a seat about ten rows behind the Detroit bench and you could feel the tension building even higher. Ten seconds into the game, I got hit by the first egg thrown by someone in the Forum crowd. That was my welcome to the National Hockey League.

The crowd kept getting angrier and angrier, especially with the Detroit team scoring four goals in the first period. At the end of the first period there was this gentleman who was sitting along the promenade, at ice level, who walked over to where Clarence Campbell was sitting, which was two or three rows above ice level. He put his hand out as if to shake hands with the league president, and as Mr. Campbell put out his hand, this gentleman slapped him right across the face.

This fellow had been followed by Jimmy Orlando, a very rugged hockey player who once played for the Red Wings. As soon as this gentleman slapped Mr. Campbell, Jimmy Orlando turned him around and just drilled him. There were teeth flying in all directions.

All hell was breaking loose, and seconds later a tear-gas bomb was thrown. People were hacking and coughing and scrambling for the exits. I stood there and asked myself, "Is this what the National Hockey League is all about?"

Five or ten minutes later I was outside the Forum where it seemed like thousands of people were milling around. They were starting to break windows. Somebody shot a gun and put a bullet through one of the windows at the Forum. Cars were being overturned and it was getting really ugly.

I went to a pay phone in a restaurant a couple of blocks away, called my paper, and told the city editor, "Hey, there's a hell of a riot going on outside the Forum. And it's going to get worse."

The city editor said to me, "Okay, kid, go back and mingle with the crowd, then come to the office and write your story." And I said to the city editor, "Why don't you come down here and mingle. I'm not going near that crowd."

I went back inside the Forum and talked to people like Jack Adams, the Detroit manager, who by this time was ranting and raving that Maurice Richard was a disgrace to hockey, etcetera, etcetera. It was quite an introduction.

With the March 17th game forfeited to Detroit, the Wings were two points ahead of the Canadiens. Detroit had one game to play, against Montreal the following Sunday. The Canadiens played the New York Rangers at the Forum on Saturday and won 4–2. But the next night in Detroit the Red Wings whipped them 6–0 to finish in first place, ninety-five points to ninety-three.

During the Saturday game Bernie Geoffrion scored a goal and an assist to give him seventy-five points, one more than Maurice Richard. So Geoffrion won the scoring championship and at the same time became the target for unbelievable abuse from a large segment of Montreal hockey fans. Geoffrion had done the unthinkable, he had won a championship they felt belonged to their beloved Rocket. Many would never forgive him. What should have been a happy accomplishment for the twenty-four-year-old Boomer turned into a nightmare.

BERNIE GEOFFRION

Was it bad, what the fans did to me? Yeah. It really hurt me, and I'll tell you why.

It wasn't my fault that Rocket got suspended for what he did against Hal Laycoe. What do you want me to do? We were going at the time for first place between us and Detroit. I got a goal and assist in Montreal on the Saturday night and I passed Rocket.

We had to play in Detroit on the Sunday night for first place. Don't forget, for first place. I remember Doug Harvey and Big Jean saying to me, "Hey Boom, that doesn't mean that when you get the chance to score you miss the net just because it's Rocket."

So on the Saturday night Béliveau got a goal and I got the assist because I gave him the puck, and I passed the Rocket.

Afterwards, it was awful. My wife got threats, and they threatened my kids and my house in St. Laurent. I had to call the cops to protect my wife and my children.

That summer, it really hurt me. I didn't want to go out. I didn't want to face nobody. Thankfully my kids were young and they couldn't understand exactly what was going on. But it was terrible.

Like the boys said, we weren't going for second place or third place. We were going for first place. It's not my fault.

Following the chaotic events of the final week of the regular season the wheels were turning in the Forum's front office as Selke, Reardon, and Irvin tried to settle things down to normal for the playoffs.

Fortunately, the Rocket-less Canadiens met a weak Boston team in the first round and had little trouble winning the series in five games.

There were two items of interest in that series. In the second game, trying for some publicity to deflect the post-riot stories that were still dominating the papers, my father alternated two goaltenders. Jacques Plante, the team's regular goaltender, and Charlie Hodge shared the duties and the Canadiens won 3–1. But the experiment lasted for just that one game.

The series was also the setting for what has become the most famous one-game career in NHL history. In one of the games at the Forum the Bruins dressed a defenceman called up from the American League. It would be his first and last appearance in the NHL as a player. Today, any hockey fan who has been within hearing range of a television set in the last ten years knows that the player's name was Don Cherry.

DON CHERRY

Norm Corcoran and I were brought up from Hershey after we had been put out of the playoffs. Warren Godfrey hurt his wrist, so I got the call.

I'm tellin' you, before the game I'm so excited I can hardly talk. The Forum dressing rooms were different then, bigger and longer, and we're in the room and I'm sitting there almost peein' my pants.

Milt Schmidt came in and told us that there was going to be a presentation before the game to Richard and Geoffrion. Suddenly I hear Hal Laycoe at the other end of the room say to Schmidt, "You mean I have to stand there while that guy gets a prize? He hits me over the head and cuts my head and I have to stand at attention?"

Schmidt said he'd have to do it and then Laycoe went nuts. He threw sticks all over the place and kicked stuff, and I remember the oranges flyin' and he's yellin', "This is horse shit!" I'm tellin' ya, it was unbelievable.

Then we go out on the ice and I remember standin' there and they introduce the Rocket and they went crazy. The fans are yellin' and hollerin' and screamin'. Then Geoffrion skates out to get something for winnin' the scoring and they booed him and threw things on the ice. And I'm standin' there thinkin', "This National Hockey League is really something. Is it like this every night?"

For the second straight year the Montreal Canadiens and the Detroit Red Wings played in the Stanley Cup finals. For the second straight year the series went seven games. And for the second straight year the Red Wings won game seven, at the Olympia.

The home team won every game. Somehow that made it seem even more inevitable that Detroit would beat the Canadiens again. The absence of Maurice Richard hung over the entire series. The Canadiens surprised everyone by doing as well as they did without their best player.

BERT OLMSTEAD

Our rivalry with Detroit was a good one and I think they were the best games at that time. I tell you who hurt us the most was that Lindsay. Howe could never score on Plante. He was usually my assignment and we never really worried too much about him. Lindsay was the guy against us.

It was tough losing those two years to them in the finals. In that series when Leswick got the goal, we were by far the better team. But we just couldn't get that goal. We always felt we were going to get the goal that would win it, but they got the lucky goal. That's what counts, luck.

A lot of people say we would have won the Cup the year we took them to seven games when the Rocket was suspended. I've heard you say it, but I'm not too sure about that. Dick could handle things like that pretty well.

We were without Rocket one time when he had a stomach muscle pull. I don't know how many games we went without losing, but we had a good streak going. The Rocket came back and we couldn't win. So I don't know about things like that.

When the Detroit Red Wings were winning the Stanley Cup with a 3–1 victory on April 14, 1955, my father was coaching the Montreal Canadiens for the last time. The Canadiens' front office had tired of the team losing so often in the Cup finals. After the Richard Riot, Senator Raymond and Frank Selke made up their minds that someone else should coach the Rocket, and their hockey team.

They offered my father a lifetime job in the front office. Instead, at the age of sixty-two, he signed to coach the Chicago Black Hawks, a pathetic team that had finished a distant sixth in the six-team NHL. He coached in Chicago for one year, then retired because of illness. He passed away May 16, 1957.

During the interviews I conducted for this book I never asked anyone a specific question about my father. But when talking with those from his era his name came up many times. I'm enough of my father's son to want to put a couple of unsolicited stories on these pages.

RED STOREY

Dick was quite a needler so it was good to get back at him. I was in the lobby of the Leland Hotel in Detroit with Sammy Babcock, one of my linesmen. Dick came along and said, "Mr. Storey, what would you do if I started the game and every player had two sticks?"

I said, "I wouldn't start the game."

Dick said, "There's nothing in the rule book that says I can't do it."

So I came back, "Well, you've done such a lousy job of coaching them with one stick I wouldn't try it with two if I was you."

He took off right away and didn't speak to me for a couple of weeks.

BERT OLMSTEAD

Let me say something about your dad. When I first went to Montreal, players would tell me a little about this. Many of them told me that Lach, Bouchard, Richard, Durnan, Blake, and Chamberlain all said they'd never have been the hockey players they turned out to be if it wasn't for Dick Irvin. And I can say the same thing. Even today, when I go back and I'm day-dreaming while doing a job or I have some sort of a problem, I can always relate to Dick.

People ask me who was my best coach and of course I have to say Toe Blake, because we won all those Stanley Cups with him. But in the next breath I say that it's only because he was taught by your dad.

I remember, I'd be in a slump and he'd have me go one-on-one against Harvey. I could never go around Harvey, but Dick would tell him to let me get by him to try and get my confidence back. He knew more about me than any sports psychologist ever could. I tell these guys today that Dick and Toe were psychologists, father, brother, coach, you name it. Now you see three coaches standing behind the bench. What do they do?

III

Five in a Row:
The First Dynasty

Within a few weeks after his team's 1955 Stanley Cup victory, Detroit Red Wings general manager Jack Adams had traded seven players off his roster, including Terry Sawchuk, the game's best goaltender. Adams said he shook things up so his team wouldn't become complacent after three championships in four years. I am writing these words thirty-six years later and the Red Wings haven't won the Stanley Cup since, so it is safe to say complacency hasn't been a problem in Detroit for a long time.

Through the last half of the 1950s upcoming superstars making their NHL debuts included Bobby Hull, Stan Mikita, Henri Richard, Pierre Pilote, Frank Mahovlich, and Glenn Hall, who succeeded Sawchuk as the goaltender in Detroit. Among those playing their final games were future Hall of Famers Bill Mosienko, Butch Bouchard, Ted Kennedy, and Bill Quackenbush.

Prior to the 1957–58 season a group of players headed by Ted Lindsay of the Detroit Red Wings tried to set up an association to bargain with team owners. Hockey's establishment didn't take kindly to the move and shortly after it began Ted Lindsay was with the Chicago Black Hawks. In due course most of the players who were initially involved were traded. It was one of the reasons Frank Selke, Sr., dealt Doug Harvey to the New York Rangers in 1961. The Lords of Hockey who tight-fistedly ran their cosy, six-team operation then must be spinning in their graves now, considering the current situation involving the NHL Players Association and the owners of the league's far-flung twenty-two teams.

The televised version of *Hockey Night in Canada* was firmly entrenched as a national institution in both languages by the time the 1950s drew to a close. When René Lecavalier broadcast the first televised game at the start of the 1952–53 season there were about 146,000 TV sets in Canada, a figure that represented only a small portion of the country's population. By 1960, 80 per cent of Canadian households were plugged in to at least one black-and-white receiver. Saturday night was hockey night on CBC-TV, either from Maple Leaf Gardens in Toronto or the Forum in Montreal. When the playoffs were on it became Tuesday and Thursday nights as well.

For five straight years, beginning in 1956, the last television image of the hockey season was that of the Montreal Canadiens being presented with the Stanley Cup. And each time front and centre in the victory celebration was Toe Blake, who is still the only coach ever to win the Stanley Cup five years in a row.

12

Toe Takes Over

As I write these words, Hector "Toe" Blake resides in a health care home in a suburb of Montreal, a victim of Alzheimer's disease.

Toe Blake is as much a part of this story as anybody. Except for a few years in the early 1950s when he coached the Valleyfield team in the Quebec Senior Hockey League, Toe has been employed by the Montreal Canadiens since February 27, 1936, when he signed his first contract with the team. Even today, Toe Blake is still on the Canadiens' payroll.

Blake first played in the NHL as a seldom-used twenty-two-year-old rookie with the Montreal Maroons. He joined the Maroons late in the 1934–35 season, appearing in eight games with no goals scored. The Maroons won the Stanley Cup that year, but Blake dressed for only one playoff game. The following season the Maroons gave up on him during their training camp and he found employment with Providence in the American League. He returned to Montreal when the Canadiens signed him late that season.

Toe Blake was an intense, profane, competitive man on and off the ice. He was once barred from a pool room that operated within the Forum building because of his foul language. After he retired as the Canadiens' coach he would watch games from the press box, where he often became involved in violent shouting and swearing matches when someone rubbed him the wrong way in regard to judging the hockey game and, in particular, the Canadiens. He could also be a pleasant and generous companion at lunch or

*dinner and a great guy to be around when he was in a good mood,
which was most of the time. But with Toe, you were never quite sure.*

*After a broken leg ended his playing career in the 1947-48 season
the Canadiens sent Blake to Houston to coach one of their minor-
league teams. He was on crutches for the balance of the season, and
his team won the league championship.*

*The following season they moved Toe up to coach their American
League farm team in Buffalo. But he couldn't get along with the
team's manager, Art Chapman, and quit halfway through the season. He returned to Montreal, coached the Valleyfield team with
great success, and was an obvious candidate for the Canadiens'
coaching job when my father left the scene.*

KEN REARDON

Frank Selke didn't want to bring Toe Blake back. He never
wanted Toe as coach. He said he did, but he didn't. Selke wanted
to bring in Joe Primeau. The French press wanted Roger Leger.
My father-in-law [Senator Donat Raymond, the team's owner]
wanted Billy Reay. And I held out for Toe Blake.

I told Selke that the year Toe broke his leg and didn't play
again, we didn't make the playoffs. That's when Toe went to
Houston to coach, with his leg in a cast. Then the next year he
went to Buffalo. But he couldn't stand the guy running the team,
Art Chapman, so he quit.

Then he went to Valleyfield and had a lot of success. But when
he was there he gave Selke a lot of trouble, and that's why he
didn't want him as coach. The Forum ran the Royals' team, and
pretty well ran the league, too. The Royals would always want the
best dates for home games and all that. Blake would say, "Tell the
Forum to go fuck themselves." He would go to the Senior League
meetings and give Selke all kinds of trouble. That's why he never
wanted him as coach. So I said, "If he gives you that much trouble
working against you, imagine how it would be with him working
for you."

When Toe retired he said on television, "I want to thank Kenny
Reardon for the chance to coach the Canadiens." So Toe made it
good.

If the personality of a good coach dominates the atmosphere surrounding his team, then the transition from Dick Irvin to Toe Blake didn't lead to any major changes in the Canadiens' dressing room. In many ways both men were cut from the same cloth. Both were what could be termed, even then, "from the old school."

FRANK SELKE, JR.

Toe and Dick were very similar in many ways, which is why there wasn't that much of a change in the operation of the team when Toe took over. Both of them had a very caustic tongue and they didn't hesitate to use it. They could cut a guy to ribbons in about ten words.

I can remember Toe giving a lot of tongue lashings to guys who were pretty high-calibre hockey players who would stand there and take it because they knew he was right.

They were both good teachers. I watched a lot of practices and scrimmages and they would stop the play when something went wrong or somebody did something stupid. They would tell the players what was expected and what they should be doing to get it right. A lot of coaches today don't seem to do that. They seem to let the players go, shift after shift, making the same dumb play, and never talk to them about it.

Toe coached the way he played. He was all business. When there was going to be some fun, an optional practice, say, Toe would buzz off and wouldn't be there. But in the main it was serious business, from the time he arrived in the dressing room until the time everybody went home.

In the late 1950s only two members of the Montreal media, Red Fisher and the late Jacques Beauchamp, travelled with the Canadiens on a regular basis. (Today as many as ten travel with the team during the season and twice that many in the playoffs.)

Given the cosy nature of the situation it was inevitable the writers and the coach got to know one another very well and friendships developed. However, once in a while there were exceptions.

RED FISHER

If there was one dominant figure on the team that won five straight Stanley Cups I think it would have to be Toe Blake. This guy was a kindly old coach, a gentleman, and a son of a bitch, all in the same sentence.

He was the kind of a guy who would take the two media guys travelling with the team, me and Jacques Beauchamp, out to dinner and would absolutely, steadfastly refuse to let us pay for the meal. The only time he would allow us to pay was at Christmas, but that was it. I'm sure the money came out of his own pocket, not the hockey team's.

On the other hand, that same guy was a mean-spirited individual who could lose his temper in such a way that there were moments when you literally hated being around him.

Hey, there was a time when I didn't speak to him for eight months, eight months, after he humiliated me in a room full of people because he was upset about something I wrote. I had called the Forum to talk with him and the secretary told me Blake wasn't there. I had a feeling he was, so I wrote what I thought was a fun piece about him not wanting to answer his telephone. But it wasn't funny because at the time he was taking his wife to the hospital. So he didn't find it funny at all.

There was a game at the Forum the next night and before the game he came into the press room. I should say he charged into the press room. I was sitting there with about thirty people in the room and he came right at me. He stood in front of me and he couldn't say anything for a few seconds. His fists were clenching and unclenching. Finally he said to me, and I don't think I've heard the word since, he said, "I should biff you one."

I looked up at him, adjusted my glasses, stood up, readjusted my glasses, and said to him, "Go ahead. I could use the money."

His fists were still clenching and unclenching, and he's glaring at me, and finally he said, "You're so goddamn cheap you probably would sue." He turned on his heels and stormed out of the room and for a minute it looked like he was going to walk right through the door without opening it, he was so mad.

So I just quit speaking to him and it lasted for eight months and we had been very close for a long time. Mrs. Blake called me about it a few times and I told her I would speak to her husband again when he apologized to me for humiliating me in front of a lot of people.

But the ice was finally broken after the eight months because my wife and my son were in a traffic accident when they were riding in a cab. My wife broke her shoulder and my son cut up his knee. A few days later Blake called to ask me how they were, and we started speaking again.

But it lasted eight months. Not only didn't we speak, I never mentioned his name in the newspaper either. And during that time he won another Stanley Cup.

When Toe Blake began coaching the Canadiens there were two players on the team who had been his teammates when his playing career ended seven years before. One was Maurice Richard, who would play for Blake through the next five Stanley Cup-winning years.

The other was Butch Bouchard, who hardly played at all for Blake. Big Butch was at the end of his career. He had brought stability to the team on defence, and a lot of class on and off the ice right from the time he joined the then struggling franchise in 1941.

In Blake's first season as coach Bouchard played in only thirty-six regular-season games. He wasn't used at all during the playoffs until the night of April 10, 1956, when the Canadiens took to the ice against Detroit, at the Forum, leading the Stanley Cup final series three games to one. Blake, sensing that the Stanley Cup would be won that night, wanted to give his team captain the chance to accept the Cup in his Canadiens uniform rather than in civilian clothes, which is exactly what happened. Butch Bouchard never played another game.

BUTCH BOUCHARD

I was ready to retire. In fact, I had wanted to retire before that season because I was not too sure I would play. I told Toe, "If you need me, I'll play. But if you don't, I think I'll retire."

But he said he needed me, that he wanted me to keep playing

because at that time Talbot was a rookie, the fifth defenceman. I got hurt about halfway through the season and I never came back. Talbot played very well, and nobody got hurt. They brought up Bob Turner around that time as well.

I wanted to retire when I wasn't playing but Toe insisted I stay around in case he needed an extra man. So when that season was over I was ready to retire. It's never easy to do something like that, but I had a good life.

Then later on, my son Pierre played with the Canadiens and I felt part of the team again. It was the first time a father and son had played for the Canadiens and for me it was a great honour. I felt that in some way he had taken my place. And he played on five Stanley Cup-winning teams.

PIERRE BOUCHARD

If you look in the book you'll see that Bouchard scored seventy-nine goals for the Montreal Canadiens. That's both of us. And it took us twenty-seven years to do it. I stuck right beside Ken Dryden and I guess my father stuck right beside Bill Durnan. We were what you call "defensive defencemen." Very defensive.

I was born in 1948 so I saw very little when it came to watching my father play hockey. I remember going to a few games and I used to blackmail my mother. If she wouldn't buy me ice cream or peanuts, I would cheer for the other team. But even though I don't remember how he played, as far as I am concerned my father was the best.

13

The Players

Butch Bouchard's last game had been the final step in year one of what became a five-year dynasty by a Montreal Canadiens team that has been called the greatest of all time. Not everyone says that, myself included, but it's hard to dispute those who do.

Starting in 1956 the Montreal Canadiens finished in first place in the six-team NHL four times in five years. Their first-place winning margins were 24, 19, 18, and 13 points. In 1956–57 the Canadiens finished in second place, six points behind the Detroit Red Wings. But the Red Wings were beaten in the first playoff round, again, by the Boston Bruins, another example why the Detroit teams of that era can never be classed as a true dynasty.

In the playoffs leading to their five straight Stanley Cups the Canadiens played forty-nine games, winning forty, losing nine. Only twice in ten series were they forced beyond five games. They swept three of the ten in four straight. In 1960, the final year of the five, the Canadiens didn't lose a game, demolishing their opposition with eight straight victories.

Their team stats were matched by an impressive list of individual accomplishments. During the five years, Montreal players were voted to either the first or second All-Star teams twenty-five times and won fifteen individual trophies. In each season the Canadiens gave up the fewest goals, which meant Jacques Plante won the Vezina Trophy five consecutive years. Doug Harvey won the Norris Trophy as the outstanding defenceman four times in those five years.

The year Harvey didn't win it, 1959, his teammate Tom Johnson did.

Dickie Moore won the scoring championship twice, Jean Béliveau once. Ralph Backstrom was rookie of the year in 1959. Surprisingly, in their five years of total domination a Canadiens' player won the Hart Trophy as MVP only once, Béliveau in 1956. In three of the other four years the writers took the easy way out and automatically voted for Gordie Howe. In 1959 Andy Bathgate of the New York Rangers won the Hart Trophy, even though his team finished out of the playoffs, twenty-seven points behind Montreal.

When they won their fifth straight Stanley Cup, in 1960, the Montreal Canadiens reached a hockey pinnacle that had never been reached before, has not been reached since, and likely will never be reached again. Yet one member of that dynasty likes to point out that what the Canadiens did then was just short of being much more impressive.

TOM JOHNSON

Everyone talks about us winning five in a row. I often think how close it was to eight in a row.

We won in 1953. In 1954 we lost in Detroit in overtime in the seventh game. The next year we lost again in the seventh game. The score was 3–1.

So while we won five straight, when you think about it we were just two or three goals away from winning the Stanley Cup eight straight years.

Tom Johnson was one of twelve players who were on all five Cup-winning teams. The others were goaltender Jacques Plante, defence-men Doug Harvey, Bob Turner, and Jean-Guy Talbot, and forwards Jean Béliveau, Dickie Moore, Bernie Geoffrion, Maurice Richard, Henri Richard, Claude Provost, and Donnie Marshall. Three of the twelve, Plante, Harvey, and Provost, are now deceased.

My father said that of all the players he coached, the one who enjoyed hockey life the most was Toe Blake. Certainly Blake had every reason to enjoy life as an NHL coach right from the start, with five Stanley Cups in his first five years. Mind you, there was some pressure. Crusty old Dick Irvin, gone from the Canadiens' scene and not too happy with his long-time employer, predicted before Blake's first season that the Canadiens would finish first by at least ten points. Irvin was criticized for putting that kind of a hex on the rookie coach. When the season was over, Blake's team had finished in first place by twenty-four points.

Along with the Canadiens' rookie coach, there were four rookie players who were destined to win five Stanley Cups in their first five seasons. Long-time NHL stars like Bill Gadsby and Dean Prentice played for over twenty years without ever being on a Stanley Cup-winning team. But 1956 Montreal rookies Bob Turner, Jean-Guy Talbot, Claude Provost, and Henri Richard got their names engraved on the Cup five times in five years.

Of the four newcomers, Henri Richard drew the most attention. For starters, he was Rocket Richard's nineteen-year-old kid brother. Henri was a little guy whose style was far different from that of Maurice. But by the time his career ended in 1975 he had played in more seasons and more games than anyone in the history of the Montreal Canadiens, and on more Stanley Cup-winning teams, eleven, than anyone in the history of hockey.

KEN REARDON

We were at training camp in Verdun because there was something going on at the Forum. I would set up the workout in the morning, go back downtown and have lunch with Mr. Selke, then go back to Verdun and run the workout in the afternoon. At lunch he would say things like, "Send me Bob Turner this afternoon to sign." So I would do that and he would be conducting that kind of business at the Forum, and I would be watching the training-camp games in Verdun.

The camp was mainly games between four teams I had organized because we had that many players. Team A would play Team B, then C would play D. Every night when I would go back to the Forum and Mr. Selke would ask me what was going on, I would be saying, "That Henri Richard, nobody can get the puck away from him." Selke would say, "Yes, but he's small," and I would agree with him. Then the next day I'd go back to the Forum again and the first thing I'd do was tell him the same story, that nobody could take the puck away from Henri Richard.

Late in the camp I was coming out of the arena at the end of the day and Maurice Richard came up to me and said, "What do you think of my young brother?" I said, "Jesus, Rocket, the kid is sensational. I've told Selke that but we both think he's too small. Let's leave him in junior for another year. We don't want him to get hurt."

Rocket said to me, "How can he get hurt more playing pro than he does playing junior? When he goes into Barrie and Niagara Falls and some of those other rinks, they try to kill him because he's my brother. Those juniors hurt you more than a pro does. They're cross-checking him and high-sticking him all night." That was out of Rocket's mouth, and it was true. When Henri would go into Quebec City to play, it was murder.

So when I got back to the Forum I repeated to Mr. Selke what Rocket had said to me. And finally Selke said, "I guess that's right." The kid had a great training camp, and we kept him.

HENRI RICHARD

I really wanted to make the team at that first training camp. I expected to play that year. But during the camp they sent me back to junior for a few days. Then they called me back and I played an exhibition game against their senior team, the Royals, and I got a couple of goals. I guess that was the night I made the team.

I always remember, I went up with Maurice to see Mr. Selke in his office. He asked Maurice if I was ready and Maurice said, "Sure. He's ready to play and he's ready to sign."

So I signed, but they gave me a two-way contract. If I didn't make it I would be sent to the Royals for less money. I was always a centreman in junior but right after I start with Canadiens Boom Boom Geoffrion got hurt and I played ten or twelve games on right wing on a line with Jean Béliveau and Dickie Moore. After that I always played centre until the playoffs in 1971 when I played right wing again with Jacques Lemaire when they wanted both of us on the ice to check Bobby Orr.

I never thought I would be on a team that would win five Stanley Cups in my first five years. I would have to say that team was the best team there ever was, but I really can't prove that.

I can't remember that going for number five was anything special. The team had been winning, winning all the time. We really didn't talk about it, going for a record or something. But I would have to say that one of those teams, somewhere along the line, must have been the best team I ever saw.

Two names dominate my thinking about the team that won five straight Stanley Cups – Jean Béliveau and Doug Harvey.

In the late seventies I was working a Hockey Night in Canada *telecast at Madison Square Garden in New York. Just as the game was about to begin I noticed the fans sitting below us were starting to applaud someone, and pretty soon all the fans in the section were on their feet applauding. I immediately thought it must be a show business celebrity, or maybe a big-name Big Apple hero from another sport. I was wrong on both counts. They were applauding Jean Béliveau as he walked up the steps to his seat. Several years after he had played his last game, hockey fans everywhere still wanted to salute Big Jean that way.*

There may be one or two former hockey players who can command the same kind of respect Jean Béliveau does today. Perhaps Bobby Orr. But not many.

ALAN EAGLESON

When I was forming the players' association in 1967 I went to Montreal to meet with the Canadiens. Bobby Rousseau arranged for the players to meet with me in my room in the Mount Royal Hotel. My big fear was that Jean Béliveau wouldn't want to join.

I gave them my talk and then, nervously I guess, asked Béliveau if he would be part of it. I said, "Mister Béliveau, are you interested?" I was only thirty-three years old and it seemed natural to call him "Mister."

I don't think he knew my name. He said, "Mr. Lawyer, hockey has been good for me. If this is going to be good for hockey, then I'll join."

I was pretty happy, let me tell you, and the rest of the guys couldn't wait to get in line with him.

A few weeks later the Canadiens were playing Toronto in the Stanley Cup finals. After one of the games I went out for a beer with Bobby Rousseau and Ralph Backstrom. I asked them how things were going and said that Béliveau's help had meant a lot. One of them said, "He's not only a great player, he's a great person."

That's still true today. It's a treat to visit the Forum just to see him for a little while.

During the five years the Montreal Canadiens won the Stanley Cup five times, Jean Béliveau was awesome. He scored a total of 186 goals and 210 assists in regular-season play. He added 28 goals and 27 assists in 41 playoff games. He played in only three playoff games in 1959 because of injury.

In those five seasons Béliveau led or tied the Canadiens in goals scored three times, led the team in assists once, and led in points three times. He won the NHL scoring championship in 1956, the same year he won the Hart Trophy.

Béliveau was also the Canadiens' leader in penalty minutes twice in those five years, including a then team record total of 143 minutes in 1955-56. Jean Béliveau? You can look it up. It's in the book.

JEAN BÉLIVEAU

I think the organization at the time had all the ingredients to make a great team. You can start with the owners, the Molsons. We knew them. They were very much part of the game. Mr. Selke, and Toe, the coach.

You can take any position. Jacques Plante in the nets and the defence as a group, led by the great Doug Harvey. We had two good offensive lines plus a third line that was very good defensively. One night when one line had a problem, the other would pick up the slack.

We had great players. And it was very important that we also had the day-to-day kind of guys you could count on when we played on the road. I remember a guy like Bob Turner, who was a defenceman, but who would move up to play as a forward on many occasions.

Billy Hicke, Ab McDonald, Claude Provost, André Pronovost. I think that as a whole we had all the elements you have to have to make a championship team.

Here in Montreal, fans saw a lot of great hockey. I'm not just talking about the five years. I'm talking here of decades, starting with the arrival of Maurice in the early 1940s.

I think the players were certainly dedicated to their responsibilities. They knew they were following other players who had given the team everything and had won Stanley Cups. It was a dream then, and I'm sure for many still today, to wear the Montreal Canadiens' uniform.

When you first get here, all of a sudden you realize where you are, surrounded by veterans on the team, and the tradition that has been transferred from generation to generation. I remember when I was the young one. I tried all along to help keep the good family atmosphere.

If you ask me what I am missing today, there is no doubt I am missing the action on the ice. But I am also missing the family atmosphere we always had on the Canadiens. We had a lot of fun, especially when we were winning. It's more fun when you are winning.

But those five years, and more, went so quickly. It's hard to believe it's all behind me.

One of the best examples of the home-grown nature of the Canadiens' dynasty was found on left wing, where Dickie Moore became a standout. A product of a blue-collar area called Park Extension in Montreal's north end, Moore became known as "Digging Dickie" as a hard-working, intense star with two Memorial Cup-winning junior teams Frank Selke and Sam Pollock put together at the Forum in the late forties and early fifties.

Park Extension borders on the more affluent Town of Mount Royal. The two are separated by a long, heavy wire fence along

L'Acadie Boulevard. Several years ago Dickie was able to move to the Mount Royal side of the fence as the result of his ownership of a successful equipment rental business. But long-time residents of Park Ex are still fiercely proud of Dickie Moore, their contribution to a great Canadiens' team.

Shortly after Maurice Richard retired the city of Montreal built an arena and named it the Maurice Richard Arena. A few years later a new arena built in Park Extension was named the Howie Morenz Arena.

Some of Moore's old pals felt it should have been named after their buddy who had grown up just a few blocks away. One of them called City Hall and was informed that arenas were only being named in honour of men who had died. When Dickie's buddy yelled back, "When did Maurice Richard die?" the politician hung up in his ear. Rules were always different for the Rocket.

Moore played on six Stanley Cup winners, was a three-time All-Star, and won the scoring championship in 1958 and 1959. Moore fans like to recall how their man took one of those titles while playing about half the season with a broken wrist.

Dickie Moore graduated from junior hockey in 1951. When he arrived at the Canadiens' training camp that fall the cocky kid from Park Ex was confident he was going to make the big jump to the big team.

DICKIE MOORE

Boom Boom made the jump right from junior to the NHL, but I didn't. Mr. Selke didn't think I was ready and during the training camp he called me in and told me he was sending me to the Royals seniors. I didn't like it but I had no choice. But he did promise me I would be up with the Canadiens before the year was out, and I was.

I had been on two Memorial Cup teams so it was disappointing when I didn't make it. I wasn't a big goal-scorer in junior – Béliveau and Boom Boom ran away with that. What I did do was play on winners. But to be honest, I did enjoy playing with the Royals. I was young and green and it seasoned me. I played on a

Howie Morenz, the Canadiens' legendary star of the 1920s and 1930s. *(Mac McDiarmid Collection)*

Dick Irvin, Sr., signs on as coach of the Montreal Canadiens, the worst team in the NHL, April 16, 1940. General manager Tommy Gorman is on the left, owner Senator Donat Raymond on the right.

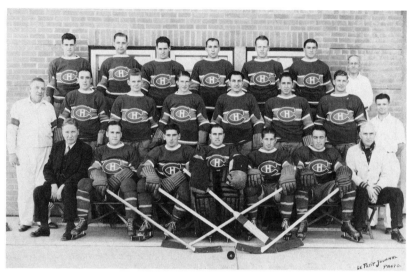

The 1940-41 Canadiens, my father's first Montreal team. Back row, l. to r.: Johnny Quilty, Alex Singbush, Charlie Sands, Tony Grabowski, Cliff Goupille, Ken Reardon, Ernie Cook; middle row, l. to r.: Bill O'Brien, Louis Trudel, Ray Getliffe, Jack Adams, Joe Benoit, Doug Young, Murph Chamberlain, unknown trainer; front row, l. to r.: Frank Patrick, Paul Haynes, Tony Demers, Bert Gardiner, Elmer Lach, Toe Blake, Dick Irvin.

Empty brown seats at the Forum as the Canadiens lose to Boston, 5-0, February 15, 1941. The Canadiens on their feet, left to right: Charlie Sands, Jack Portland, Cliff Goupille. The Bruins are Woody Dumart, Dit Clapper, and Bobby Bauer. *(Mac McDiarmid Collection)*

The Punch Line: Maurice Richard, Elmer Lach, Toe Blake. Their one-season points per game record still stands. *(Mac McDiarmid Collection)*

The Punch Line puts pressure on Boston goalie Frank Brimsek during the second game of the 1946 Stanley Cup finals. Lach is on the left, Blake near Brimsek, and Richard where he usually was, in front of the net. *(Mac McDiarmid Collection)*

Fans in New York called Ken Reardon "horse face." He posed
with fellow westerner Elmer Lach to show how much the name
upset him. *(Mac McDiarmid Collection)*

Dressing room, 1947. Standing, l. to r., Glen Harmon, Billy
Reay, Butch Bouchard, Toe Blake, Roger Leger, Bill Durnan,
Elmer Lach, Maurice Richard. Wrapped in blanket are Ken
Reardon and Bob Fillion. *(Mac McDiarmid Collection)*

Bill Durnan makes a save in the 1947 Stanley Cup final against Toronto. Glen Harmon and Bill Ezinicki are the players with high sticks. *(Mac McDiarmid Collection)*

Elmer Lach and the Rocket, 1949.

Bill Durnan receives a replica Vezina Trophy from NHL president Clarence Campbell on opening night of 1949-50 season. It was Durnan's fifth Vezina win.
(Mac McDiarmid Collection)

Team owner Senator Donat Raymond, in second row on the right, made a rare dressing-room appearance as the Canadiens celebrated their upset win over Detroit in the 1951 playoffs. Goalie Gerry McNeil shared top billing in the series with Maurice Richard.

The Barilko goal: Bill Barilko scores on Gerry McNeil to win the Stanley Cup for the Toronto Maple Leafs. Cal Gardner is the Maple Leaf behind Barilko. Howie Meeker and Tom Johnson are behind the net.
(Hockey Hall of Fame and Museum)

A typical scene in a Canadiens-Maple Leafs battle in the early 1950s. Maurice Richard and Fern Flaman are trying to stage the main event, while linesman Sammy Babcock holds back Flaman. Bert Olmstead is on the left, Butch Bouchard on the right.

February 14, 1952: The Canadiens surprised a battered Bernie Geoffrion with a post-game cake on his twenty-first birthday. They had just beaten Toronto 3-1.

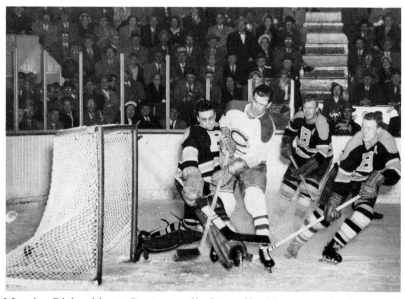

Maurice Richard beats Boston goalie Sugar Jim Henry to win the seventh game of the 1952 Cup semifinal. The Rocket had been KO'd earlier in the game and was still groggy when he scored on a brilliant end-to-end rush. *(Mac McDiarmid Collection)*

line with two good guys, Les Douglas and Cliff Malone. They taught me a lot. Maybe if I'd gone up right away I would have had a few problems.

I didn't play much my first two full seasons with Canadiens because of injuries, First it was my knee, then my shoulder. But I never missed the playoffs.

The first year I won the scoring was the year I broke my wrist. We were playing in Detroit and Marcel Pronovost hip-checked me. My stick jabbed into him and I fractured my wrist. The wrist was hurting me but I kept on playing. They took x-rays but they didn't show anything until later on when they took some more and it showed the fracture. They said that either I could have an operation right then or they could put a cast on it and see what happens. I chose for the cast.

Toe let me play although I did ask him to have a meeting because I felt I was hurting Henri Richard, who was my centre-man. We were one and two in the scoring at that time, with Bathgate close behind. So Toe had a meeting on the train and told Henri and a few of the other guys it was up to them. I had told Pocket I thought it was unfair if I was hampering him by staying on his line but he said it was okay. He told me not to worry and to keep playing. So I was pretty happy.

For the rest of the season I had a lot of help. My left wrist was the one that was broken so on the power play they switched me over to right wing so I could play with the one hand and catch the puck and then bring it over and shoot it or deflect it. Like I said, I was never a big scorer in junior so I never expected anything like that to happen, that I would be going for a scoring championship. But when it was all over, I had won.

All the teams have their own mix when it comes to the personalities of the players. On the Canadiens of that era Henri Richard was a silent type. Toe Blake was asked if Henri could speak English. Blake replied, "I don't even know if he can speak French."

Toe never had a problem hearing Bernie Geoffrion, in both languages. The Boomer was constantly front and centre in the noise department – in the dressing room, on the bench, and at parties where he would sing whether his teammates wanted him to or not. (It was usually not.) And Boom Boom has never been shy about expressing an opinion or two.

BERNIE GEOFFRION

I have to say that was the best team that ever played hockey. With all my respect to Toe Blake, he didn't have too much to do. I can tell you that right now.

But I will say that Toe Blake was a man of discipline. He knew how to handle the guys, what to tell the guys, but he never, never pushed anybody to the wall. He would grab a guy and talk to him. I remember him giving hell to Doug Harvey. He didn't give a damn who you were.

I have to say that the team we had, it was the best. And I'll tell you something, we should have won the sixth one, the one we lost in '60-'61 against Chicago. That's when Rudy Pilous was their coach.

First of all, we had a couple of guys hurt, including me. And I don't think that we had the same desire to win the sixth one as we did the fifth one, when we were going for the record.

But the five in a row? Man, what a team that was! What a team!

While Béliveau, Moore, and Geoffrion were putting the puck in the other team's net, Jacques Plante and the defence in front of him were keeping it out of theirs. It is no coincidence that when hockey teams reach the "dynasty" level they not only have the best goaltender in hockey but the best defence as well.

Four of the twelve players who were on all five Cup-winning teams played on defence. Doug Harvey was, of course, the leader. He is in the Hall of Fame, and so is Tom Johnson, a Manitoba native who first joined the team in the early fifties.

The other two were Bob Turner and Jean-Guy Talbot. Turner is a westerner who played junior hockey in his native Regina with the Pats, a team owned by the Canadiens.

Talbot was a product of the Quebec Junior League. He once had to sit out an entire season as his penalty for inflicting a career-

ending head injury on an opposing junior player named Scotty Bowman.

TOM JOHNSON

I was in Buffalo for two years. When I came up to the Canadiens they more or less said I had to play real bad not to stay. At that time there were a few defencemen retiring, like Kenny Reardon and Glen Harmon, and they traded Hal Laycoe.

I played with Butch Bouchard as my defence partner until he retired. Then it was Jean-Guy Talbot. Butch was a real steadying influence for me. He knew the players and he knew the league. And he liked me. I used to room with him. He's a top person.

My first season was '50-'51 and that was the year we played those two long overtime games in Detroit. Four overtime periods and then three in the next game. I had never been through anything like that. But you didn't seem to run out of energy. You didn't know where that energy came from but it was still there. You seemed to be skating better near the end of the game than you did part way through the game.

You say that Howie Meeker complained that I had him up against the glass when Barilko scored. Well, I had my man (laughs). Unfortunately, the other guy scored the goal.

When it came to the team that won five straight Stanley Cups, we had so much talent we never worried. We never thought we'd lose. There was a real confidence factor on that team, plus we got the great goaltending from Plante. We never even thought of losing.

I wore number ten. When I first came up we would play a lot of exhibition games all around Quebec, even during the season. They would introduce the players in the order of their numbers, and of course the Rocket was number nine. The cheer he got would last a long time. I always say I used to skate out at the end of the Rocket's cheer. They could never hear my name, so not too many people in those towns ever found out who I was.

A goaltender has been close to the bottom line of every championship hockey team that has stood a longer than usual test of time.

Think of Durnan, Broda, Sawchuk, Bower, Parent, Dryden, and in the case of the Canadiens' dynasty under review, Jacques Plante. Talk to the players who had goals taken off their sticks by them and you sense lingering frustration. Talk to their teammates and you hear rave reviews.

BOB TURNER

Jacques Plante is my guy when you ask about a key player on that team. As far as I'm concerned, he's the best goalie of all time. People talk about Sawchuk or Dryden or Fuhr and I just laugh. I don't care, Plante was the best.

Remember how he played when we played Toronto in that last series and beat them four straight when we won our fifth Cup? He stoned those buggers. They had chances and some breakaways, and he stoned them.

I was there in New York the night Bathgate hit him in the face with a shot. He was really cut, blood all over the place. That's when Toe finally let him start using his mask. How many of those others would have come back after something like that? He was the difference so often, it wasn't funny.

JEAN-GUY TALBOT

In that first year Henri and I were the only two rookies starting the season. Then there were some injuries and they brought up Turner and Provost. I was the fifth defenceman for the first twelve games and I got on the ice maybe just one or two times. Then Butch Bouchard got hurt and I got my chance to play.

I remember going to training camp and there was about fifteen defencemen. Montreal owned so many teams, in Buffalo, Cincinnati, the Royals, and Shawinigan where I played.

If you notice the Montreal team down through the years, they have always made sure they had a lot of good defencemen. Even when we were winning five Stanley Cups they traded Dollard St. Laurent. Then after they won five Cups they traded Doug Harvey. Then they traded Tom Johnson and Bob Turner. I was the only one left. I wondered what I was doing there.

New ones came along and they were good – Jacques Laper-riere, J.C. Tremblay, Ted Harris, and Terry Harper. Then they traded them, too, and along came Robinson and Savard and Lapointe. In my case, I went to Minnesota when the expansion came in 1967.

We had some great forwards, but the emphasis was on defensive hockey. They were always looking for good defencemen and good goalies. It's been their style. We had enough good scorers. They told us to stay back and make sure they don't get any against you. That was the main thing in those days.

I played when we won five straight Stanley Cups and I was still there to play on the next two, 1965 and 1966. The style of hockey we played then was just about the same. Toe was still the coach. I ended up playing for many coaches but I played the longest for Toe. He was a really good coach, tough but honest, and that was the difference. He never put down any players, in the paper or anywhere. He would tell you, but he wouldn't tell anybody else. And if somebody said something against any of his players, he was behind us all the time. After a game if a reporter or somebody came to him and asked him why somebody played bad, Toe would say, "What do you mean he played bad?" He would never agree. When a coach does that, it makes you work a little harder.

In assessing the strengths of the team that won five straight Cups, Jean Béliveau always points out the value of the team's defensive forwards. There were two in this category who played on all five winners, Donnie Marshall and the late Claude Provost.

In later years Provost would gain fame for the job he did shadowing Bobby Hull. Nicknamed "Joe," he was one of those unsung hard workers – a grinder – who did his job game in and game out without too many people noticing him. He died of a heart attack while playing tennis in the mid-1980s.

Donnie Marshall was an outstanding player with Sam Pollock's Junior Canadiens in the early 1950s. Marshall served his professional apprenticeship for a few years in Cincinnati and Buffalo, where he was again a high-scoring centreman. But when he finally joined the Canadiens during the 1954-55 season, his on-ice role was changed.

DONNIE MARSHALL

I had a defensive-type role because of the number of players on the team who were good scorers. So I had to fit into the overall scheme from a defensive standpoint.

Toe Blake was very strong on an overall plan on how he wanted us to play the games. I always felt his strongest belief was in a team concept, yet he did allow his players to play their own style of hockey provided it fit into his overall system. Toe realized that his players' individual talents had brought them to the Canadiens and he wasn't about to suppress those talents.

Of course, he was never happy when we lost. He was a hard loser, a very hard loser. But he was fair. He criticized you when you deserved to be criticized.

But my main memory about the way Toe ran the team was his emphasis on a system. In our meetings on the mornings of the games he didn't talk very much about the other team. He always emphasized the system we were going to use that night. To him, that was the important thing and we had to think that way, too.

During the glorious years from 1956 to 1960 there were changes to the team's lineup, but not many. Although the Canadiens were a model of consistency, a few familiar faces did disappear.

Butch Bouchard's retirement came after the Cup win in 1956. Veteran centre Ken Mosdell's last Stanley Cup was also in 1956. Floyd Curry, who had first arrived at the Canadiens' training camp as a fifteen-year-old in 1940, retired after the second Cup victory in 1957. Defenceman Dollard St. Laurent was traded to the Chicago Black Hawks after the third straight win. Bert Olmstead closed out his career with the Canadiens in the Cup-winning game in Boston, April 20, 1958.

BERT OLMSTEAD

I left Montreal after we won the Cup in 1958 because of a torn knee ligament. Blake and Selke told me in Boston on the afternoon of the last game that the medics told them I would never skate again. I told them I didn't believe that, but they insisted the reports all said my knee was shot.

They told me I could coach any team in their system except the big team. I told them I didn't want to coach because I thought I could still play. Six hours after that conversation we won the Stanley Cup. I played in the game, on one leg.

Toe said he could trade me to Chicago but I didn't want to go there because that was where I had started. I said I would go to Toronto, and in June that's where I ended up. A doctor there, Jim Murray, handled me just great and I played every game the next season. I was with Toronto for four years and I was really happy. One thing I can say is that we won the Stanley Cup the last game I played for Montreal, and the same thing happened in Toronto.

I talk to people now who were with other teams when I played, mainly in the United States, and they tell me the way things were with their organizations. I can't even relate to them. I wonder if we were even in the same league because I spent most of my life in Montreal and Toronto, first class all the way. When I hear their stories I tell myself they shouldn't have beaten us the way they were acting and, let's face it, they didn't beat us.

I played thirteen years, was in the playoffs twelve, and played in the final game for the Stanley Cup eleven times. I think that's pretty good.

It is truly remarkable how few changes there were during the five Cup-winning years. But the familiar faces that did disappear had to be replaced.

New forwards who were part of the lineup by the time the fifth Cup had been won included Marcel Bonin, Ab McDonald, Bill Hicke, André Pronovost, Phil Goyette, and Ralph Backstrom, who won the Calder Trophy as the NHL's outstanding rookie in 1959.

The lone significant addition on defence, to go along with the regular four, was Albert "Junior" Langlois, who came up from the minors just in time to be part of the Cup-winning team in 1958. Langlois played the next three seasons and then was traded to the New York Rangers in 1961 in the shocking trade that involved Doug Harvey.

JUNIOR LANGLOIS

I played my junior hockey in Quebec City and when I turned pro I was with Rochester. We had played our last game of the season in Cleveland on a Saturday night. We had to wait after the game to see if Buffalo won because if they did we were out of the playoffs. Kenny Reardon was there that night from the Canadiens' front office. I guess he was supposed to inspire us or something. Anyway, Buffalo won so we were going to have a party. I was coming into the hotel carrying a case of beer under each arm and our coach, Roly McLenaghan, saw me and said, "You'd better go easy on that stuff. The Canadiens have just called you up." I thought he was kidding but the trainer was there with my skates and a bus ticket to Detroit. They wanted me to go there and play with Canadiens in their final game of the season. So that's how I started. I played in the game in Detroit and in the playoffs, too.

That same year when I went to sign my contract Mr. Selke told me I had played well enough to make the team but if they kept me I would be the last defenceman and wouldn't play very much. I was a little worried about playing in Montreal before the crowd at the Forum. But I wasn't too scared to ask him for an NHL contract, not a minor-league contract, and that's what happened. He gave me an NHL contract. It was for $7,500. I phoned my mother right away and said, "Hey Mom, we're going to have money for the rest of our lives. I just signed a $7,500 contract."

To tell the truth, when I got to Detroit I really didn't want to be there. It was like a dream world even though I had been to training camp a few times. But when you're there for a real game the atmosphere is so different. There I was with all those stars, Béliveau, Boomer, Harvey, everybody. I kept staring at the floor when we were getting dressed for the game. I was too scared to look them in the eye. But the guys treated me just fine. Then in the playoffs Dollard St. Laurent broke his cheekbone when Leo Labine hit him, so that gave me a chance to play pretty regularly.

When you are a rookie joining a team like that there can be a real confidence problem. Toe Blake was a hell of a guy in that regard. I asked him, "Coach, how do you want me to play?" A lot of coaches would try to change a guy's style, but not Toe. All he said was, "Play exactly the same way that got you here. If you do something wrong, I'll tell you."

I'll always remember the dressing room. Right across from me was the guy with the laser eyes, Rocket. I never wanted to look over that way at all. I was given a place between Tom Johnson and Doug Harvey. I look across the room and I see the Rocket and Henri and Béliveau. Every once in a while I'd say to myself, "What am I doing here?"

I was on the team when we won eight straight games in 1960 for the fifth straight Cup. That was something special and we treated it as something special. We weren't going to fool around.

I think the best moment for me was the first time I stepped on the ice in that game in Detroit. I mean, it was a dream I had when I was a kid but I never thought I would attain it. At the time you won those Cups you don't realize how important it would be to you for the rest of your life. The one thing I would have never dared is what they do today, when you see all the guys grab the Stanley Cup after the last game to get their pictures taken with it holding it at arm's length over their head. I would never have done that, and I don't think anybody else on the team would have either. There was too much respect.

I remember I used to look around at those great players and say to myself that they won the Cup. I was just a player. Oh, I contributed I guess, but it was just to give them a rest. But they still remember me in Montreal, which tells you something about playing for the Canadiens. I live in L.A. now and go back just once in a while. Yet I can still walk down Ste. Catherines Street and people will yell at me, "Hey, Junior! Comment ça va?" They remember me, and I wasn't a star. It's amazing.

Greatest team ever? Absolutely. Don't forget that they had to change the rules because of their power play. That tells you something. To be able to play there at that particular time was the greatest thrill of my life.

The Canadiens' dynasty in the late fifties was mainly home-grown. Almost all of the players on the team had come up through the Montreal farm system. One exception was Marcel Bonin, a hard-working journeyman forward who turned pro with Detroit and played on the Red Wings' Stanley Cup-winning team in 1955. He went from Detroit to play one season in Boston and another in the Quebec Senior League with the Quebec Aces before the Canadiens signed him. He was a member of the last three teams in the five-in-a-row streak.

Marcel Bonin is a colourful Quebecer who had a strange reputation that preceded him into the NHL. By the time he joined the Red Wings he was known as "the Bear Wrestler."

Marcel Bonin

A big circus came to town in Joliette and I wrestled a bear. Believe it or not, Joe Louis was the referee because he would do anything then to make money to pay his taxes.

They offered a thousand dollars to anyone who could put the bear down. I start like a boxer and give the bear a real punch on the jaw. So right away the guy told me, "Hey, the bear is not a boxer, he's a wrestler." I was not afraid, but the bear beat me.

I also eat glass sometimes, when I would go on the road and have supper in Chicago or Detroit with Maurice Richard and some of the boys. We would have lots of fun.

When I was growing up as a kid I used to listen to hockey on the radio. I always would hear about the lines. Abel, Lindsay, and Howe in Detroit, and in Chicago they had the Bentleys and Mosienko. And of course in Montreal, the Punch Line, which had Toe Blake, Elmer Lach, and Maurice Richard.

Maurice Richard was always my idol. Before I play in the NHL, I never see Maurice Richard in my life. First time I play against him was in Detroit and that was the first time I see him. Before the game, in the warmup, I skated over to shake hands with Maurice and I said to him, "You always been my idol." He didn't say anything. He just look at me with those big black eyes. Then I say, "I'm going to check you tonight." And he say, "It's going to take two guys like you to check me tonight." (laughs)

When I was playing with Canadiens I scored the winning goal for the Stanley Cup in 1959. But what I remember most about that team was the boys. We were like brothers. When we go out after

154

the game, everybody go together. Not two guys go here, and three guys go there. My best hockey memory is about the friends I made on that team.

Detroit was very good when I played there and they always seemed to finish first. But everyone on those teams played with their heart, for the fans, and for the coach, too. If the coach told us to do something, we do it. We'd never answer back to him. I never saw a guy in the room answer back to the coach. What the coach told us, that stayed in the room. Today it seems different. Everybody talks. Everybody wants to make a press conference.

Marcel Bonin was a colourful character and the memories of some of his exploits, on and off the ice, still cause his former teammates to chuckle. Here is Dickie Moore's favourite Marcel Bonin story.

DICKIE MOORE

I thought Marcel Bonin was an important addition to our team. He added a lot. He fit right as a player and off the ice he always had a lot of spirit and helped us have a lot of fun.

One time, in Boston, we'd had our team meal the day of the game and we were all sitting around watching a football game on TV. Marcel was there and he saw how, in the football game, they'd knock a guy down and then pick him up, help him up to his feet even though he was playing for the other team.

So that night Marcel gets in the game and he hammers a Bruins guy and down he goes. Then Marcel leans over and he helps him up. Toe pulled his hat over his head and he really let Marcel have it when we got back in the room.

Marcel said, "Hey, coach, in football they do dat. So I do dat too." At the time he couldn't understand why Blake was so mad.

During the Canadiens' cup-winning stretch a Montreal native, Connie Broden, scored a hockey first. Broden played on a World Championship winning team for Canada, then returned from overseas and joined the Canadiens in time to play for a Stanley Cup winner the same year.

Connie Broden

I grew up in the NDG [Notre Dame de Grâce] area of Montreal and used to line up at the Forum for fifty-cent tickets to the rush end. We'd stand there a long time and then when they'd open the wickets adults would come along and push us out of the way and get the best seats.

I played junior and senior for the Canadiens' organization for many years. When I played in Cincinnati in the International League we set a record for consecutive wins that wasn't broken for about forty years. Donnie Marshall was on that team with me.

I quit hockey in 1957 and went to work for Molson's. A month later I got a call from the Whitby Dunlops senior team. They were looking for players to take overseas for the World Championships. Senator Molson thought it was a good idea, so after working at the brewery for only a month I was back playing hockey.

When I got back from overseas the Canadiens had me start practising with them and I played a few games in the season and in the playoffs. In those days they would pay you a hundred dollars for suiting up and another twenty-five dollars if you played in a game. So when a player would limp off after being hit by a shot or something I wouldn't wait, I would jump on the ice right away so I could get credit for playing in a game.

One time Toe Blake pointed to me between periods and told the guys that I was real eager to play and had the kind of spirit he wanted everyone to have. Little did he know that I did what I did so that my pay for the night would go up by 25 per cent.

After the 1958 playoffs I went back to Molson's and was with them for thirty-three years until I retired. I didn't get too much money playing for the Canadiens, but I got my name on the Stanley Cup.

As I write these words thirty-one years have gone by since the Montreal Canadiens became the only team to win the Stanley Cup five years in a row. The Pittsburgh Penguins won in 1991, so unless Mario Lemieux and company win it in each of the next four years, the Canadiens' record is safe until at least 1996. Something tells me it will endure long after that – like, maybe forever.

The men who played on that Montreal team are modest when you ask them about their amazing feat. But when talking with them I got the impression that, deep down, they agree with people like Danny Gallivan and Frank Selke, Jr., who rank that team as the greatest of all time. And why shouldn't they? Who among us can come up with a definitive argument to prove otherwise?

DICKIE MOORE

The greatest team? It's hard to go back in time. Every team that wins is a great team. But how can you look back and try to match up great teams from different years.

At the time there is no doubt we were the best. We had everything. We had a hell of a power play. But there were times we could have been beaten. Detroit had some great teams. And Boston had us on the ropes. There, I credit the confidence and the experience and the winning feelings that we had.

You need a great goaltender, regardless of who you are, and we had Plante. Nobody wins the Stanley Cup without great goaltending, and we got it. Boston used to hold us in our end sometimes for about eight minutes. Plante would make all kinds of key saves, then we'd go down and pump one in on them.

Another Montreal native, Phil Goyette, played on the last four of the five straight. Goyette was a centreman who became a regular after being called up late in the season prior to the 1957 playoffs.

Goyette played in Montreal until 1963, when he was traded to the New York Rangers as part of the deal that involved Jacques Plante and Gump Worsley. He played in the NHL a total of fifteen years and won the Lady Byng Trophy in 1970 when he was a member of the St. Louis Blues.

PHIL GOYETTE

I was a standby on the first team, a young stud waiting on the sidelines. It wasn't easy to break into a club of that calibre. When I was given the opportunity I said, "I'd better make it now or I never will."

We had great confidence, but there was also pressure. It was there after four in a row when we played Toronto in the finals going for number five. They were an up-and-coming team and there was always a big rivalry between Montreal and Toronto.

There was pressure before the games, but after they started it was all go. Our winning attitude and experience helped when the Toronto series got going. We said, "Let's get this over fast." And we did.

I don't want that record broken. I hope it stays for as long as I'm alive.

14

As Others Saw Them

Part of the mystique of the Montreal Canadiens stems from the fact that when Toe Blake's boys were winning five straight Stanley Cups, the television version of Hockey Night in Canada *was making its earliest impact from coast to coast in Canada.*

Danny Gallivan became the English-language voice of the Canadiens in the fall of 1952. During the regular season the CBC would alternate games from Montreal and Toronto on the Saturday night national network. During Danny's first six years in the booth the Canadiens were involved against either Boston or Detroit in the Stanley Cup finals, and he had the airwaves all to himself. In 1959 and 1960 the Canadiens played Toronto in the finals. That meant the Hewitts, Foster and Bill, broadcast the games played in Toronto.

But Danny was almost always there when the Canadiens were on their record-setting streak of five in a row. To this day he maintains that was the best team ever.

DANNY GALLIVAN

Number one, the team won five Cups in a row. No one has ever done it. If you could pick one team out of the five as being better than the others, I'd take the '58-'59 team.

You have to look at the number of players from that team who are in the Hall of Fame. And they had the depth to go with it. One year somebody got hurt in the playoffs, it might have been Béliveau, so they put Phil Goyette in the lineup. He hadn't been playing. What happens? In his first game he gets three goals.

Pride is always a part of Montreal hockey teams. But it has never been greater than the pride that team had, and how it would build, after two Cups, three Cups, four Cups, five Cups.

They were good, and they knew it, but not in a negative way. By that I mean they never got overconfident to the point of sloppiness. During the 1960 playoffs, when they won eight straight games, they played in Chicago and won the game 2–0. That had to be the most perfect hockey game ever played, I would think.

There's a cute little anecdote about that game. Jim Norris, the Chicago owner, was sitting with Frank Selke. After the second period Norris asked Selke if he was going to go to the Canadiens' dressing room. Selke said he wasn't. So Norris said, "Do me a favour. Go down there and ask your boys to let us have the puck."

I like today's hockey. The players are very talented. I think that if you picked the best 120 and put them in a six-team league it would be way ahead of the six-team league of the fifties and sixties. I may be living in the past, but considering what we have today with so many teams, I still look back to the team that won five straight and say that hockey was the best hockey.

An all-time great team gets that way because of all-time great players, and certainly the Canadiens' first dynasty had no shortages in that department. When people who were close to the team name their choices as to the main contributors, it's like listening to a roll call at the Hockey Hall of Fame. It is not surprising that there is a variety of choices in the selection of the dynasty's first star.

RED FISHER

Toe Blake is my choice as the dominant figure on the team that won five straight Stanley Cups and Dickie Moore is my second choice. Moore had more desire, character, courage, and talent than most players I've seen. I know a lot of people pick Doug Harvey. But as huge a talent as Harvey was, as much as he wanted to win, Dickie Moore had all of those things. What he also had was a loyalty to the organization to match it.

More than any other player on that team, Moore played with pain. I was walking alongside him one day in a hotel and I hear this noise, "Crack, crack." I said to Dickie, "What's that?" He replied, "My knees." And it was. He couldn't walk without that "Crack, crack." I mean, here's a guy who won a scoring championship with a cast on a broken wrist for most of the last half of the season.

KEN REARDON

I put Jacques Plante very high on that team. When we'd play on the road in those days, in the first period we'd be battling for our lives and he'd kick out everything. Then in the second period we'd get one and we'd be on the way. The game might finish 4-1 or 5-1, but if you'd seen the first period we should have been down 2-0. Plante used to hold us in the game until we got going.

When you look at that team you have to say the Rocket was the luckiest player of them all. When you get old you look around the team you're on for some help. If there's no help, they're going to get rid of you because you're not doing your share.

But with Rocket on that team, here's a guy surrounded by Béliveau, Geoffrion, Moore, Harvey. I guess any hockey player, if he's in his last years, with talent like that on the same team, he's going to get a year or two more out of it. He doesn't have to be the big gun anymore.

At the end Rocket was playing at over 200 pounds. Toe didn't even bother with his weight at that time. Rocket wouldn't even get on the scales. I saw somewhere where Rocket admitted that he played at over 200 at the end. But as usual he covered himself by saying he felt a lot stronger. (laughs)

The term "widely respected" is often overdone when referring to pro athletes. But in the case of long-time defenceman Harry Howell, it is well merited.

Howell played twenty-one seasons in the NHL, seventeen with the New York Rangers. He holds Ranger records for most seasons played and most games played. He's in the Hall of Fame. But everyone in hockey is genuinely sorry a good guy like Harry never played on a Stanley Cup-winning team.

Harry Howell broke in with the Rangers in 1952 so was very familiar with the Canadien dynasty of the fifties.

HARRY HOWELL

There is no doubt they were the best team I ever played against. What I remember most of all is their power play. It was just devastating. They had Doug Harvey and Boom Boom Geoffrion on the points. And they had so many guys who they could play up front. Béliveau, the two Richards, Dickie Moore, Bert Olmstead.

I always thought Henri Richard was underrated just a bit. He was the toughest of them all for me to stop. You always knew what he was going to do. He always cut to his backhand. But it didn't matter, he could still beat you because of his speed.

I think the tradition of the Canadiens had a lot to do with their success. I know a lot of people don't go for that kind of stuff, but I always thought it was very important. It seemed they just wouldn't lose when it really counted.

I remember one year, in the playoffs, we had a goalie named Gordie Bell. In the first game of the series, right in Montreal, he shut them out. Two nights later, no way. They whipped us. Bell's mystique didn't last past that first game. Once they got going, you couldn't do much about it.

In another playoff game we had them down 4-1 for a long time. They made it 4-2 but we still had the game under control. Then Béliveau got going in the third period and the goals started to go in. They beat us 6-4. We outplayed them for fifty-five minutes but we lost the game in the other five minutes. That team would do that to you all the time.

We had some great battles with them in the old Madison Square Garden in New York. I used to hate it during the national anthem when they would sing about "The Rocket's Red Glare." The fans would yell at the Rocket when they sang that and you could see his eyes light up. You knew something was going to happen.

Lou Fontinato was our tough guy on defence. He hated the Canadiens. I thought it was funny when they traded him to Montreal, knowing how much he had hated them when he played against them.

One night there was a big riot in New York. Fontinato got into a fight with the Rocket. Lou pulled Richard's sweater off and then jumped on it with his skates and cut it up pretty bad. Richard went wild when he saw that happen. A couple of weeks later Lou got a bill from the Canadiens for $38.50.

During the 1950s the Boston Bruins experienced total playoff frustration at the hands of the Canadiens. Beginning in 1952 the teams met in the playoffs six times in seven years and the Canadiens won every series. That meant Boston centre Fleming Mackell, a native of Montreal, had to suffer through the obligatory post-series handshakes with the victors from his home town six times in seven years.

FLEMING MACKELL

The thing that bothered me most about the Bruins and the Canadiens was that we could never beat them for the Stanley Cup. You know that something like this really carries on into your life. All my kids, all of us, we really disliked the Montreal Canadiens. We hated Montreal.

You can see now, when you look back, and understand why. But when I looked back I couldn't believe how often we lost to them . . . how many series we lost to them. They were a good team. But the Bruins were a good team, too.

We came the closest in 1958. The final series went six games. Boom Boom Geoffrion was supposed to be hurt and I remember saying to Leo Boivin and Leo Labine that we had a good chance to beat Montreal with Geoffrion out. But he played, and they beat us.

In the fifth game we went into overtime. The series was tied and on TV Frank Selke said the Rocket would score the winning goal. He did, but we were really stupid. When I think of it now we should have had somebody stay with him. We should have thrown a real checking blanket over him. But we didn't. Imagine, letting the Rocket go, for God's sake. And he scored. It always went that way it seemed.

Why did we lose all the time in the playoffs?

This is hindsight, but I think the Canadiens' team had a little edge in coaching against us. First there was your dad. And then there was Toe Blake.

We had Milt Schmidt, who was a great hockey player but to me not a great coach. We also had Lynn Patrick, who was a pretty good coach.

Even after I was through playing and I was watching the Bruins it was the same thing. They had Harry Sinden and others and there were times when the Bruins had better teams than the Canadiens. But they always lost to Montreal in the playoffs.

Dryden beat them one year. I remember talking to the Bruins a week before the playoffs when Dryden had just come up in Montreal where I was living at the time. I told them about him. I told them that even though he had hardly played he was very good. The Bruins' guys acted as if it would be no problem. But he beat them. And there was another year Rogie Vachon beat them.

When I played it was the goalie, too. Jacques Plante was the big difference on the ice . . . big saves against us at the right time. Always those big saves.

Another Montreal-born player who got away from the Canadiens was a goaltender who eventually made it to the Hockey Hall of Fame, Lorne "Gump" Worsley. One of the game's most loquacious and colourful characters during a career that spanned twenty-two seasons, the Gumper played his junior hockey in the Montreal area and was signed by the New York Rangers.

Worsley broke in with New York in 1952-53, played fifty of the Rangers seventy games, and won the Calder Trophy as rookie of the year. The following season he never played a game in the NHL. Gump may be the only rookie award winner to be sent to the minors before his sophomore year even began. Johnny Bower beat him out of his job in New York, so in 1953–54 Worsley tended goal for Saskatoon in the Western Hockey League. But he was back on Broadway the next season and stayed there until 1963, when the Rangers traded him to the Canadiens in exchange for Jacques Plante.

Gump is famed for his one-liners. One of his best came when he was backstopping a weak New York team and he was asked which team gave him the most trouble. He quickly replied, "The Rangers."

During those years, Gump Worsley had a bird's eye view of the Montreal powerhouse of the late 1950s.

GUMP WORSLEY

There's no comparison with that hockey club. I don't think there's one around right now. They just had everything. It was tough to be in the nets against them, because everybody could score goals. They didn't have too many guys who weren't good goal scorers. When you played them you spent 80 per cent of the time in your own end of the rink.

Don't forget, the first couple of years was when they didn't have that rule where a guy comes out of the penalty box once a power-play goal is scored. It was tough playing against them at a time like that. We had a guy like Lou Fontinato who liked to run people. So he would, and he'd get a penalty, and the next thing you know we're down 2–0. But after they changed the rule, they just continued on anyway.

Everybody that played them had to chase them. There wasn't anybody on that hockey club who was a non-skater. They could skate all night and never slow down. That was the thing.

For a goalie looking at them, Geoffrion had the big shot, of course. But guys like Béliveau and Moore, they didn't overpower you but they could do it all. Look at the centremen they had. And Plante. I mean, what can you say about Plante? He had a goals-against average of about zero. They just had too much power for everyone. They had a super hockey club.

When the Montreal Canadiens were in the process of winning five straight, Frank Mahovlich broke in with the Toronto Maple Leafs. The Big M won the rookie award in 1958. In the following two years he played against the Canadiens in the Stanley Cup finals.

FRANK MAHOVLICH

They dominated. When we would get a penalty and they'd put out Geoffrion, Béliveau, Maurice Richard, Doug Harvey, and Dickie Moore on the left side, why, that was a lineup that made them change the rules. It was the best team I've ever seen to control the puck.

Our teams in Toronto after that, when we won four Stanley Cups, we struggled to get through the season. We ended up in fourth place one time and still won the Cup. I think the reason was that Punch Imlach just kind of drove us into the ground. He whipped us too much. But we won the Cup four times and I have to say that Imlach was kind of an inspirational guy when that happened.

I played a couple of years for Scotty Bowman in Montreal. Bowman had the ability where he could get his team to a peak and keep it there. Punch couldn't do that. He couldn't keep his team at a nice pitch. It was always up and down and struggle, struggle, struggle. Seems to me those Canadiens teams in the fifties didn't have to go through that, or Bowman's teams in later years.

One of the most famous games the Canadiens played during their era of five straight Cups was in Chicago on April 4, 1959. It turned out to be the final game of a playoff series as Montreal eliminated the Black Hawks, and the final game in the long officiating career of the man in the middle during a wild night in the raucous Chicago Stadium, Red Storey.

After the game, which had featured some controversial calls and non-calls by Storey, NHL president Clarence Campbell spoke in disparaging terms about Storey's handling of the game to a newspaper reporter from Ottawa, Bill Westwick. Campbell never told Westwick his remarks were "off the record" and they appeared in print the next day. Storey quit in protest over this lack of support from his boss and never refereed again in the NHL.

RED STOREY

It all started when Marcel Bonin went in to check Eddie Litzenberger. Bonin put his stick flat on the ice to trap the puck and Eddie stepped on his stick and went flying in the air. The Chicago players hesitated because they thought I was going to call a penalty, but there was none. By the time they got their composure back the Canadiens had scored a goal.

Then Junior Langlois hit Hull and knocked him flying. It was a good hip check, but here again the Hawks thought I was going to call a penalty, but I didn't. Then Claude Provost scored and all hell broke loose.

A guy jumps out of the seats onto the ice and threw a cup of beer in my face. I grabbed him, and Doug Harvey grabbed him from the other side. Doug realized I was going to hit the guy so he yells at me, "Red, you can't hit a fan. You can't hit a fan." And, bingo, he drives him. Doug could see I was still mad, so he hits the guy again. We let him go and he staggered off the ice. Doug never left me. He stood right with me at centre ice.

Another guy had jumped over the screen on the other side. I didn't see him coming across the ice but Doug did and he hollered "Look out." The guy jumped on me from behind, so I dipped my shoulder and flipped him up in the air. Doug hit him with his stick and cut him. I think the guy needed about eighteen stitches. Nobody else came on the ice after that.

That was an example of something I often try to tell people, that the only friends a referee has when he's in trouble are the players. I know it's hard to believe, but when push comes to shove the players will back you up and protect you. At least in my case, I always knew the players were my best friends when there was trouble. Harvey was that night, for sure.

KEN REARDON

Do you remember the Red Storey Riot in Chicago? I do.

Bonin tripped the guy and we went in and put the puck in the net. I turned to Mr. Selke and said, "There's no goal, Mr. Selke. Red must have blown the whistle. There must have been a whistle because everybody stopped." So not only did we not get a penalty, we got a goal.

In the game Red worked before that one, somebody ran Henri Richard into the end of the rink and bloody near killed him. Red stood over him, like a referee in a boxing ring when a guy is down, and I swear it looked like he was going to start counting, one, two, three. Henri got up, and Red said, "No penalty." I don't know what he would have done if Henri hadn't got up. That was the worst call in the whole series, that particular call, not the one that he missed on Bonin.

You know, referees carry it in their own mind that they want to even something up. I think he tried to even it up on the Bonin play.

During the Canadiens' record Stanley Cup run the team's managing director, Frank Selke, Sr., received just praise for his role in building the club to heroic proportions. All the while his son, Frank, Jr., was working down the hall in the Forum's public relations department. Old-timers from that era still call Frank (and me, too) "Junior." Among Frank's most vivid memories is his father's team that won five straight Stanley Cups.

FRANK SELKE, JR.

I know other people have other feelings. I know you feel very strongly about the Montreal team that won Cups in the seventies. But the team that won five in a row is, to my mind, the greatest team there ever was.

The player that struck me the most of any I have ever seen was the Rocket. I know I have to remember that when I first saw players like Richard, Blake, Lach, Durnan, Reardon, I was a very impressionable young man. As you get older I guess you are not quite as gullible, if that's the right word, but I don't ever remember seeing anybody play the way the Rocket played. He wasn't the best hockey player, but he was the most unpredictable and certainly the most exciting player I ever remember. He would do things in a way you thought would never happen, but it did.

He would do the unexpected, but then he could rise to the occasion and do what was expected of him, too, as high as those expectations might have been. There was the time in 1958 when they went into overtime against Boston and the TV people were scrambling for an intermission guest. They hauled my dad into the studio for an interview with Tom Foley.

Tom said, "Mr. Selke, you've seen a lot of overtime games. What do you think is going to happen?" My dad said, "Well, Tom, the Rocket hasn't done anything for us tonight so I wouldn't be the least bit surprised if he's the one who wins it for us." And about five minutes into the overtime, he did.

There were only about thirty players who performed for the team through that era. There were very few changes made where someone who came in for any length of time proved to be just as good as the guy he replaced.

They were a powerhouse. But when Rocket retired in 1960, he not only took his talent and skills away with him, he took his heart, too. I think maybe that had more to do with the team not being able to win the next year, win a sixth straight, than anything else. It wasn't the same team without his fire.

I did a little bit of counting recently about the years I worked at the Forum. During the time I was there, from 1946 to 1967, I actually worked with thirty-five men who are now in the Hockey Hall of Fame. Those are players and builders, like your dad and my dad. Not very many men get the chance to grow up in an environment like that. It was all very exciting for me.

15

Doug

In the fall of 1989 newspapers across Canada carried a photograph of hockey legend Doug Harvey, a gaunt, sick, dying Doug Harvey. It shocked hockey fans.

Harvey was sixty-four years old and had been hospitalized for almost a year for treatment of cirrhosis. He knew the end was near and had sneaked out of the hospital to take his grandson to a Canadiens practice at the Forum. That's when the photograph was taken. I talked with several of Harvey's former teammates and opponents while conducting interviews for this book. Many were dismayed that the photograph received such widespread exposure. They felt it was a sad and unnecessary last look for hockey fans at one of the game's all-time greatest players. Harvey passed away the day after Christmas, 1989.

Doug Harvey must be front and centre in any summary of the Montreal Canadiens team that won five straight Stanley Cups. Today, when hockey people are asked to select their all-time All-Star team, the selections for the defence positions are almost unanimously Bobby Orr and Doug Harvey.

That sort of thing keeps Harvey's name alive in the minds of today's generation of hockey fans, who never had the pleasure of seeing him play. His hockey skills are well known. What isn't as well known is the fact that he was one of the greatest all-around athletes in the history of Canadian sport.

Harvey played a season of Double A professional baseball for a team in Ottawa and won the batting championship. In the 1940s he played for the Montreal team in the Quebec Rugby Football Union, which was part of the Canadian Football League. I once asked him what sport he would choose if he could play only one. He answered me with a story.

"I was playing football for Montreal against the Toronto Argos. I played sixty minutes as a running back and a defensive back. After the game the owner of the team came into the dressing room and handed me twenty dollars. I asked him what it was for and he said the deal was, twenty dollars if we lost, twenty-five dollars if we won. I thought I had been playing for nothing."

Doug would do almost anything, anywhere, with almost anybody, for nothing or almost nothing as long as it was fun. At the peak of his hockey career there were always Doug Harvey stories. But they were mainly happy stories, about the pranks he pulled while he and his teammates were enjoying the good times. Doug would explain his actions by saying, "Just trying to keep the boys loose."

Doug always had fun being "one of the boys," something he could never get away from or grow out of. After the Canadiens traded him to the Rangers in 1961 he had a very successful season as playing coach in New York. He won another Norris Trophy as the league's top defenceman, and the Rangers made the playoffs for the first time in four years.

The Rangers were anxious for him to remain as playing coach. When he balked they said they would be happy if he just coached and offered him a long-term contract. But Doug didn't want to be a coach, no matter how good the job or how big the contract. He told me once that coaching tore him up inside because he couldn't join the boys after a game for a few drinks at their favourite watering hole. "I hated it," he said, "when we'd get to the corner outside the rink after a game and they'd go one way and I had to go the other." So he quit as a coach in the National Hockey League and for the next seven years drifted from pillar to post as a player in the NHL and the minor leagues. He played his final NHL game with the St. Louis Blues when he was forty-four years old.

For most of the final twenty years of his life the stories about Doug Harvey weren't fun-filled anymore. He was a sucker for opportunists. At the end of a season with the Rangers, as he was set to return home to Montreal, he fell in with the crew of a Canadian naval vessel and set sail with them from New York. He was talked into opening a restaurant in Montreal, Chez Doug Harvey. It was a disaster. So was a venture as a candidate in municipal politics. He drifted from job to job, some of them in hockey. He was an assistant coach in Los Angeles, a scout for Houston. Nothing lasted very long.

At times his behaviour was bizarre. When he was to be inducted into the Hockey Hall of Fame in 1973 he didn't show up at the ceremony. While helping run a hockey school he walked onto the ice in his bare feet to instruct young players. There were reports of him sleeping in a railway boxcar during the time he was working around the barns at a race track in Ottawa. In the late seventies he showed up at the Montreal Forum for a special ceremony honouring Canadiens greats from the past wearing blue jeans. That night, instead of walking directly to the presentation table when his name was called, Harvey wandered about the ice talking to players of both teams who were lined up across the blue lines.

Times were better for Doug in the mid-eighties. He returned to the Forum to be honoured as one of the Montreal Canadiens' all-time All-Stars and behaved well. On October 26, 1985, the Canadiens retired his sweater Number 2. At the same time team president Ronald Corey welcomed him back to the organization by hiring him as a scout. It was a humane gesture by the team, and Doug appreciated it. He lived a much better life and kept that job until his past caught up with him and he entered hospital, where he remained for most of the last year of his life.

Today, when you talk to those who played hockey with Doug Harvey and knew him well, they remember the good times.

When Hal Laycoe joined the Canadiens in 1947 Doug Harvey was a rookie defenceman. The two men became good friends. Hal Laycoe lives in Vancouver and it is obvious he is still very much a Doug Harvey fan.

HAL LAYCOE

I helped Doug build his house in the west end of Montreal. He had me and his two brothers, Howie and Alf, working on it, with

Doug usually doing a lot of planning and talking and us doing most of the work. He was the kind of guy who thought anything was possible. He would always think of a way. A friend of his who was in the construction business dropped by one day and when he saw some of the beams we amateurs had lifted and put into place, big heavy ones, he said we should all have had a hernia for the rest of our lives. But when Doug thought something could be done, it usually got done.

When Doug was in his first year they booed him at the Forum. They had never seen anybody play hockey like Doug Harvey. They had never seen anybody fool around in front of his own net the way he did, with total disregard for checkers. Dick got very upset and warned him that if he ever lost the puck that way and the other team scored, it would cost him $100. That was big money in those days, like maybe $1,000 today. I know that Doug never had to pay the hundred, and I know he never changed either. I think the more agitated the fans got, the more he'd do it.

Nobody could control the puck like Doug Harvey – forwards, defencemen, anybody. One of his favourite ploys was to slow the game down. If some team was going like hell against Canadiens it was like he'd say, "Hey, this game isn't supposed to go this way," and he'd slow the game down so they could get back into it again.

If the score was 8-2, Doug might have a goal or an assist. But if it was 3-2 he'd have two or three points. He could pace himself and he was so skilful at that he was able to play until he was forty years old.

One of the best Harvey stories I remember is the way he'd negotiate his contract. Frank Selke would call him in at the start of a season, the way he did with everybody. Selke would always start off by telling you all his troubles. His favourite cow had died on the farm, or one of his kids was sick, stuff like that. He would spend fifteen minutes getting you to feel sorry for him, then he'd say, "Well, I've got your contract here," and he'd open his desk drawer and slide it across the desk at you.

When he'd do that with Harvey, Doug would just sit there and not say a word. He'd look at it, then slide it back at Selke without saying a word. Selke would usually excuse himself, saying he had something else to do, and a week or so would go by before he'd call Doug in again. He'd go through the same ritual and Doug would look at the contract again, say nothing, and slide it back to him again. Finally, after four or five times, Doug would sign it. Likely the contract was exactly the same as when he first looked at it, but that was the way Doug operated.

You know, he would always play better hockey with a lesser defenceman. They would often put the weakest defenceman on the team with Doug, and he would carry him. Oh, you can think of so many things when you talk about him. He should never have left Montreal. He didn't deserve what they did to him. He didn't deserve to be traded.

RED FISHER

We were staying over in Detroit and Toe wanted to promote some togetherness within the ranks. So he arranged to take the boys on a tour of the Ford Motor Company. The game had been on a Sunday night, and this was Monday morning, and the boys got on the bus around 10 a.m.

The bus took off for Ford with one quick stop, at the Detroit Olympia. Doug Harvey, who was sitting at the back of the bus, yelled to the front of the bus where the coach was sitting, "Hey, Toe, why are we stopping here?"

Toe said, "The Red Wings players are coming with us."

From the back of the bus came Doug Harvey's voice again saying, "Those guys were trying to cut my head open on Sunday night. If you think that on Monday morning I'm visiting the Ford Motor Company with them, you're out of your mind." So he walked down the aisle and got off the bus. Blake, who now realized he had made a mistake, didn't say a word.

We were leaving that night for Toronto on the midnight train. It's almost midnight, and all the players are on the train, but there's no Doug Harvey. I kept saying to Dickie Moore, "Where's Doug?" and Moore kept answering, "Don't worry about Doug. He'll be here."

Thirty seconds to midnight, here comes Doug Harvey, a suitcase under each arm, staggering down the platform under the weight of his luggage and the weight of whatever he had been drinking since he left the bus at the Olympia. The train starts moving and Harvey starts running, and the boys are at the door yelling, "Come on, Doug!"

Finally, he just makes it as a couple of the guys reach out and haul him up onto the train. And Moore looks at me and says, "See? I told you he'd make it."

Why was he traded? I don't think Frank Selke ever forgave Harvey for being part of that pre-NHL Players Association group that banded together in the late fifties. Many of the players who were part of that original group, Harvey, Ted Lindsay, Tod Sloan, they were all traded.

I'm certain that Selke had promised himself, somewhere along the line, that he was going to trade him. They had won five straight Stanley Cups with Doug Harvey, then they didn't win in '60-'61. In Selke's mind that was likely ample reason to trade the guy.

I think Selke was also thinking he wanted a lot more toughness on the team. There was nothing panty-waist about Doug Harvey, but I guess he wanted a real tough guy. So he traded Doug and got Louie Fontinato from the Rangers.

TOM JOHNSON

When you look back to the great Canadiens teams in the fifties, there were a lot of good players. If you name a dominant person, besides the coach and the general manager, I think the dominant person on the ice was Doug Harvey. Doug was just a team man. He wasn't selfish at all. In fact, he taught a lot of people how not to be selfish.

There are a lot of Doug Harvey stories, but Doug was Doug. And he was that way, he never changed, right through to the end. When I went to see him in the hospital, and everyone was so worried about him and feeling sorry for him, Doug wasn't feeling sorry for himself. He was just talking about the old days and talking about his future, which didn't last too long, unfortunately.

Bob Turner

We had lost two straight at the Forum, which we weren't supposed to do. We were having our regular Saturday morning meeting in the dressing room the day of the next game and Toe told us that Mr. Selke was coming in to talk to us, which he hardly ever did.

So we were all tense as hell. A lot of us thought the old man was going to tell us we were going to be sent down. My spot was behind a big post at one end of the room, so we're all sitting there and Mr. Selke comes into the room.

Before he even started to talk, Doug stood up and said, "Mr. Selke, Bob Turner wants to know how come our meal money is only seven dollars a day. That's not enough. We can't eat on that now."

Old Doug was making it up as a joke on me, and to cut the pressure for the guys. It took me by surprise so I yelled out, "I didn't say that."

I don't think Mr. Selke heard me and he said, "Well, you know, Bob, I think we're going to up that to ten dollars. I'm glad you brought that up."

By now I'm trying to hide behind the post. Mr. Selke never said another thing. He just turned and walked out of the room. We never got the pep talk.

Doug was always the ringleader. We were in Chicago one night on a Sunday. The night before in Montreal we had beaten them 11-1, then the next night they beat us 7-1 or something like that and Toe was really steamed at us. We had to catch a train around midnight. All the defencemen used to ride in one cab and we're looking for a place to have a drink. Doug said we'd have time for two beers and sure enough he tells the cabbie to take us to a bar that Toe knew about and didn't want us to go into. Toe used to tell us he'd fine anybody a hundred bucks if he caught him in there.

So we're sitting at this long bar and I'm on the very end, right beside Doug. I see him looking over my shoulder at somebody and he says to me, "Hey, Bob, turn around. Look at the blonde that just walked in. She's really something, just gorgeous."

So I turned around and who's standing right there in front of me but Toe. Scared the hell out of me. Toe took one look at us, turned around, and walked out of the bar. Old Doug had suckered me again. But we didn't get fined, not that time anyway.

EDDIE MAZUR

It seemed like the Canadiens were always playing in Toronto on Grey Cup day. Dick didn't want the players going to the game, being outside in the cold all day and all that, so he had a fine of $500 for anyone who went.

I come on the scene, a big kid from the West, and the first year I remember Doug comes on the train carrying a big parka. Tom Johnson laughed and said, "What do you need that for, Doug?" And Doug said, "You never know, it might be cold in Toronto."

Everyone knew Doug was going to go to the football game. So he goes, and then gets a goal and an assist that night, and Dick fines him the $500. The next year we were back on Grey Cup day and Doug is doing the same thing.

So I found out it was a regular thing. Doug would always go to the Grey Cup game, and Dick would always fine him $500.

A summer or two after we moved to Montreal I was with my father in our garage in the Town of Mount Royal. It was in the evening and I, as usual, was watching him work with his electric saw, or whatever, doing my best to avoid helping out with the project he had under way. Suddenly, Doug Harvey arrived, unannounced. Except for the housewarming party my folks gave when we moved in, Doug had never paid a visit.

A look from my father got a message across to me quickly, and I left. The two men sat talking in the garage for a couple of hours. When their conversation was over I naturally wanted to know what it had been about.

Doug had come to see Dad, hoping his coach would intercede on his behalf with Frank Selke. Simply, Harvey was broke and wanted an advance on his next season's contract. He knew Mr. Selke would turn him down. Likely, he had already tried.

I don't know if my father ever said anything to Mr. Selke about it or what the eventual outcome was. But it was, typically, Doug.

Floyd Curry

We were playing in one of those long overtime games in Detroit in the playoffs in 1951. That was the series when the first game went into the fourth overtime period and in the next game we went into the third overtime period. We won both games and Rocket scored the winner both times.

I remember sitting in the dressing room between periods in overtime. I don't recall which game it was or what overtime it was, but we'd been playing a long time. We were all just sitting there trying to get our breath and nobody was saying anything. Then Doug pipes up and says, "Geez, will somebody hurry up and score and end this thing. The bars are all closing pretty soon."

Gordie Howe

I didn't know Harvey very well when we played. We used to try and get guys to go to their backhand because for most it was weaker than the forehand. We found out pretty quick that Harvey was just as good, if not better, with the backhand. He used to follow through when he would shoot the puck and put the stick right in your face. That led to a lot of interesting conversations in the corners.

When I played in Houston, in the WHA, Bill Dineen was running the club. He gave Harvey a job as a scout because he was down on his luck or something. He did things his own way. The scouts had to make written reports after their trips. Harvey came back from a long trip and Dineen asked him where his report was. He pointed to his head and said, "In the computer, right here."

He used to tell stories to the players. He told them that every city he went to as a scout was one where, sometime or another, he had been in the jail bailing out his buddies. My sons, Marty and Mark, were playing and they were kind of disappointed. They didn't like to hear that kind of stuff from an old hockey hero. They asked me if what he was saying was true. I told them if it came from Doug Harvey, it probably was.

He got traded from Montreal because of that business about the new players' union. The old guys running the teams in those days, Adams, Selke, Smythe, were tough birds who didn't like you upsetting their establishment.

Frank Selke used to send me a nice telegram whenever I would reach a milestone. But after I went to the WHA he wouldn't speak to me.

JUNIOR LANGLOIS

I have the set of videos they put out about the five straight Stanley Cup years. There's no doubt Doug Harvey was the key guy. It has to be Doug. You watch those games and it seems that nothing happens until Doug makes it happen. It's amazing.

I've had people at my house and I ask them if they want to see a real hockey player, and I show them the videos. They look and say, "Oh my Lord, this is unbelievable." I'm talking about people who know the game and that's a word I've heard them use, "unbelievable."

When it was time to open up, when we were one down, say, Doug would head down the ice and make that perfect pass to whoever was cutting for the net. He would just take over. Don't get me wrong, there were a heck of a lot of great players on that team. It was Star Alley. But I have to think he was the main man in the overall scheme of things.

I was traded to New York with Doug in 1961. I was working for Massey-Ferguson, in Cookshire, Quebec, in the off-season. I was through work and going home and I turned on the five o'clock news on my car radio. That's when I heard that I had been traded.

Doug had tried to call me before that to tell me about the trade. He wanted me to go with him because he said he would be playing and coaching and if I was there it would help him a lot. We had played together quite a bit with the Canadiens so we knew each other and that would make it easier.

They traded Doug because of that players' union thing. Look how every one of them ended up getting traded. I mean, really, how can you trade Doug Harvey?

Harry Howell

I played for Doug the year he coached the Rangers. I remember him telling me he was in the best shape he'd been in for about ten years.

He was very quiet that season, very serious. Believe it or not, he led by example. I learned a lot from him that year and it was the biggest shock of my career when he quit as the coach of the team.

He behaved himself when he was the coach. I couldn't say that about him the rest of the time he played in New York. But he was a good coach and we had a good year.

Scotty Bowman started coaching in the National Hockey League with the St. Louis Blues during the first season of expansion, 1967–68. The playoff format assured that one of the six new teams would reach the Stanley Cup finals. Bowman's Blues made it, but they might not have had Doug Harvey not arrived on the scene, at the age of forty-three.

Scotty Bowman

We hired Doug that year to be the playing coach of our farm team in Kansas City. We played Philadelphia in the first round. In the sixth game, in St. Louis, we were leading 1–0 when they tied it up with fifteen seconds to go. If we won that game we would win the series but we lost in the second overtime period. A defence-man named Ray Fortin went to stop a shot and it went off his glove into our net, just like Doug did that year in Detroit. Now we have to go back to Philadelphia for the seventh game, and that was the worst I ever felt in hockey. We'd won a game in their building but I didn't think we could win another one.

That same night Kansas City was playing at home in the playoffs against Fort Worth. They usually won their home games, but that night they lost and were eliminated. In those days you couldn't bring up players from your minor-league team as long as they were still in the playoffs, and we had a few guys who were hurt.

So at midnight I called Doug and he said, "I got three guys who are ready to go – Gary Veneruzzo, Craig Cameron, and me. I'm ready."

They practised with us the next day and then we flew to Philadelphia. We couldn't get in because of fog so we had to stay in Hershey. We had a hell of a time getting rooms, and I roomed with Doug.

We won the game 3-1. Doug got the first star, Al Arbour the second, and Glenn Hall the third. Doug played about forty minutes and as far as I'm concerned he won the game for us. He played a terrific game. And he was forty-three years old. Imagine.

DICKIE MOORE

I was with Gerry McNeil today and we were reminiscing about old times and talking about Doug and how sad it was his life ended up the way it did. Doug wasn't that kind of a guy when he played. Gerry said he was our leader, and that's true. Everybody went to him for advice.

I blame the trade. He should never have left Montreal. But that's water under the bridge and as far as he was concerned he had a good life. He told me that two days before he died. And when you look back to the things he did, it's amazing. One time he got into the scooter business. He showed up at training camp and drove a scooter right into the dressing room.

When Dick was coaching he was always after Doug about the way he would handle the puck around our goal crease. One night in Detroit, Dick went after him pretty good on the bench. The next shift he gets out and cuts in front of the net and nearly lost the puck to one of their guys, but he didn't. He kept carrying it along by the boards, passed by where Dick was, and said, "See, coach, he missed me." And this is right in the middle of a game against Detroit. We all started to laugh, and so did Dick. How many guys would do that?

Doug chose his own way of life. He would tell us not to worry about him, to worry about ourselves. And he really did do a lot for other people. Near the end the Canadiens did a lot for him.

Ronald Corey and Serge Savard brought him back into the organization as a scout and I think Doug really appreciated that. He didn't touch a drink his last two or three years.

When that picture of him looking so poorly appeared in all the papers a few weeks before he died, I didn't feel that bad about it. Knowing Doug, if he hadn't wanted that to happen he wouldn't have been there. He was very proud of his grandson and he wanted to be seen with him. Doug was a very modest guy. He never wanted to take any praise. But I think at the end he appreciated it. . . . He wanted some appreciation for what he had done.

IV

The 1960s

For those of us who like to delve into hockey's history, the "good old days" ended in 1967. When we talk about expansion, and we still are, that was the year the big one hit. Suddenly there were twelve NHL franchises, not six, and teams were travelling to places like Los Angeles and Oakland in the West and Philadelphia and Pittsburgh in the East.

The Chicago Black Hawks won the Stanley cup in 1961, their only victory in the last fifty-three years. For the rest of the 1960s, both before and after the newcomers arrived, the Stanley Cup was the exclusive property of the Montreal Canadiens and the Toronto Maple Leafs. The Canadiens won it five times, the Maple Leafs four.

Bobby Orr arrived in Boston in 1966 and the art of playing defence has never quite been the same since. Orr, Phil Esposito, and the rest of the big, bad Bruins were poised to become champions as the decade ended, although the word "dynasty" would never quite describe their team.

The 1960s ended with the Canadiens having won the Cup

four times in five years. The decade had begun with the history-making fifth straight Cup victory, their last until 1965. By that time the team at the Montreal Forum had a distinctively new look.

16

The Old Gang Breaks Up

The Montreal Canadiens won their fifth straight Stanley Cup at Maple Leaf Gardens, in Toronto, the night of April 14, 1960, when they defeated the Maple Leafs 4–0. Jean Béliveau scored two goals in that historic game while Henri Richard and Doug Harvey each scored once. Jacques Plante got the shut out.

The Canadiens had reached what is still the highest peak in Stanley Cup history twenty years after Senator Donat Raymond had decided to keep the team alive when it had plummeted to the lowest point in its long history. But in 1960 another senator, Hartland de M. Molson, occupied the office of president of the Montreal Canadiens. Senator Raymond had sold the hockey team, and the Forum, to Senator Molson and his brother Tom in September of 1957.

On the morning of September 15, 1960, during a scrimmage at the Canadiens' training camp at the Forum, Maurice Richard scored four goals on hockey's best goaltender, Jacques Plante. When the scrimmage ended the club advised the press that a news conference would be held at the Queen Elizabeth Hotel at two o'clock that afternoon. It was then, in a room packed with reporters, the mighty Rocket announced that his hockey career was over.

Maurice Richard's timing was right. He was bowing to the inevitable. Hockey is supposed to be a young man's game. On August 4, 1960, Richard turned thirty-nine. Injuries had caused him to miss eighty-nine games the previous three seasons. In his last two playoff years Richard had scored just once in twelve games.

He also had problems with his weight. In recent years he has freely admitted that by 1960 he was not willing to work at keeping himself in proper playing condition. A few years after Richard's retirement some of Toe Blake's cronies were arguing about how much the Rocket had weighed during his last couple of seasons. They called Blake, who told them, "I don't know. He would never get on the scale." It was a surprising statement from a coach who constantly carped at his players about how much they should weigh.

So the Rocket was gone, with then-record totals of 544 regular-season goals and 82 playoff goals. His record of six playoff over-time goals still stands. In the hearts and minds of those who were privileged to watch him play – and with all due respect to a base-ball pitcher in Boston and a football wide receiver in Toronto, the highest-paid professional athletes in their sports today – there will never be another "Rocket."

During the 1991 Stanley Cup playoffs I was part of the Hockey Night in Canada *crew broadcasting the Wales Conference final between Boston and Pittsburgh. During one of the games in Boston my partners in the booth, Bob Cole and John Garrett, talked about a couple of "Rockets." One was football player Raghib "Rocket" Ismail, who had recently signed a multimillion-dollar contract with the Toronto Argonauts. The other was Roger "Rocket" Clemens of the Boston Red Sox, another millionaire who had been the winning pitcher that afternoon at Fenway Park. When they were finished I butted in with the last word by saying, "Come on, you guys. There's only been one real 'Rocket,' and he didn't play football or base-ball."*

It was thirty-one years after Maurice Richard had played his last game, yet I am sure almost all of the HNIC *audience knew who I meant.*

When the 1960–61 season began the Rocket was the only absen-tee from the Canadiens' lineup that had swept to the Stanley Cup with eight straight victories the previous spring. They were, again, the unanimous choice in pre-season polls to finish in first place and were picked to win a sixth straight Stanley Cup. They finished in first place, a mere two points ahead of a fast-improving Toronto team. But number six was not to be.

Ironically, the first season of Maurice Richard's retirement was when one of his most cherished records was equalled. Bernie Geoffrion, the man who many fans said they would never forgive for passing Richard to win the scoring title in 1955, tied the Rocket's record of fifty goals in one season. Geoffrion was the NHL's best player in 1960-61, winning the scoring championship and the Hart Trophy as the MVP.

Geoffrion scored his fiftieth goal on March 16, 1961, when he fired the puck past Toronto goalie Cesare Maniago in a game at the Forum. The ovation the Boomer received that night must have made him feel that all had been forgiven. Well, almost all.

BERNIE GEOFFRION

That was the best year in all my career.

First of all, I had great confidence. I remember Frank Mahovlich being fifteen or twenty goals ahead of me, and he stopped at forty-eight. When I passed him, he couldn't believe it. He couldn't get to the fifty.

I didn't do it by myself. There was Béliveau, Harvey, Dickie, [Henri] Richard, the whole gang. The thing I remember the most is that nobody was selfish. If I was wide open, fine. If I was not open, hey, give the puck to Dickie or somebody else.

When you have confidence, sometimes everything goes in. It's like a quarterback when he passes eighteen out of eighteen. Same thing. I was shooting the puck at an angle that was impossible. Zap, in the net.

Today I watch games on TV and I can't believe what I see with my eyes. The shooting. Half the guys can't hit the net. It's terrible.

Despite Geoffrion's career season, the Canadiens did not win a sixth straight Stanley Cup. One reason was a knee injury the Boomer carried into the playoffs. He was able to play in only three of the first five games of the semifinal series against the Chicago Black Hawks, who had finished in third place, seventeen points behind the Canadiens.

Travelling to Chicago for the sixth game, the Canadiens were down three games to two and Geoffrion's knee was in a cast. During the train ride Doug Harvey decided to play doctor and cut the cast off the Boomer's ailing knee. It didn't work. A hobbled Geoffrion tried to play but was of little value and the Canadiens' record streak of Stanley Cup victories ended when Glenn Hall blanked them 3-0. It was Hall's second straight shutout.

Game three of that series was the one Danny Gallivan says is the best game he ever broadcast. It ended on a goal by Chicago's Murray Balfour after fifty-two minutes of overtime with the Canadiens playing short-handed because of a penalty to Dickie Moore. Earlier in the overtime the Canadiens appeared to have scored, but referee Dalton McCarthur ruled the puck had been directed into the net by a high stick. When the game ended, Toe Blake charged onto the ice and slugged McCarthur. Blake was fined $2,000.

DANNY GALLIVAN

The final score was 2-1 and what sold me was the best goaltending by two goalies, in one game, that I've ever seen.

You've got three overtime periods. You've got big guns like Mikita, Hull, Wharram, Pappin, and the Canadiens with all of their big guns. They were lickity-split, going all the time. Plante and Hall were just magnificent. And it was a playoff game, with all the pressure.

As I remember the winning goal, Balfour was going in on the right side and Hull hit him with a perfect pass. It was a clean-cut goal. Incidentally, that's one thing there were more of then, clean-cut goals. It was much easier for broadcasters in those days than it is for you fellows today.

I saw Blake hit McCarthur. When the periods or the game ended, Blake used to walk along the ice toward the dressing room and hug the boards as he went. But I saw then that he wasn't headed in that direction. His hat was a touch on the angle, and his face was as red as a ketchup bottle. He walked right across the ice and he let go a wild right hand. He was such a fierce competitor, he probably would have done that in a regular-season game.

We started our broadcast at 8:30 and I think it was 1:30 when we signed off. And were they ever jammed in at the Stadium. That's the night Jim Norris said that by the time the last overtime period started, every drop of beer in the place had been sold. Norris figured if there had been another intermission, there would have been a riot at the beer stands.

The old cliché about a player coming back to "haunt" his old team applied to Ab McDonald, a rangy winger out of Winnipeg who was with the Canadiens for the final two years of their five-straight Stanley Cup record. McDonald played all the way through to the finals in his first season. After playing all but two regular-season games the following year he was not used in the playoff sweep of eight straight victories in 1960.

AB MCDONALD

I had a strange experience because I was with the Canadiens for the last two years of the five-straight streak, then was sold to Chicago and played for them when they beat the Canadiens and stopped the streak in 1961.

I grew up in Winnipeg and belonged to Montreal when I was a junior. In those days junior teams were allowed one inter-branch transfer and the Canadiens sent me to play in St. Catharines, which was a Chicago farm team. So one way or another, I kept shuffling between Montreal and Chicago.

When I played with that big team in Montreal, you always had the feeling you were going to win. That's all you thought about. We might win a game 4-1 and after the game the guys would be asking, "How did we get that goal scored against us? What was the reason? How can we stop it the next time that situation arises?" It was like that all the time.

Then I went to Chicago and the atmosphere was quite different. I was a bit down at the start because I had the feeling I had been sold by a winner. Chicago had a lot of good, young players like Hull and Mikita, but nobody thought we were going to win it that season. The Canadiens were the big favourite, and that was only natural. But Glenn Hall was great in the nets and we surprised them.

I think the Canadiens were at the end of an unbelievable stretch and they had lost that little bit of extra drive that you need. Anyway, I went from one Cup-winner to another, and it was a good feeling.

Another who went from a Montreal Cup-winner to a Chicago Cup-winner was Dollard St. Laurent, although he didn't make the trip as quickly as McDonald did.

St. Laurent was an outstanding defenceman with the Montreal Royals seniors who joined the Canadiens in 1951. He played for the team until the 1958 Stanley Cup win, after which he was traded to the Chicago Black Hawks. He does not have pleasant memories of the way the deal was handled.

DOLLARD ST. LAURENT

I was traded because of my work with the players' association. I was at the meeting in Florida when the players tried to get together with the owners to see what was going on. The following year I was traded. Harvey and Olmstead were there, too, and they both got traded. When I got to Chicago you could see how many guys on that team had been part of trying to form the association. Tod Sloan and Jimmy Thomson were there from Toronto, Lindsay from Detroit.

I thought I was still doing a good job for Montreal but Frank Selke got rid of me just the same. He said Chicago wanted me, and this and that. He told me he had reorganized my contract with Chicago. When I got there Tommy Ivan told me that Selke had nothing whatever to do with any contract I would have with Chicago. I tried phoning Selke every day and I couldn't speak to him.

I couldn't get together with Tommy at all. We couldn't agree on what I should be paid. Just before the season he told me that they wanted me to go to Montreal to play for the All-Stars in the All-Star game. He said that when I got there I was to check with Jim Norris, who owned the Black Hawks. So I did and he asked me how much money I wanted to play in Chicago. I told him and he said that was okay with him, and that was that.

When we beat the Canadiens in the playoffs it was a thrill. They had some injuries. Boom Boom was hurt and so was Billy Hicke. Big Jean didn't get a goal against Glenn Hall. Hall held us in and we kept working. I remember telling Ab McDonald, Billy Hay, and Reg Fleming that if we worked hard and beat Montreal we would have the Stanley Cup. And that's exactly what happened.

The break-up of the dynasty began when Maurice Richard retired. It continued for a period of four years, during which the Canadiens did not win the Stanley Cup. That was the longest the team went without a Cup victory in the twenty-six years between 1953 and 1979. When the Canadiens won again, in 1965, only five regulars remained from the 1960 Cup-winners.

A few weeks after the 1961 semifinal loss to Chicago another superstar left the scene. Doug Harvey was traded to the New York Rangers for defenceman Lou Fontinato. Harvey became the Rangers' player-coach, and another era had ended at the Forum.

KEN REARDON

We were finished with Harvey. Selke didn't want him. We couldn't handle him anymore, mostly off the ice. Looking at it from the standpoint of an employer and an employee, Harvey had become a real pain in the ass. You know, when you win the Stanley Cup, for a few days after you're drunk and you're tired, but you have to go to City Hall to sign the Golden Book. Harvey could never make that. He was a troublemaker.

He didn't play that well the last year we had him. We were looking for a way to trade him, but we wanted to trade him up, as you always want to do with a star player. I phoned Muzz Patrick in New York. We started to talk about "haves and have nots" and Patrick wondered how he could get a guy like Harvey. Selke and I had been talking about how we could get rid of Harvey.

I said to Patrick that Harvey could be available but he would have to be traded up, not just as a player. He said, "I'd make him player-coach." I said to myself, "Here's our chance."

You always come to a point when you've got to unload your captain. That comes through time, and attrition, and he's usually an older guy who is almost finished. You don't want to keep him and sacrifice a good rookie. With Harvey, our chance to get out of it was when Patrick said he would make him player-coach, and we made the deal.

The year the Montreal Canadiens lost their five-year grip on the Stanley Cup was also the year Jacques Plante lost his on the Vezina Trophy. Toronto's Johnny Bower took over.

When the 1961–62 season began the Canadiens had a new-look defence in front of Plante. Junior Langlois went with Harvey to New York and Bob Turner had been traded to Chicago. Replacing them were rookies J.C. Tremblay and Jean Gauthier, plus Fontinato from New York and former Toronto defenceman Al MacNeil. Tom Johnson and Jean-Guy Talbot were holdovers.

The Canadiens' 1961 training camp was held in Victoria, B.C. A vote was held to elect Harvey's successor as captain. Jean Béliveau was the winner even though Bernie Geoffrion thought he would be. Geoffrion threw a temper tantrum when the result was made known.

The camp in Victoria was the scene of a bizarre off-ice incident that the boys of that era still recall when they get together to talk over old times.

MARCEL BONIN

One day after practice at our training camp in Victoria we were going back to the Empress Hotel, a bunch of us, walking. There were parking meters on the street and I thought I would have some fun, so I hit one of the parking meters with my fist. And I broke my wrist.

We didn't say anything to Toe Blake. The next day I went to practice and my wrist was so sore somebody else had to tie my skates when Toe wasn't watching. When we got on the ice one of the boys gave me a body check right away, and I fell down and said I hurt my wrist. So when they told Toe Blake that Bonin had a broken wrist, he thought I had got hurt in the practice.

Far from being dismayed by the absence of the great Doug Harvey, Plante said he would show everyone how good he was by winning the Vezina Trophy back again. And he did just that, plus winning the Hart Trophy as the league MVP. *Many felt it was the best year of his career.*

The Canadiens finished first in 1961–62, thirteen points ahead of the Maple Leafs. In the Stanley Cup semifinal against Chicago they won the first two games, then lost four in a row. Again, Glenn Hall was the main culprit in their demise. The Canadiens scored only seven times in the four Chicago victories. Hall blanked them 2-0 in the series clincher.

The Canadiens stood fairly pat with their lineup the next season. The only notable absentee was defenceman Tom Johnson. His thirteen-year career in Montreal ended when the Canadiens did not protect him and he was drafted by the Boston Bruins. Johnson played the next two seasons in Boston, then retired to the Boston front office where he still resides. He coached the Bruins to a Stanley Cup in 1972.

The six-team NHL *had one of its closest finishes in 1962-63. Toronto finished in first place, one point ahead of Chicago, three ahead of Montreal, and only five up on the fourth-place Detroit Red Wings.*

The playoffs belonged to Punch Imlach's team at that time. They had defeated Chicago in the finals in 1962 and would defeat Detroit in the finals in 1963. In the semifinals they disposed of the Canadiens in five games, as Toe's boys were shut out in the deciding game for the third straight year. Johnny Bower did the deed in 1963. In the five-game series, the Canadiens scored just four goals.

When Bower was blanking the Canadiens 5-0 at Maple Leaf Gardens on April 4, 1963, Dickie Moore and Jacques Plante were playing their final game in a Montreal uniform. One month later, Moore announced that he was retiring. His final season had been a frustrating one. At one point, one of the Montreal Canadiens' all-time great competitors had come close to quitting.

RED FISHER

It was about four or five days before Christmas. We were in Chicago and that night Dickie Moore had either not been in uniform at all, or if he was he hadn't played very much. We had one more road game on the trip, two nights later, in Detroit.

Dickie knocked on my hotel room door about one o'clock in the morning, came in, sat down, and told me he was going home. "I can't take this anymore," he told me.

I said, "Hey, this isn't the Dickie Moore I know who's talking to me about quitting his team in the middle of the season." But he kept insisting that he wanted to go home the next day.

I tried to explain to him that, while he was in the twilight of his career, it would be a terrible way to end his career. I asked him to stay with the team and play in Detroit. Then, if things were still the same, at least he could go back to Montreal and talk to management. I told him that if he took a train or a plane home the next day, that would be the last thing people would remember about him.

What was really bothering him was that he had stopped scoring. I told him he had stopped scoring because it seemed all he did when he was on the ice was pass the puck to Henri Richard. I used the old line, "If you don't shoot, you don't score."

Anyway, he went to Detroit and, sure enough, Blake puts him in the starting lineup. Henri Richard wins the opening face-off, the puck goes to Moore, he takes one or two steps past the centre-ice red line and shoots the puck. It goes right under Terry Sawchuk's arm and into the net.

Moore wheeled around, looked up at the press box, and waved his stick at me. Later in the game, he scored another goal.

He ended up finishing the season. But I'm convinced that if he hadn't come to my room that night he would have quit, because that's the way he was. He was very stubborn, and very proud. He just couldn't accept not playing for the Montreal Canadiens.

DICKIE MOORE

Things hadn't gone too well for me and they talked about trading me. I said nobody was going to trade me, that I could make a living in business and I was going to retire. But Mr. Selke talked me into going to the training camp in the fall.

I couldn't see that things were any different then, so I went upstairs, thanked them for what they had done for me, and told them I was going back to my decision to retire because I couldn't play for anybody else. I still had the feeling they were going to try to trade me.

As I came out of the office Toe grabbed me and said, "Dick, don't retire. Don't be silly because you'll be sorry. You're gonna be out a long time and you're gonna miss it."

I told him that was okay for him to say because he was making a lot of money. That's when he told me how much they were paying him – $16,000, that's all. I couldn't believe it but I had to because it came from Toe and he was a pretty honest guy. I always thought coaches made a lot more than players. So there he was making that kind of money and he'd coached five Stanley Cup-winning teams.

Toe was right, I did miss the game. But I stayed out of it that winter and that's when I fractured my kneecap in an accident in my workshop. Mr. Selke called me and asked if I could come back and play in the playoffs. But I couldn't skate because of my kneecap. So I couldn't make a comeback even though I really wanted to. I couldn't wait to get back, but I couldn't skate.

The Canadiens knew I wanted to play again but they didn't protect me. I was sitting in my office when King Clancy called and told me Toronto had drafted me. The Canadiens thought I had talked to them before, but I hadn't talked to anybody. I told Clancy there was no guarantee I could skate but I was willing to give it a hell of a try.

When it came to me signing with Toronto, Punch Imlach and I were apart by a thousand dollars, so we tossed for it and I beat him. He hated to lose, believe me, but I beat him on a toss for a thousand. That's how we decided what my salary would be with the Toronto Maple Leafs.

Over the years the Montreal Canadiens have not made too many trades in the "blockbuster" category. But one month after Dickie Moore said he was leaving, the Canadiens unloaded another super-star from the glorious era. In a trade involving seven players they sent Jacques Plante to the New York Rangers. Going with Plante were veteran centremen Donnie Marshall and Phil Goyette. In return the Canadiens received forwards Dave Balon, Leon Roche-

fort, and Len Ronson, plus the Rangers' number-one goaltender, Gump Worsley.

While Toe Blake always maintained Jacques Plante was the greatest goalie he ever saw, he had little use for him as a person. Whatever was left of their relationship was over when the 1963 playoffs ended. While Canadiens watchers weren't too surprised to see Plante leave, the other goaltender in the deal was very surprised to be heading back to his native Montreal.

GUMP WORSLEY

How did I feel? Shocked.

I was with Muzz Patrick at the NHL meetings the night before at the Queen Elizabeth Hotel. We were in the press room having a few suds and I asked him if they were thinking of trading me. He said, "Never."

The next day, the very next day, I got a call from one of my buddies and he said I'd been traded. I said, "Yeah, sure." He told me to turn on my radio and I heard it on the radio. A few minutes later you called me from your radio station, and then I got a call from Mr. Selke. To this day I'm still waiting for a call from the Rangers to tell me they traded me.

The big thing for me was wondering if I was going to be accepted. I was coming in to take over from a guy who had a goals-against average of about zero. So acceptance was the big thing for me.

I got hurt early in that season, in Toronto, and I wondered then if I would ever be back with the team. I was thirty-four years old and I had torn my hamstring. So when I was ready to play they sent me to Quebec to get in shape. Ken Reardon told me they'd bring me back in three weeks. I'm still waiting for his call, too. I played the rest of that year in Quebec City.

The reason the Gumper languished in Quebec City was Charlie Hodge, a pint-sized goalie who had been bouncing around between the Canadiens and their various farm teams for seven years. When he took over after Worsley's injury, Hodge played in the Canadiens' remaining sixty-two games, had eight shutouts, and won the Vezina Trophy.

Hodge was known as "Little Charlie." He measured five-foot-six and as a kid had a tough time convincing people running junior hockey in Montreal that he deserved a chance to make a team.

CHARLIE HODGE

I was scouted when I was playing minor hockey in Lachine by a chap named Frank Mahoney. He told me the junior Royals wanted me to try out. So I packed up my equipment and took the streetcar to their practice. When I got there some old guy was standing in the dressing room and he said, "Go home, kid. You're too small."

So I went home but then the next day I went back on the streetcar. That time I got my pads on and this old guy comes along again and tells me to go home. So I did.

I went back again the next day, lugging all that equipment on the streetcar, and that time I was all dressed and going on the ice and this same old fart, whose name I never did know, yelled at me again and told me to take a hike because I was too small.

Sam Pollock was running the junior Canadiens teams and right after that his B team lost a game quite badly. He called me and asked me to come and play for that team. I did, and I was with Sam from then on.

It was no big deal trying to fit in with the big team when I got there to stay. They all knew me because I'd been up and down so often. And because of the junior hockey set-up in those days you were part of the organization much earlier.

I played along with Plante when Dick alternated two goalies in one game in the playoffs in 1955. I thought it was great but Plante wasn't too thrilled. When I finally was there to stay I won the Vezina Trophy in my first year and played with Gump when we won the Stanley Cup the next year. I got a shutout in the finals. Those were my best years and my best memories.

Little Charlie backstopped the Canadiens to a first-place finish in the 1963-64 season, one point ahead of Chicago. They played the

THE HABS

defending Cup champion Maple Leafs in the semifinal. Hodge blanked Toronto in the first game and after five games the Canadiens had a 3-2 series lead. But their old nemesis Johnny Bower did it to them again. Bower blanked Montreal 3-0 in the sixth game and stopped seventeen shots in the third period of the seventh game at the Forum to preserve a 3-1 Toronto victory. Dave Keon scored all three Toronto goals. The Leafs went on to win their third straight Stanley Cup.

Game seven of the Toronto series was the last in a Canadiens' uniform for another of the superstars from the five-in-a-row era, Bernie Geoffrion. The Boomer missed fifteen games that season because of injuries and felt he was getting a message that the Canadiens were intent on making more changes to the old guard. His relationship with the team was good when he retired, but it didn't stay that way for too long.

BERNIE GEOFFRION

The year after I score the fifty goals I only score twenty-three. They thought I was finished. But in those days there were only six teams. Twenty goals was like hitting .300 in baseball. Today, with twenty-one teams, guys get fifteen goals and think they're big. Anyway, I don't live in the past, and I'm glad for them.

They asked me what I wanted to do so I told them I wanted to coach the big club. What really hurt me is that they promised it to me. At the time Floyd Curry was coaching the Quebec Aces but he didn't speak French. That didn't go too big there. So they told me, you retire and go to Quebec City for a couple of years to get experience. Then come back, and you'll get the big club.

I talked it over with my wife, Marlene. [Marlene Geoffrion is the daughter of Howie Morenz.] This was 1964 and I was only thirty-three. But we decided to think of our future. So I signed my papers and went to Quebec to coach for two years. I finished first both years.

After the second year was over I had dinner with the owner, Mr. Martineau, and he told me I would come back and coach there another year. That was okay. So Marlene and I start driving home

198

to Montreal, and we stop for a coffee. Just before I pull over, I open the radio and I hear, "Boom Boom Geoffrion just got fired." I say to Marlene, "How can that happen when I had dinner with that guy last night and he tells me I got my job, no problem?"

Anyway, I was fired because they wanted to rehire Phil Watson. When I got back home in Montreal I sat in my chair waiting for the phone call from the Montreal Canadiens. No phone call at all. So I go to the Forum to see Dave Molson, who was now president of the team. He told me the only job he had for me was to coach the Canadiens' juniors.

Now I really got mad. I just finished coaching in the American League and instead of going up I'm going down. So that's when I told them, "I'm going to come out of retirement, and I'm going to come back to the Forum, and I'm going to beat your ass!"

Harold Ballard heard about it and offered me a four-year contract to go to Toronto. I hadn't played for two years and I was not a free skater. I had to work hard at it. But the New York Rangers had finished last and they had the first pick. Emile Francis was running the team and he told me I'd never pass by the New York Rangers. I tried to talk him out of it, told him I had a bad back and bad knees, because I wanted to go to Toronto. But he didn't listen, and he drafted me.

That summer I trained like heck but after two weeks at training camp I called Marlene and told her I wasn't going to make it. But then I started to get my second wind and I stayed.

I went to the Forum and I got two goals against the Canadiens. [John] Ferguson was watching me and I was joking to him, "Tell Toe he's got to be kidding. You gonna watch me?"

So I pop two goals that night. Jim Neilson on defence gave me a beautiful pass up the middle and put me on a breakaway. I put a big deke on Charlie Hodge, sent him out for a cup of coffee with cream and sugar. I was jumping in the air. Oh man, that was one of the biggest goals of my life.

There was another major change to the Montreal Canadiens in the summer of 1964. The man who built the dynasty, Frank Selke, Sr., and his right-hand man, Ken Reardon, left the organization on the same day. Mr. Selke was asked to retire. Reardon was relieved of his duties. The operation of the hockey club was now in the hands of Sam Pollock.

Mr. Selke was seventy-two years old but had no intention of retiring. At the news conference announcing the changes he began a short speech by saying, "When Senator Molson asked me to retire, I was shocked."

But the Molson family was in charge, and the old guard in the front office was gone. Now in place was an organization that would lead the Montreal Canadiens to ten Stanley Cup championships in the next fifteen years.

17

More New Faces,
Two More Cups

When Bernie Geoffrion played his final game for the Montreal Canadiens on April 9, 1964, there were a few teammates remaining from the club that had won a fifth straight Stanley Cup four years earlier. Big Jean and Henri were still there. So were Backstrom, Talbot, Hicke, and Provost. But all the other names above the lockers in the Canadiens' dressing room had changed. Now they included Laperriere, Harris, Ferguson, Rousseau, Harper, and a couple of Tremblays. They were the nucleus of a team that would win the Stanley Cup four times in the next five years.

Some referred to Sam Pollock as "Trader Sam." But in addition to his wheeling and dealing in hockey's flesh market, Pollock's determination to maintain and strengthen the Canadiens' scouting system was just as important, if not more so. This was especially true in the province of Quebec, where Pollock and his staff knew about every young hockey player who might someday become a Montreal Canadien. A few, like Rod Gilbert and Jean Ratelle, slipped away. But not many.

A prime example of how a native Quebecer was nurtured to stardom on the Montreal Canadiens was Gilles Tremblay. A solid two-way left-winger, Tremblay played his way through the system to graduate to the Canadiens during the 1960–61 season. His career was cut short in 1969 by a chronic asthma condition. Gilles Tremblay is now a widely respected colour commentator and analyst on both the radio and TV versions of La Soirée du Hockey.

GILLES TREMBLAY

I come from Montmorency Falls, a small town near Quebec City, and I played kids' hockey there at my school and in juvenile. I was lucky two ways. I was one of the best players, and as we were only five miles from Quebec City my juvenile team was able to play there in the bigger rinks. So scouts watching games there saw me a lot more than if I had just been playing in Montmorency Falls.

The following year they formed a new league, Quebec Saguenay, for kids my age all through our region and northern Quebec. That's when I played against J.C. Tremblay. My brother Ludger was a senior hockey player. He had played with Jean Béliveau, in Quebec City, and he told me to go with a team called Victoria. That was a weak team but my brother said it would be better because I would get more ice time for better experience. And he was right.

The next year they made two teams from that league to play in Montreal in the Metropolitan Junior League. That was better for me, to be seen playing hockey in Montreal.

During the Christmas holidays we were playing at the Forum on a Friday night. We won 3–0 and I got all three goals. After the game our owner, Paul Dumont, came to me and said, "Do you know who was watching you tonight? Sam Pollock, and he wants to talk to you."

So I talked with Sam and he asked me if I was ready to move up to play for his team, the Junior Canadiens. I was only sixteen and a half. That was the year Sam had the Junior Canadiens playing in three different leagues, Junior A, Senior A in Ontario, plus the Quebec Professional League. He told me he wanted me to play for him the next three games, and I did. So in less than a week I played in four different leagues, Sam's three plus my own league where he first saw me.

When I had played in Montreal I thought we were going right back home so I had no extra clothes, no toothbrush, nothing. I slept in Montreal, bought a suit and some things the next day, then left for Kingston and played there that night. Sam was the coach and Scotty Bowman was there, too, as his helper.

Ralph Backstrom was the big star of that team. Also on the

team was a big, tough defenceman named Bingo Ernst, who had been around for many years playing senior hockey. In that game he jumped over the boards and took a run at a guy. He missed him and by mistake hit Backstrom and knocked him out. He nearly killed him. Sam took Bingo off the ice right away and told him to go right to the train station and go back to Montreal. He was that mad. That was the last we saw of Bingo Ernst, and that was my initiation into senior hockey.

I played the next night in Ottawa against the Toronto Marlboros and after that in Shawinigan in the Quebec League. Sam asked me to stay with his team and he arranged for me to change schools. I have been with the Montreal Canadiens ever since, playing, and now broadcasting.

In my second year, 1957, they put me at training camp with the big team. They would do that with a few kids to make enough players for the camp, and also to give us a chance to get the feel of the big team. I went to the camp for the rest of my junior years.

After my last year junior, Sam organized a new league, the Eastern Professional Hockey League. He said he didn't want his kids going to the American League where there were a lot of old pros, drinking and all that. During that year, as I found out later, the Canadiens turned down two trades for me. The first offer was from Lynn Patrick, in Boston. He offered Jean-Guy Gendron, who had scored twenty-five goals the year before, and $25,000 for me. Sam said no because two of his left-wingers were having problems. Bonin had a sore back and Moore had a bad knee.

Then I also found out from Emile Francis that he offered to trade Rod Gilbert to the Canadiens for me. Gilbert was playing junior for New York's farm team in Kitchener. And Sam said no again. So he kept me in the organization, and I went up to the big team after playing in the Eastern Pro League.

I learned one thing in those days about the Montreal Canadiens. They really cared about the kind of players they signed. Sam came to my home in Montmorency Falls just to meet with my father and my brothers and get an idea of where it was I came from. I saw a lot of pretty good young hockey players leave the organization in those years because they were bad livers, or coming from bad families. When we were just kids they made sure we dressed properly, wore ties on the road, things like that. You learn fast, and you appreciated it in the long run.

During interviews for this book there were two subjects often brought up by many of the former players. One was how they began their careers in the NHL. Another was money. They would mention how much they, and others, earned during their playing eras. Nobody went out of his way to complain about what the players earn today. But they seemed to want to make sure I knew how times had changed.

GILLES TREMBLAY

It was tough to make it when there were only six teams, especially in Montreal with the team winning five straight Stanley Cups. Even when I was at the camp as a junior they didn't take it easy on you. A guy like Bert Olmstead, for example, a real tough hockey player even in practice. I don't blame them. As far as they were concerned, you were a young guy trying to take away a job. But once you made the team they accepted you right away. They figured you were a good hockey player, one of them.

I played my first game against Detroit at the Forum, November 12th, 1960. Early that week Mr. Selke and Sam asked me to come up and watch the game on Wednesday, against Boston. Mr. Selke had seats right behind the goal and I sat with him for that game. He said he wanted me to get a good look from close up, to see how fast it was and how rough it was. So I watched that game with the big boss. He told me I would play the next game, against Detroit, and that I would be checking Gordie Howe.

I practised the next two days and then on Saturday night I was in the starting lineup. They put me on a line with Béliveau and Geoffrion. During the national anthem I was not feeling too good. Across the ice from me, there was Howe, with Alex Delvecchio and Parker McDonald. I would rather have been playing on the line with Ralph Backstrom and Bill Hicke. But there I was, against Howe, and I was against him when we played Detroit for the rest of my career.

Howe tested me a couple of times at the beginning of the game.

But afterwards he told me that as soon as he saw how I reacted in that game, he knew I was in the league for good.

I have to laugh when I look back to what happened when we were first signing our contracts in those days. I played that first season for $100 a game, so I made close to $7,000. The next year we had our training camp in Victoria. Mr. Selke tried to sign everybody before we left for camp and only one guy didn't sign. Bernard Geoffrion. The year before he had scored fifty goals. He was only the second guy ever to score fifty . . . . Geoffrion wanted a $5,000 raise. He didn't go to camp right away but showed up a week later. He got a raise of $3,500 and he was the only fifty-goal scorer in the league at that time.

That year I signed for $7,500. They had traded Bob Turner to Chicago for a guy named Fred Hilts. Mr. Selke told me that whoever had the best camp, me or Hilts, would make the team. He said if Hilts made it I would lose my job and they would trade me. I had a terrible camp, but Hilts was worse. So I made the team and scored thirty-two goals that year.

Mr. Selke told me at Christmas time not to worry about money, that he would fix me up at the end of the year. He kept his promise and gave me a bonus of $3,500. I scored thirty-two goals and got the same bonus as Geoffrion when he scored fifty.

The Calder Memorial Trophy is named after the first president of the NHL, Frank Calder, and is awarded annually to the league's outstanding rookie. The Canadiens' farm system produced three winners in six years starting in 1959 with Ralph Backstrom. Three years later Bobby Rousseau was the winner, and two years after that it was defenceman Jacques Laperriere. Since then the rookie award pickings have been slim. After Laperriere in 1964, the lone Montreal winner was Ken Dryden, in 1972.

Like Gilles Tremblay, Rousseau and Laperriere were products of the province of Quebec. As teenagers both were standouts for the Montreal Junior Canadiens. Bobby Rousseau was a right-winger who played on four Canadiens' Stanley Cup-winning teams. He was rookie of the year in 1962 on the strength of twenty-one goals and twenty-four assists in seventy games. In those days, that was good enough.

BOBBY ROUSSEAU

I was one of Sam's boys. After I played junior he had me play for Hull-Ottawa in the Eastern Pro League. The Canadiens brought me up for fifteen games in '60-'61. They had some injuries. I scored my first NHL goal then, on Jack McCarten, who was playing for the New York Rangers. The funny thing about that was that I had played against him at the Winter Olympics in Squaw Valley the year before. Sam had loaned me to the Canadian Olympic team. The Americans won that year and McCarten was their big hero, just like Jim Craig was when they won in 1980. I didn't score on him at the Olympics, but I got my first NHL goal against him a year later.

If you're asking me about highlights with the Canadiens I guess there are two. The first would be my first Stanley Cup, in 1965. I played on four, but that was the best. We beat Chicago in seven games in the finals. I was playing on a line with Jean Béliveau and Dick Duff. In the seventh game we had them down 4–0 after the first ten minutes or so. Our line had three of the goals and I had three assists.

The other is the night I scored five goals in one game against the Detroit Red Wings. The goalie was Roger Crozier, and it was in February of '64. At that time my wife was expecting our second child and it was getting kind of close for her. The doctor told her to stop going to the hockey games. So on the morning of that game I took her to the bus terminal and she got on the bus to go to her home in Ste. Hyacinthe to stay at her mother's place, close to the hospital.

After I put her on the bus I went home and I ate four or five doughnuts, maybe even more. That was all I had to eat. I packed my suitcase and left for the Forum. So on a day when I had doughnuts for my game meal, I scored five goals.

I had thirteen goals before that game. In those days twenty goals was a good season, and suddenly there I was early in February with eighteen. I finished the year with twenty-five. I scored one goal in the first period, two in the second, and two in the third. I got the fifth goal at about the seven-minute mark of the third period. After that I must have got on the ice maybe twice. I remember being kind of disappointed because Toe was keeping me on the bench. There must have been some penalties. I don't really recall. But as I look back, it was a great feeling.

An important member of any hockey team's official family is the team doctor. For over twenty-five years Dr. Doug Kinnear has been the club physician of the Montreal Canadiens. Dr. Kinnear joined the team in the early 1960s and immediately learned that hockey players are a special breed.

DR. DOUG KINNEAR

I was covering the first game of my hockey career and Claude Provost got cut by a high stick. They signalled to me from the bench so I went into the clinic and saw that he had a deep laceration on his forehead. The cut was about two inches long.

It was my job to do the stitching and the first thing I did was ask for the freezing. Bill Head was the therapist in those days and he shook his head to give me the signal that hockey players do not require cuts to be frozen.

I swallowed hard, took the needle and the sutures, and proceeded to sew up the laceration. Then I said, "Claude, you'd better go next door, lie down and rest for a while." He said, "Thanks Doc," jumped off the table, headed back to the bench, and was on the ice for his next shift. That was a revelation to me.

Later in his first year with the Canadiens, Doug Kinnear was involved in the most serious player injury ever seen at the Montreal Forum.

On March 9, 1963, Lou Fontinato crashed head first into the boards at the south end of the Forum while trying to check Vic Hadfield of the Rangers. Fontinato fell to the ice and didn't get up. Somehow you knew this was not a normal hockey injury. In all my years of going to hockey games I have never heard a crowd as silent as that one was looking at Lou Fontinato lying on the ice at the Montreal Forum, with his neck broken.

Dr. Doug Kinnear

It happened right in front of me. I was sitting behind the glass at the south end of the Forum. Vic Hadfield had his back to me, right up against the glass, and he had the puck. I saw Fontinato coming in to nail him on the boards, and Fontinato put his head down. Hadfield sidestepped, and Fontinato went head first into the boards, right in front of me, and just dropped to the ice.

The thing that I still remember was that there was a total hush in the building, nothing but silence. Even before I got onto the ice I knew that something very major had happened.

I went out on the ice and Lou was saying, over and over again, "Don't roll me over. Don't touch me. Don't move me." Lou knew his neck was broken. He was quadriplegic, with no movement at all in his arms or legs.

We got him onto the stretcher, using the appropriate precautions. At that time the security men at the Forum were the ones who came onto the ice to take the stretcher off. They lifted the stretcher and were taking him off when one of the security men slipped. I was walking beside the stretcher, and the stretcher rolled. I grabbed it and stabilized it, or Lou would have rolled off. I shudder to think what could have happened if I hadn't been right there. Ever since then we have had players on skates take a stretcher off the ice.

Lou Fontinato

I think that players who have other kinds of injuries, like knees, and keep hoping they can come back feel it more than I did. You get an injury like I got, you know you're not coming back.

I was entertaining thoughts of maybe retiring in a year or two. I kind of looked after a few of the bucks I made and I bought a farm and built an apartment building.

I was the kind of guy who ate, slept, drank hockey. I took it pretty tough even though I was looking forward to only playing another year or two and then calling it quits. I never shied away from work. With my farm and my apartment building, if I couldn't make as much as I could in the National Hockey League there was something wrong.

It was unfortunate it happened, but you can't win 'em all, and you can't lose 'em all either. I have never looked back. I might look a little older, but I tell you, I feel good.

I meet the odd guy who says, "You're Louie Fontinato. You broke your neck playing hockey." So I just swivel my head around from side to side, which I can do now, and say, "No, you got the wrong guy."

Now that I'm a farmer it comes in handy sometimes. I'll hear a weather forecast and he'll say it's going to rain tomorrow. I'll say, no it isn't, because I can feel it in my neck when it's going to rain. (laughs)

I got the nickname "Leaping Louie" because of my Italian temperament, I guess. They'd give me a penalty and I wouldn't agree. So I'd take a jump in the air and yell at the ref, and that's how that came about.

They weren't paying too many dollars when I started. In my first year pro I went out to Vancouver where Coley Hall was running the team. He liked money better than I did. I signed for $3,500, but I was so anxious to play and loved it so much I told people that Hall was crazy. He could have signed me for $2,500. You didn't walk right into the NHL as a kid in those days. A lot of good players served apprenticeship in the minors.

I played pro hockey for twelve years and right to the end I was never sure of my job. In my last year in Montreal they had a guy like Jacques Laperriere coming up. We never played out our option, like they do today. Then the option was a train ticket to the minors. One bad game, well, okay. Second bad game, you were called up to the office. Third bad game and you might get your option, that train ticket to the minors.

After a while, with a family and the farm life and when I could have afforded it, I could have left it. But I loved playing hockey. The life was like prestige, spelled "money."

When Lou Fontinato's hockey career came to a tragic end, the Canadiens replaced him with twenty-one-year-old Jacques Laper-

riere. He played six regular-season games to close out the 1962-63 season and five more in the playoffs. The following season Laperriere became a regular, and he remained one until a knee injury ended his career in 1974.

Jacques Laperriere was another of Sam Pollock's highly regarded French-Canadian prospects who lived up to his advance billing. Laperriere won the Calder Trophy in 1964 and the Norris Trophy as the NHL's outstanding defenceman in 1966. A gangling type, he played on five Stanley Cup-winning teams and was elected to the Hockey Hall of Fame in 1987. "Lappy" has been an assistant coach with the Canadiens for the past several years. When the NHL entered the jet age of airplane travel, Laperriere had to struggle with a very serious fear of flying.

JACQUES LAPERRIERE

I was brought along by Sam, you know. First when I played for St. Laurent, in the Metropolitan League. Then I played for him with the Junior Canadiens and then with Hull-Ottawa.

When you were one of Sam's gang, you were taught to do things the right way. We had to wear a hat at all times, and a shirt and tie. First class, that's how he trained us right from the start. If you forgot your hat when you got to the bus, then you go home. He wouldn't bring you to play the game. If the guys were smart, they learned a lot about how to act and about discipline. It was very important to his system when you were a young player. They watched how you reacted. Sam was very strict, but on the other side he was very fair. He treated you pretty good and I learned a lot when I was still very young.

When I first started to play we travelled by train. But when we started to fly everywhere I was scared. We didn't have the planes that we have today. It wasn't that I was afraid to fly, but when they closed the door it seemed like I was in a prison. I couldn't move and it would start to build up and build up. There was no way I could get out.

Today, with the planes we've got, you don't feel anything. I must say that at times I'm still scared, but I have no choice. I've got to work, so I've got to fly.

One reason the Montreal Canadiens stopped winning Stanley Cups in the early 1960s was a lack of toughness. Or so the story goes when Habs fans talk about the arrival onto their scene of John Bowie Ferguson. Ask me my choice of the ten most popular players in the last fifty years of the Montreal Canadiens, and Fergie would be near the top of the list.

John Ferguson is a native of Vancouver who joined the Canadiens for the 1963-64 season and played on five Stanley Cup-winning teams in his eight seasons in Montreal. Along the way he has had a most interesting career, on and off the ice. His wife, Joan, was a skater in the Ice Follies, hardly Fergie's milieu when you think about it. When his playing career ended he became a businessman in various enterprises, including horse racing and the garment trade. He was an assistant coach for Team Canada in the famed 1972 series against the Soviets. In 1977, six years after he retired from playing, Fergie became the coach and general manager of the New York Rangers. Later, he was GM with the Winnipeg Jets. But he is best remembered as a hockey tough guy.

John Ferguson played junior hockey in Melville, Saskatchewan. From there he made stops at Fort Wayne in the International League and at Cleveland in the American League, earning the reputation as a player who could score goals and win fights. Fergie was playing for Cleveland when Frank Selke brought him to Montreal.

Toe Blake put Ferguson in his starting lineup for the 1963-64 opener, against Boston. His linemates were Jean Béliveau and Bernie Geoffrion, which wasn't a bad way to start. Twelve seconds after the drop of the puck Fergie was in a fierce fight with Bruins' tough guy Ted Green. Later in the game he scored two goals. As far as Canadiens fans were concerned, it was love at first sight.

JOHN FERGUSON

Jim Hendy owned the team in Cleveland and he brought me there. Jack Gordon was running the club and he called me in one day and said he had a chance to sell my contract to Boston, New York, or Montreal. The Canadiens seemed the most interested and he asked me if I would like to go to Montreal. I said I certainly would. I was coming off a year when I led the American League in goal-scoring and penalties and made the All-Star team. So the Canadiens made a working agreement with Cleveland and bought my contract.

When my first training camp was over I remember Blake saying to me, "I'm going to play you with Geoffrion and Béliveau. Both of them are getting older. Look after them." People ask me if the Canadiens ever told me they wanted me to fight. What Blake said then was really all anyone ever said to me. So I took the initiative. The team did need some toughness, yes. Terry Harper and Jacques Laperriere started that year, too. And that was the year of the big trade, when they got Gumper for Plante, Marshall, and Goyette.

The Canadiens had class. I remember we used to wear shirts and ties to practice. It was all hockey. When we'd practise everything was done at a high pitch. Even in the Claude Ruel years. We would shoot, shoot, shoot pucks all the time. The speed was there. You never had a chance to relax in practice.

I had a lot of fights and it's hard to say who was the toughest going against me. I always thought Reggie Fleming was tough, but he didn't want to go too often. I didn't let myself associate with players from other teams. I would never play in the golf tournaments. I wouldn't instruct at hockey schools unless it was a school of all Canadiens. That's the way I was taught.

There was tremendous pride in those days. Those teams we had in the sixties, we all got along so well together. We played for the sweater. They don't do that much anymore. Ownership is a reason. They trade top players. When Gretzky got traded there were no holds barred after that. Look at the games against the Russians these days. I can remember when everybody wanted to play against them. Now they bring up farm team players because a lot of the guys can't be bothered. There's no pride.

When I broke in I was making $125 a game. Sam said he'd pay me that either in the minors or the majors. It worked out to $8,750 for the season. It makes you cringe when you think of it now.

John Ferguson may have let his non-fraternization guard down just a bit for Gerry Cheevers, the long-time goaltender for the Boston

Bruins. Like Fergie, Cheevers has become very involved in horse racing.

GERRY CHEEVERS

Fergie was probably the most fierce competitor I ever played against. In many ways he was the Canadiens' leader.

We're both in the racing game. We love horses. This particular year there was a real hot horse for the Triple Crown. His name was Hoist the Flag. He might have been one of the greatest horses ever.

When you played against Fergie you were always prepared for a confrontation or a bumping match, even a goaltender. He never let up. This game was at the end of the season. I think we had clinched first place and there was nothing at stake, a meaningless game. But Fergie would never acknowledge that. In the warmup I'd look at him and he'd look at me, as fierce as ever. We might have bought each other a beer at a race track some time in the summer, but that never mattered in the hockey season.

In the game a guy took a shot from the right point and out of the corner of my eye I saw Fergie coming in for the rebound off the backboards. I know there's going to be a hit, a collision, so I've got to prepare for it. I'm saying that I'm finally going to lay this guy out for a change, right on his keister. So I turned quickly, I go right at him, and suddenly he yells, "Cheesy!" I stopped, and he says, "Hoist the Flag broke his leg this morning!" Which he did. I said, "What?" but he kept right on coming and laid me out flatter than a pancake.

That was the only time he ever talked to me in his whole career. He told me about Hoist the Flag breaking his leg.

GILLES TREMBLAY

One year I was going to play left wing on a line with Fergie. At the training camp they would mix things up, so one day I was in the stands watching the practice and Fergie was on the ice. There was a rookie in the camp, Danny Grant, who had been a terrific junior at Peterborough. There were some people who thought he would be able to take a spot on the big team.

I know Fergie's job wasn't in danger, but even so he told me he was going to test Grant in the first practice. Grant cut in front of the net and Fergie gave him a cross-check, right in the face, and sent him to the hospital with a concussion. I think he was in hospital for about a week.

I'll give Grant credit. He came back and made the team, for a little while. They traded him to Minnesota where he was rookie of the year. But that's just to show you again how hard it was to take a job away from somebody on the Montreal Canadiens.

During John Ferguson's first season with the Canadiens another product from Sam Pollock's junior hockey factory made a brief appearance in the Canadiens' dressing room. It would not be his last.

Yvan Cournoyer was another in a long line of outstanding play-ers with the Montreal Junior Canadiens who seemed to be a sure bet to graduate to the big team. During the 1963-64 season the Cana-diens called up the twenty-year-old Cournoyer for a five-game NHL trial. He scored four goals in the five games, impressing Frank Selke to the point where he wanted to sign Cournoyer to a professional contract right then and there. When that didn't happen, Mr. Selke started to get the feeling that perhaps his days in the Canadiens' front office were coming to an end.

FRANK SELKE, JR.

The plan was for Senator Molson's cousin, David Molson, and his brothers, Peter and Bill, to take over the team from the Senator after that season. My dad knew nothing about that. He wanted to sign Cournoyer but they wouldn't let him do it.

My dad found out after the fact that David had told the Senator it was imperative they have Cournoyer with them, as a rookie, the next year. They felt they could win the Stanley Cup with him in their first year, and they wanted to look good.

That always stuck in my dad's craw, and he was a little con-cerned about the Senator's decision in that case.

YVAN COURNOYER

Mr. Selke used to tell me he would have won the Stanley Cup one more time if they had listened to him and let him sign me when I first came up. I don't know about that, but it made me feel good when he would say it. I guess they didn't want to sign me because then they would have had to protect me for the next year. The other way, I could come up as a rookie.

When I was young I knew I was going to be a hockey player. It was in my blood. I would do anything, any sacrifice, to be a hockey player. I used to shoot the puck in my garage all summer. Some guys think they're going to get better in the winter. In the winter you play hockey. In the summer you work to improve to be a better hockey player. For me, that is where it all started, shooting the pucks in our garage.

In my first year I didn't play very much. People talk about Toe Blake using me only on the power play. But I was young and he thought I could do that kind of a job. I still feel he did the right move. I was just glad to be on the team. I think the other team was scared sometime when they saw me come on the power play because they figured that this guy's going to score some goals. I was respected by the other teams.

I only had one penalty shot in my career and that was when I was a rookie. It was in Toronto. The fans were mad at the referee and they threw all kinds of things on the ice. I had to wait about ten minutes before they could clean off the ice. Johnny Bower was the goalie. When I started to skate at him I was afraid I would lose the puck. I think I had that more in my mind than scoring the goal. I was just glad I made it all the way to the net.

Bower stopped me and that was the start of my problem with him. Every time I would score on him I would look at him and say, "Now I got you." But he'd look at me and say, "Well, you don't score too often." But I always had problems against him.

We won the Stanley Cup the first year I played. In the finals it went to seven games against Chicago and the last game was at the Forum. I remember that morning my mother called me and said, "Somebody stole your car." For me, my car was very precious. But the Stanley Cup was the ultimate. Never mind about the car. I had a big hockey game that night and I was very nervous.

I scored a goal and an assist in that game. We were ahead 4-0 after the first ten minutes. After that, I don't think I got on the ice again. But we won the Stanley Cup. That was my first and I'll never forget that night.

The flashy Cournoyer, nicknamed "the Roadrunner," didn't exactly burn up the NHL in his rookie season. After scoring four times in five games as a junior call-up, he scored just seven times in fifty-five games as a full-time rookie. But the best was yet to come.

Cournoyer played on a team that finished second in the 1964–65 season, four points behind the Detroit Red Wings. In the semifinals the Red Wings were upset by Chicago, while the Canadiens ended Toronto's string of three straight Stanley Cups in a rough six-game series.

The 1965 Stanley Cup final was strictly a home-ice affair. The Canadiens won it in game seven, becoming champions for the first time since 1960 with an outburst of four goals in the first ten minutes. Jean Béliveau scored on Glenn Hall after just fourteen seconds of play. After the game, Béliveau was named the first winner of the Conn Smythe Trophy as the MVP of the playoffs. Big Jean totalled eight goals and eight assists in thirteen games.

It was the first of several Stanley Cup wins for a group of players brought to the Canadiens by Sam Pollock that would dominate the playoffs for all but one year through to the end of the 1960s. Defencemen J.C. Tremblay, Ted Harris, Jacques Laperriere, Terry Harper, and Jimmy Roberts all played on their first Cup-winner in 1965. So did forwards Bobby Rousseau, Yvan Cournoyer, John Ferguson, Dave Balon, Gilles Tremblay, and Claude Larose.

Veteran forward Dick Duff had been an important addition to the team in December, coming over from the New York Rangers in exchange for Bill Hicke.

But the fresh new faces made the difference. Sam Pollock's team had arrived.

CLAUDE LAROSE

I came up through Sam Pollock's system, first in junior, and then he brought me and Barclay Plager up to Ottawa in the Eastern

Pro League for the playoffs. That team had guys like Cesare
Maniago and Al MacNeil and we won the championship. It was a
great experience for me.

My first year with the Canadiens was when we won the Cup in
'64-'65. In those years the team was rebuilding. Toronto had won
the Cup the three years before.

The leaders on that team were Jean Béliveau and Henri Richard. You're lucky to be a rookie when there are leaders like that.
It's tough for a kid to come up with a team that doesn't have one
or two experienced leaders. A lot of good young hockey players
get with teams like that. They get into a bad groove with a losing
team and it's tough to get out of it. For kids coming to the Canadiens in those days it was a lot easier. Not many guys got to play a
few years with Béliveau and Henri, but I did.

*The 1965–66 season saw the Gumper chalk up another personal
first, the Vezina Trophy. Worsley and Charlie Hodge combined for
the lowest goals-against total in the league. It was a far cry from
Gump's days behind the porous defence of the New York Rangers.
Worsley played in forty-eight of the Canadiens' seventy games.
Hodge worked the others. The Canadiens finished in first place and
won the Stanley Cup, just like in the good old days.*

*Henri Richard is not the member of the Richard family who is
famous for scoring goals. But the Pocket Rocket got one in Detroit
to win the 1966 Stanley Cup that, while not in the sensational
category like many of his brother's classics, is still well remembered,
especially in Detroit.*

*The Canadiens swept the Toronto Maple Leafs in the semifinals
and were leading the finals 3-2 going into game six at the Detroit
Olympia. The game was tied 2-2 at the end of regulation time.*

*Early in overtime Richard and his linemates, Dave Balon and
Leon Rochefort, rushed into the Detroit zone. Richard fell reaching
for Balon's pass and slid toward the Detroit net. Both the Pocket
Rocket and the puck ended up over the red line behind goalie Roger
Crozier. The Wings and their fans howled that Richard had knocked
the puck into the net with his hand. Referee Frank Udvari didn't see
it that way, and the Canadiens had won a second straight Stanley
Cup.*

HENRI RICHARD

I play a lot of old-timers' hockey with Norm Ullman, who was on that Detroit team, and we were talking about it the other day. I always have to say I didn't knock that puck in with my hand.

I never saw the bloody puck. It was underneath me, under my arm. If Crozier had've played it like any other goalie would, if he had tried to protect me from hitting the post, the puck would never have gone in.

The puck was under my elbow. So when I got to the goal I lifted my elbow to try and miss the post. I did miss the post, and that's when the puck went in the net. That's what Ullman says, too.

The 1966 final series started with the Red Wings winning the first two games, in Montreal. Bill Gadsby was a popular Detroit defenceman who was playing in his twentieth, and final, NHL season. Gadsby had never played on a Stanley Cup-winning team. A lot of fans were pulling for him when it seemed he would finally be rewarded at the end of a fine career. But Bill Gadsby was denied a hockey player's crowning moment of glory one more time.

BILL GADSBY

I'm feeling good these days. Have a bit of arthritis, but I'm running hockey schools and enjoying life.

Memories of the Canadiens? Yes, a helluva lot of memories. I wrote an article about a year ago and said I had never seen a bad skater on the Montreal Canadiens. I never played against any or seen any since. I always thought they had the best skating club in the league. I think they all learned on the St. Lawrence River. They could all skate, even a guy like Butch Bouchard. Old Butch wasn't fast but he got around.

I always enjoyed playing. I enjoyed the competition and the rough going. Along those lines I have to think of Rocket Richard. He was so strong. I had never run into anyone like him. I remember the smoothness and the polish of Jean Béliveau. Henri Richard came to play 110 per cent every night. He never tailed off in all the years I played against him. I thought he was underrated. And of course he got that big goal against us in my last game.

I remember Dickie Moore being chippy, and a little goofy, but he came to do a job and he did it well. Doug Harvey has to stand out in my mind. I thought he was so good back of the blue line getting plays started. I tried to learn from him. He was one of the reasons they changed the rules because their power play was so strong.

1966 my biggest disappointment? Very much so. We played pretty well. After we won the first two games, we didn't get cocky that I remember. We had a job to do, but Montreal ended up playing better than we did. A couple of breaks decided the series. Nothing I can do about it now.

GUMP WORSLEY

After they beat us in the first two games in Montreal we went to Detroit and we won the third game, beat them pretty good. After the game I talked with Gadsby. He and I had played together in New York. Poor Bill. He had never won a Stanley Cup and after we beat them that first game in Detroit, he knew. He said, "We're gonna go down again." He figured that if they won the third game they'd have us, and he was right. But Bill knew what was going to happen after that.

That series really proved to me how tough it is to play in Montreal. After we lost the first two games at the Forum I went over to the golf course where I lived, in Beloiel, to play a few holes before we left for Detroit. I got there and suddenly there are guys giving me shit. You know, "What's wrong with you guys? . . . You're lousy. . . . It's fixed." Then after we win the next four in a row I go back to the golf club and all I hear is, "I knew you could do it. You're terrific."

That's the kind of pressure I remember most in Montreal. It's not so much the pressure to win, it's the pressure out on the street. The Canadiens have the tradition of win, win, win. You just can't lose. You can be in one of the best games ever played, 2-1, 3-2, close like that, and if you've lost it, you get it from everybody.

Your kids get it at school, and your wife gets it, too. "What's wrong with your father's team? What's wrong with your husband?"

That's the pressure you don't get playing in a place like New York. Down there, you go a block and a half from the rink and you're away from all that. Go into a restaurant and nobody knows who you are. You can't do that in Montreal.

18

The Leafs' Last Cup, Then Two More for the Habs

The 1966-67 season was the final one for the six-team NHL. On February 9, 1966, the NHL had announced an expansion that would double its size. Beginning with the 1967-68 season the league would have teams operating in Los Angeles, Oakland, Minneapolis-St. Paul, St. Louis, Pittsburgh, and Philadelphia.

A bid from Vancouver, with Foster Hewitt as one of the backers, was turned down. This slight to a Canadian-based bid sparked righteous indignation from hockey fans, the media, and opportunity-seeking politicians from, as Foster might have put it, coast to coast in Canada. Vancouver finally got its franchise four years later.

The 1966–67 season belonged to the Chicago Black Hawks, who finished in first place for the first time in their forty-year history. In 1965-66 Chicago's sensational left-winger Bobby Hull had scored fifty-four goals, breaking the single-season record of fifty he shared with Maurice Richard and Bernie Geoffrion. In 1966–67 Hull scored fifty-two, by far the most goals scored by a player that season. The Black Hawks set a record for goals scored, with 264, and Glenn Hall and Denis DeJordy shared the Vezina Trophy. However, once the playoffs began the Chicago team, as usual, came up short. They were beaten in the first round by the Toronto Maple Leafs, a team that had finished nineteen points behind Chicago in the regular season.

The Canadiens finished second, two points ahead of Toronto. They swept the New York Rangers in the semifinals, with John

Ferguson scoring the series-winning goal in overtime. Then the Canadiens lost to Toronto in a six-game final.

The 1967 playoffs remain a vivid and nostalgic memory for staunch Maple Leaf fans because their team hasn't won the Stanley Cup since. What is still a vivid memory for members of the losing Canadiens is the goaltending of Toronto's Terry Sawchuk. It's surprising they don't mention Johnny Bower, too. After the Canadiens whipped the Leafs 6-2 in the series opener, Bower blanked the Canadiens 3-0 in the second game. Two nights later he stopped fifty-one shots in an overtime marathon to give his team a 2-1 lead in the series. Bower was injured in the warmup before game four, and Sawchuk took over. The Canadiens won that game 6-2. But the Leafs won the next two with Sawchuk giving up just two goals in the two games.

Toronto centre Dave Keon won the Conn Smythe Trophy as the playoff MVP. But because of what he did to them in the final two games of the series Terry Sawchuk, who snatched the Cup away from Montreal in the seventh game of the 1954 finals in Detroit, is the guy the Canadiens remember when you ask them about the finals of '67, against Toronto.

GUMP WORSLEY

We had a good team in those years, really good. I remember one year we were at the bottom of the league at Christmas and we finished first and won the Stanley Cup. They don't talk about that team of the sixties like they do some of the others because we didn't win four in a row, or five in a row. We won two, then lost to Toronto, then won two more.

We should have won five straight. It was only one guy who beat us. One guy. Sawchuk. We just dominated them. You know what happens when you have a good goaltender in a short series. But I can be biased talking about something like that. (laughs)

DAVE KEON

For seventy games in the regular season we were right where we should have been, a third-place team. Then, for the four or five weeks of the playoffs, we played as well as we could. We got great goaltending, for sure, and Terry Sawchuk did play very well. But so did Johnny Bower.

In the games they won they really outplayed us. But in the games we won, we did the same thing to them. They had three or four days off because they won their first series in four straight. They were waiting while we went six games against Chicago.

We weren't supposed to beat Chicago. But in that series we kept getting more confident as the games went on. Against Montreal, it was the same thing after we won the second game.

I think that maybe, to a certain degree, they had convinced themselves that they should win it, that it really should be theirs. Expo 67 in Montreal, and all those things. But it didn't turn out that way. Our goaltenders got hot. Those things happen.

JEAN BÉLIVEAU

We had no business losing in '67 to Toronto. You always mind losing, but when you are beaten by a better team, or a team that played better than you did, you can understand.

Terry Sawchuk was the reason. I remember walking in on him all alone in a game in Toronto, I think it was the last game, and how he stopped me, I still can't figure it out. I always had the feeling that if I score on that play, if he doesn't make that tremendous save, it very easily could have been another five Stanley Cups in a row.

The first two years of the expanded NHL were dominated by the Montreal Canadiens. They finished first overall both years and won two more Stanley Cups. The first post-expansion Cup came easy. The second took a bit more doing.

The NHL now had two divisions, East and West. The Original Six stayed together in the East. There were a few games between the old and the new during the regular season, then the teams played within their own divisions in the first two playoff rounds. The divisional winners met in the finals. In this way the new kids on the block wouldn't feel totally left out in the cold.

In the 1968 playoffs the Canadiens defeated the Bruins, Black

Hawks, and the Scotty Bowman-coached St. Louis Blues. The next year they disposed of the Rangers, Bruins, and the Blues again in the finals. In the two years the Canadiens' playoff record was twenty-four wins, three losses.

In 1968 Montreal swept Boston in four straight. In 1969 they needed six gruelling games to beat the Bruins, who were just two points behind them when the regular season ended.

When the Boston Bruins skated onto the ice for the 1968 series against the Canadiens, it was their first playoff appearance since 1959. (They haven't missed the playoffs since.) A rebuilding job was in full swing in Boston. Phil Esposito was there, via Chicago. So was a young defenceman named Orr, from Parry Sound, Ontario, although at times it seemed he had come from another planet, where they manufactured super beings, including hockey players.

BOBBY ORR

When I first came up with the Bruins it was something special to play against the Montreal Canadiens, one of the great franchises ever in sports.

The thing I remember most is never, ever did you have an easy game against them. The Forum was one of my favourite places to play, even though you always knew you were going to be in a tough game. Year in and year out, the Canadiens' organization was the toughest I ever played against.

When I first came up I used to look at the guys sitting on their bench and say, "My God." I mean, there was Béliveau. What can you say about Jean, one of the classiest individuals that I know. Laperriere . . . the Tremblays . . . Henri Richard. I never saw his brother, the Rocket, but I heard a lot of stories about him and how, from the blue line in, there was no one like him. I wish I could have seen him play and had a chance to play against him.

Those two years we played the Canadiens in the playoffs was when we really started to mature as a team, especially in 1969. A series like that was great for our team. I don't think any of us had ever been in a position like that, playing a team like Montreal under so much pressure.

Let me tell you a story about Cournoyer. We're playing them in an afternoon game in Boston and Yvan is flying. I mean, I can't catch him. Nobody can catch him. He'd come down and . . . whoosh . . . he flies by me on one side. Next rush . . . whoosh . . . he flies by me on the other side.

There was a face-off in front of our bench. Gerry Cheevers was the back-up goalie that day and he says to Cournoyer, "Hey, Yvan, take it easy. Slow down."

Yvan turns to Cheevers and says, "No, Gerry, I can't do dat. I got the big tailwind today."

The final game of the 1969 Canadiens-Bruins series was one of the best I've seen. Rogie Vachon was the Canadiens' goaltender and he and Gerry Cheevers were terrific. Vachon made a save off Phil Esposito in the first overtime period that was a classic.

The game ended in the second overtime when Jean Béliveau fired the puck past Cheevers for the only overtime goal of his great career. But please note that when Big Jean played, overtime was reserved strictly for the playoffs.

JEAN BÉLIVEAU

That's an easy one for me to remember because that was my only one. It put us into the finals against St. Louis.

I was playing on a line with John Ferguson and Claude Provost. Fergie started the play by rushing the defenceman behind their net. He got rid of the puck around the boards and Provost stopped it. I released the puck very quickly. I have a picture of it at home with Ted Green sliding in front of me. A fraction of a second more and I think Green would have blocked the shot. Cheevers reacted, but too late, and it went in. Top corner.

GERRY CHEEVERS

I remember the end we were in so it must have been the second overtime. All I remember about the play is that if I would have saved it, it would have been with a great reaction. But I reacted too late. The puck went over Green and then over my shoulder. It was a terrific wrist shot. It's hard to believe that was Béliveau's only overtime goal in his career.

It was disappointing, that game. I think we all believed later it was a great experience for us, taking the Canadiens into double overtime in the sixth game.

We win, and we go back to Montreal for a seventh. We were an inch away that year. We could have gone on to win the Stanley Cup. When there's a seventh game, you just never know.

The Canadiens followed up Jean Béliveau's series-winning goal in Boston with their second straight Stanley Cup, and fourth in five years, when John Ferguson scored the winning goal on Glenn Hall in St. Louis on May 4, 1969.

Some interesting changes had come about that season. Jacques Plante had been retired for three years when Scotty Bowman coaxed him to come back and play for his St. Louis Blues. Plante and Hall made a great statement for hockey's senior citizens by combining to win the Vezina Trophy. But when Plante played against the Canadiens that season he was not trying to beat his old nemesis, Toe Blake. As Plante was ending his retirement, Blake was starting his.

Moments after the Canadiens won the Stanley Cup in 1968, Blake said he was quitting. Not many of us believed him, but he meant it. A few weeks later the Canadiens held a news conference to announce that twenty-nine-year-old Claude Ruel, a coach and scout on Sam Pollock's staff, was the team's new coach.

When the Blake era ended at the Forum, the Canadiens had had only two coaches in twenty-eight years, Toe and my father. During that time their teams finished in first place fourteen times, and won the Stanley Cup eleven times. When the 1990–91 season ended the record for continuous service with one team among the twenty-one NHL coaches was three years. Obviously some history lessons don't get through.

Claude Ruel was a good junior defenceman when his career was suddenly ended by an injury that cost him the sight in one eye. If anyone who did not know what was going on had walked into the news conference announcing Ruel's appointment to the prestigious position as coach of the mighty Montreal Canadiens, he or she would have thought those making the announcement were discussing the death of a close friend or relative. Sam Pollock, David Molson, and Toe Blake were there, supposedly to warmly welcome the new coach. But they were a sad-looking group and there wasn't a smile to be seen. When they had said their piece the front-office types bolted from the room, leaving the confused and equally sad-looking Ruel to face a media horde all by himself.

In choosing the unknown Claude Ruel to replace the legendary Toe Blake, Pollock opted for one of his faithful company men rather than an experienced coach. There was no argument on that score. The Canadiens have never had an employee more faithful than Claude Ruel. Today he is the team's director of player development.

Ruel's appointment was surprising but it didn't rock the championship boat, at least not right away. His team was strong enough to make Ruel a Stanley Cup-winning coach after finishing in first place in his rookie season.

The Sam Pollock look to the Canadiens' lineup continued as the decade was ending. Two more outstanding Quebec junior prospects, defenceman Serge Savard and centre Jacques Lemaire, made the team in Blake's final year. Both became big stars, played on eight Stanley Cup-winning teams, and were elected to the Hockey Hall of Fame.

SERGE SAVARD

The Canadiens brought me to Montreal from my home near Amos when I was fifteen years old. I could not make Junior A, so they sent me to a Junior B club. They didn't bother sending me an invitation to camp the following year, so I thought they were very disappointed in me. But I came back to Montreal and registered at school in September, just like the year before.

Cliff Fletcher was working for Sam and he was in charge of guys like me. A couple of weeks after I started at school I called him and said I hadn't received any money. The year before I got twelve dollars a week for expense money. They always claimed it was a mistake that I didn't get invited to the junior camp, but I don't think it was a mistake. I guess they figured they were stuck with me being in Montreal, so Fletcher told me to show up. They put me with a team called the NDG Monarchs. Doug Harvey's brother, Alfie, was the coach. I made an All-Star team for a game at Christmas, so at Christmas the Canadiens paid me my expense money going back to September.

The first two years I played for the Canadiens we won the Stanley Cup. Both times we beat St. Louis in four straight, but those games were a lot tougher than a lot of people say they were. We didn't take them for granted. In the first series we won every game by one goal. The next year one of the games was 1–0. [Savard got the goal, scoring on Jacques Plante.]

They were both very tough series from the standpoint of the checking. St. Louis had an experienced team and they got terrific goaltending.

I was a forward when I started playing hockey. I was six-three, 210 pounds when I came to Montreal when I was fifteen. They told me I was too big to be a forward, so they put me back on defence. I guess that ended up to be okay for me. Jean Béliveau was my first hero, but when I started to play defence Doug Harvey was my hero. It seemed funny to play against him in the first final series we had against St. Louis.

Harvey used to do a spin-around play when he was carrying the puck. You can see it on some old film clips from the Stanley Cups in the 1950s. So I started doing it as a kid and probably did it more in my career than he did. People still remember me doing that. I picked it up from Doug Harvey.

Which brings me back to Danny Gallivan. When Serge Savard would spin into a 360 and leave a forechecking opponent in his wake, one of the most famous of the many Gallivanisms would be heard across the land. Danny and his legion of fans took great delight every time the Canadiens' defenceman pulled off a "Savardian Spinnerama."

DANNY GALLIVAN

I was in Oakland for a radio broadcast and went for a walk the day of the game. I saw all these signs, "Bowlarama" and what not. Everything was "something-rama."

I didn't deliberately think of using something along those lines that night, but I guess the phrase stuck in my mind. Savard had that neat move of coming up to a checker, stopping, and spinning around. So instead of saying "spin" I said "spinnerama."

Then a little later I thought there could be some extra alliteration, because Savard starts with an S. So I made it "Savardian Spinnerama."

"Cannonading" came quite accidentally. One night on a face-off, Béliveau drew the puck back to Geoffrion. Boom Boom had a great shot. The puck came right off his stick and I called it a "cannonading shot."

I took a lot of criticism for things like that. Some say I brutalized the language. Four or five days after I used "cannonading" I received a letter from a man who was very terse and to the point. With reference to the word, and I knew there was no such word, he wrote, "How dare you? There's no such word."

The letter annoyed me, but it was also signed. So I answered it. I kept it short. I wrote, "No such word? How dare you? There is now."

I can't match those broadcast-booth stories. Who can? But I can tell you that the first time I did a play-by-play broadcast at the Montreal Forum, Jacques Lemaire scored three goals. It was in February, 1966, and Lemaire was playing for the Montreal Junior Canadiens. The TV station I was with taped a junior game on a Thursday night for showing on Saturday. It was the first time a Quebec Junior League game was televised in English. Scotty Bowman was the Junior Canadiens' coach.

The following season we televised a series of junior games, live. My colour commentator was Jacques Plante, then retired. A couple of years later Plante was back in the NHL, playing for Scotty in St. Louis.

The night he scored his televised hat trick, Jacques Lemaire was in his final season in junior hockey. After one year with the Canadiens' pro farm team in Houston, he made the big club. But it wasn't easy.

JACQUES LEMAIRE

I played my first year pro in Houston and had a terrible season, especially at the start. I was there with guys like Serge Savard, Rogie Vachon, and Carol Vadnais. Our coach was Ray Kinasweich and he tried to make me feel good by saying I'd make the Canadiens because of how I played in the last half of the season. But I was sure I was going to play in the minors for many years.

When I went to the Canadiens' camp the next season I felt pretty good. After the first couple of workouts I was confident and never felt out of place. The team had a lot of centres at that time – Béliveau, Backstrom, Henri – so Serge Savard told me to ask if I could play left wing. And that's where I was when the season started but I didn't play much. Then Henri got hurt and they put me at centre and I stayed there from then on. After Henri came back he got mad at Toe Blake and left the team. He went up north for about a week. Toe told me not to pay attention to what was going on about him and Henri: "Just play your game." That's what he kept telling me. So I did.

GILLES TREMBLAY

Our team in the sixties had very good balance – good veterans, good kids, and good goaltending. You look at the Canadiens over the years, they've always had good goaltending. Jacques Plante was there for a while when I first came up. But when we were winning the Stanley Cup in the sixties we had Charlie Hodge, Gump Worsley, and Rogie Vachon.

We should have won five in a row. In 1967 we lost to Toronto but the only reason was Terry Sawchuk. He was terrific in the nets. We outshot them every game, I'm sure, and it was very close.

I didn't quite make it all the way to win the Cup in 1969. A couple of years before they had given us shots for the Hong Kong flu and my system reacted to it. It turned into an asthma problem and I still have it to this day. When I was playing hockey it got too bad and I had to quit. But I'll always remember my final game, for sure.

We were playing L.A., in Montreal, and I wasn't feeling too

good. I was on a line with Jean Béliveau and Yvan Cournoyer and Big Jean scored four goals in the first two periods. I had a goal and three assists.

When the third period started Ralph Backstrom was at centre. I thought that there was something wrong with Béliveau's equipment. I came to the bench after the shift and Jean told me he wasn't going to play in the third period. Claude Ruel was our coach and he had told Jean he was going to keep him on the bench in case he got injured. It was unbelievable after the way Big Jean had played the first two periods, but that was what Ruel did.

After that game I got very sick and had to go to the hospital. I never played again. But what Ruel did to Big Jean that night makes it very easy for me to remember my last game.

V

The Early 1970s

In the late 1960s the National Hockey League grew from six to twelve teams and during the 1970s the expansion beat continued. When the decade ended there were new NHL teams in Vancouver, Buffalo, Washington, and Long Island. Those teams are still around. Also during the seventies, there were a few years when travel plans included Kansas City, Cleveland, Denver, and Atlanta.

Two significant intrusions on the hockey scene occurred. One was the World Hockey Association, which was in business from 1972 to 1979. The NHL laughed when the new league was first mentioned, but the WHA made Bobby Hull hockey's first million-dollar player, gave Gordie Howe a chance to play with his two sons, and wrote Wayne Gretzky's first contract. In 1979 the NHL had to accept four of its franchises – Hartford, Quebec City, Winnipeg, and Edmonton – before the WHA finally agreed to disappear.

The other intrusion came from the Soviet Union. Their best had never played our best. But in the 1970s that eagerly awaited confrontation finally happened. Canadian hockey fans came out of it with some great memories, and with the realization that hockey was no longer, exclusively, our game.

Three different teams won the Stanley Cup in the 1960s. It would be the same story in the seventies although the final count was a bit more one-sided: Boston two, Philadelphia two, Montreal six. Through the last half of the decade another dynasty was in place at the Montreal Forum.

19

From Top to Bottom,
and Back Again

As the 1970s dawned, a funny thing happened to the team at the Forum. It didn't make the playoffs. When the 1969–70 season ended it had ninety-two points, only seven out of first place in the East Division. Ninety-two points were six more than the St. Louis Blues had, and the Blues finished first in the West Division. Still, the team at the Forum didn't make the playoffs.

The Montreal Canadiens and the New York Rangers ended the season tied for fourth place with identical records of wins, losses, ties, and points. But the Rangers had a better record in goals for and against. So New York was in, and Montreal was out for the first time since 1948.

Danny Gallivan and I broadcast the Stanley Cup finals between the Boston Bruins and the St. Louis Blues. Before one of the games at the Boston Garden I ran into Sam Pollock and commiserated with him over his team's unaccustomed absence from the playoff scene. Sam said, "Before the season, if someone had told me we'd get ninety-two points, I'd have said, 'I'll take it. Let's start the playoffs right now.'"

Sam got his ninety-two points, but the playoffs started without him. Ninety-two is the highest point total in NHL history for a non-playoff team.

When the Canadiens won the Stanley Cup in 1969, four players on the team had been in uniform in 1960 when the fifth of the five straight Cups had been won. They were Jean Béliveau, Henri Rich-

ard, Claude Provost, and Ralph Backstrom. When the Canadiens rebounded to win the Stanley Cup again in 1971, only Béliveau and Richard remained.

Pollock had begun weeding out some veterans during the 1969-70 campaign. In January Dick Duff was traded to Los Angeles for a valuable future draft choice. In late February Gump Worsley, who had played in only six games, was sold to the Minnesota North Stars. Neither had been getting along with Ruel.

In the summer of 1970 Bobby Rousseau was traded to Minnesota in return for Claude Larose, who had been traded there two years earlier. Defenceman Ted Harris was left unprotected and was drafted by the North Stars. Claude Provost, one of the best defensive forwards in the Canadiens' history, was sold to Los Angeles. Provost retired before the season began.

Late in the 1970-71 season Ralph Backstrom was traded to Los Angeles, again for a future draft pick. This was one of Sam Pollock's most famous deals. Backstrom helped the Kings stay ahead of the California Seals, who finished last overall. The Canadiens already owned California's first pick in the 1971 draft. They gladly used it to select Guy Lafleur.

As the veterans departed, Pollock's revised version of "new faces" began a long run at the Forum. Pete Mahovlich, who had played thirty-six games in 1969-70, became a regular. Before the 1970-71 season ended so had Guy Lapointe, Marc Tardif, Réjean Houle, and Pierre Bouchard.

During 1970-71 Pollock made three more very important additions to his team - Al MacNeil, Frank Mahovlich, and Ken Dryden. In various ways they would play key roles in establishing another Montreal Canadiens dynasty, one that would win the Stanley Cup six times in the next nine years.

Al MacNeil is a Maritimer who spent one of his ten years as a pro hockey defenceman in Montreal. MacNeil was hired as Claude Ruel's assistant for the 1970-71 season. By December, with his team spinning its wheels, Pollock realized Ruel was not in control and made a change. The loyal Ruel obediently went back to his scouting duties, and Al MacNeil became the Canadiens' head coach.

On January 13, 1971, as the Canadiens gathered at Montreal's Dorval airport for a flight to Minnesota, MacNeil was paged for a telephone call. Minutes later he told three of his players, Mickey Redmond, Guy Charron, and Bill Collins, that they had been traded to the Detroit Red Wings.

Everyone who plays for a Stanley Cup-winning team contributes to the victory. But the main reason that edition of the Montreal Canadiens went on to become Stanley Cup champions in 1971 was because they traded Redmond, Charron, and Collins to Detroit in return for Frank Mahovlich.

FRANK MAHOVLICH

At that particular time we were in turmoil in Detroit. I didn't feel it was the players' fault, but they kept trading players all over the place. Ned Harkness had come in to run the team, and there was quite an upheaval, right from training camp. I couldn't believe it. Pete Stemkowski was the first to go, and then they started to move everybody.

When it came to be my turn, I can remember Sam Pollock phoning me. I told him I didn't feel like going anywhere at that particular time. He asked me to go to Minnesota and play the game the next night. Then he said that when the team got back to Montreal we would get together, have a nice chat, and straighten things out. Sam was a good salesman, and he convinced me.

I flew to Minnesota, and when I got off the plane the coach, Al MacNeil, and Ron Caron, who at the time was Sam's assistant, were there to meet me. I said to myself that if they cared enough to meet my plane, then the Montreal Canadiens must be a good organization. Right then and there I knew I was going to like it.

We went on from there to win the Stanley Cup that year. That was a miracle for me, to go from a bottom-place club to the Stanley Cup in the same season.

In addition to the welcoming committee at the airport, another reason the "Big M" found happiness in Bloomington was because one of his new teammates was the "Little M," his younger brother Pete. The first thing Frank did when he got to the hotel was bunk in with Pete and have a nap.

I was broadcasting Frank's Montreal debut that night on CFCF Radio. The Canadiens didn't have a number 27 sweater with them, so Frank wore Bill Collins's old sweater number 10 for one occasion only. No one else wore it again that season. So there's your answer to the trivia question, "Before Guy Lafleur, who was the last player to wear number 10 for the Montreal Canadiens?"

Early in the first period the Canadiens drew a penalty and Frank was on the ice killing it. You didn't normally think of the high-scoring Frank Mahovlich filling that role. After the game I asked Al MacNeil why he had the Big M killing a penalty on his second shift with the Montreal Canadiens. MacNeil replied, "I looked down the bench and he was the best player sitting there. So I put him on."

The Canadiens won the game, and Frank scored a goal. It was an omen of things to come.

The Canadiens were settled into third place for the last several weeks of the season. They knew they'd finish there and meet the Boston Bruins in the opening round of the playoffs. The Bruins were running away and hiding from the rest of the league, steam-rolling their way to single-season records of 121 points and 399 goals. Phil Esposito was scoring seventy-six goals in seventy-six games, a record we were sure would stand forever. (When Espo scored his seventy-sixth, Wayne Gretzky was ten years old, Brett Hull was six, and Mario Lemieux five.)

Rogie Vachon was the Canadiens' regular goaltender, with Phil Myre as his backup. Vachon joined the Canadiens in 1967, in time for Punch Imlach to label him a "Junior B goalie" when Imlach's Maple Leafs were beating the Canadiens in the finals. Vachon had helped win the Stanley Cup in 1968 and 1969, and had shared a Vezina Trophy with Gump Worsley. But as the '70–'71 season was winding down, Pollock and MacNeil were becoming convinced their goaltending wasn't good enough.

The Canadiens' American League farm team, the Voyageurs, was splitting its home games between Montreal and Halifax. One of the team's goaltenders was a bespectacled law student at McGill University, Ken Dryden.

KEN DRYDEN

There had been rumours in the French press for several days that they were going to bring me up, but nobody had said anything to me about it. In late February we played a Sunday afternoon game, in Halifax, against Providence. Floyd Curry was coaching us and after the game he told me I had been called up. He gave me a plane ticket to Montreal and said, "Here it is. Good luck."

I flew to Montreal that same day. The Canadiens had played an afternoon game in Philadelphia and my plane landed the same time theirs did. I ran into the players walking through the airport. Phil Myre looked at me and did a real double take. I could see the expression on his face meant, "What are you doing here?"

I practised for about a week but never played and they didn't give me any indication as to when I would play. I started to wonder what I was doing there and felt I would be better off back with the Voyageurs. Then they took me on a road trip, and I played my first game in Pittsburgh.

Dryden played in six games before the season ended. He was brilliant in a 2-1 win in Chicago. That performance convinced Al MacNeil that he would start the unknown rookie against the big, bad Boston Bruins when the playoffs began.

AL MACNEIL

In the game in Chicago we hardly got out of our own end. In fact, I don't think we got out at all in the third period, but we won 2-1.

They had a powerful club, a lot of big shooters like Mikita, Bobby Hull, Dennis Hull, Pappin, and a lot of other guys. Chicago isn't an easy rink for a visiting goaltender, especially a rookie just starting. Dryden put on an amazing show. Anyone who was there that night couldn't have been surprised at him starting the first playoff game.

JACQUES LAPERRIERE

I didn't know Dryden but I heard good things about the way he was playing for the Voyageurs. It didn't take long to find out he was a very high-quality goaltender.

We were the underdogs against Boston but we pulled together and everything seemed to turn to our side. We had some breaks, plus we had Kenny in the nets. He was fantastic. When you've got a goaler who starts keeping the puck out of the net the way he did, there's always a good chance you'll win.

When the 1971 playoffs began nobody was saying to Jacques Laperriere and his teammates, "You've got a chance to win." What chance? The Bruins were twenty-four points ahead of the Canadiens when the regular season ended. But what did we know? The 1971 Canadiens' playoff year became the most dramatic and emotional of any I have covered, and I have covered them all for the past twenty-five years.

It had everything: an underdog team eliminating the best team in hockey in the first round; an unknown goaltender with six games of NHL experience winning the Conn Smythe Trophy as the playoff MVP; a revered French-Canadian hockey hero publicly criticizing his English-speaking coach, igniting a front-page media war with severe linguistic overtones. Then, as the final curtain fell, one of the Montreal Canadiens' all-time greatest superstars was carrying the Stanley Cup off the ice at the Chicago Stadium, his final act in what had been the final game of a now legendary career.

The year 1971 had it all.

The Canadiens shocked the Bruins, and everybody else, by winning the first round in the seventh game, played on a Sunday afternoon in Boston. But ask Habs fans what they remember most about the series and they'll talk about the second game. Ask those who played in the series and they'll talk about the second game.

The Bruins won the opener 3-1 and two nights later were leading 5-1 late in the second period. Final score, 7-5, Canadiens. Gerry Cheevers had played well in goal for Boston in the first game but Bruins coach Tom Johnson switched to Eddie Johnston for game two. When the series moved to Montreal the Canadiens' comeback victory was a big story. So was the fact that Al MacNeil had picked the unknown rookie goalie, Ken Dryden, to face Espo, Bobby, and company right from the start of the series.

AL MACNEIL

Before the series Boston said that Cheevers would be their goaler in the first game and Johnston would play in the second. I thought

Bernie Geoffrion's wedding day, as he marries Marlene Morenz, daughter of the legendary Howie. Left to right: Billy Reay, Maurice Richard, Butch Bouchard, the newlyweds, Dick Irvin, Elmer Lach, Ken Mosdell, Doug Harvey. Kneeling are the team's trainers, Gaston Bettez and Hector Dubois.

Maurice Richard, Floyd Curry, and Bernie Geoffrion add up their goals after a win over Chicago in 1953.

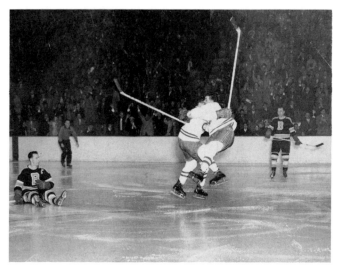

Maurice Richard broke Elmer Lach's nose as they celebrated Elmer's Cup-winning goal, in overtime, in April of 1953. Boston's Milt Schmidt looks on from ice level. Bruin at right is Joe Klukay. *(Roger St. Jean)*

The Canadiens presented Doug Harvey with a cake on his thirtieth birthday, December 19, 1954, prior to a game in Detroit. They won 5-0 and Doug was the first star.

Players and executives of the 1959-60 Montreal Canadiens, the team that won the fifth of five straight Cups. Back row, l. to r.: Camil DesRoches, Henri Richard, Billy Hicke, Bill Head, Claude Provost, Ralph Backstrom, Don Marshall, André Pronovost, Tim Condon, Red Aubut, Frank Selke, Jr.; middle row, l. to r.: Hector Dubois, Marcel Bonin, Dickie Moore, Albert Trottier, Bob Turner, Albert Langlois, Ab McDonald, Ken Reardon, Jacques Plante, Tom Johnson, Phil Goyette, Jean-Guy Talbot; front row, l. to r.: Doug Harvey, Frank Selke, Sr., Maurice Richard, Tony the Tailor (who supplied the jackets), Toe Blake, Jean Béliveau, Bernie Geoffrion.
(Courtesy Montreal Canadiens)

In the early 1980s the Canadiens honoured Toe Blake and the twelve players who were on all five Stanley Cup-winning teams, 1956-60. Standing, l. to r.: Claude Provost, Jean-Guy Talbot, Maurice Richard, Tom Johnson, Jean Béliveau, Blake, Bernie Geoffrion, Henri Richard, Dickie Moore, Don Marshall, Doug Harvey. Kneeling: Jacques Plante, Bob Turner. *(Denis Brodeur)*

Jean Béliveau in his first season as team captain.

Dickie Moore, a home-grown kid who made it with a lot of talent and a heart to match.

Rookie goaltender Ken Dryden during the 1971 Stanley Cup playoffs. The Canadiens won the Cup, Dryden was chosen the MVP, and his stance in the goal crease had become familiar to hockey fans from coast to coast. *(Denis Brodeur)*

Yvan Cournoyer against Chicago's Tony Esposito in the 1973 Cup final. The Roadrunner set a playoff scoring record and won the Conn Smythe Trophy as playoff MVP. *(Denis Brodeur)*

John Ferguson arrived in Montreal in the 1960s. Here's Fergie against the Flyers, playing the only way he knew – straight ahead.
(Denis Brodeur)

Jean Béliveau completes a hat trick by scoring his 500th career goal against Minnesota goalie Gilles Gilbert. Frank Mahovlich looks on.
(Denis Brodeur)

The Pocket Rocket, Henri Richard, with the Stanley Cup in hand for a record eleventh time, Chicago Stadium, May 10, 1973. No other player in NHL history has been on that many winning teams.
(Denis Brodeur)

Scotty Bowman behind the bench. Like all great coaches, he wasn't always liked but he was always respected. *(Denis Brodeur)*

Steve Shutt, the sniper on Scotty's dynasty. His sixty goals in 1976-77 are still a league record for left-wingers. *(Denis Brodeur)*

The dynasty of the 1970s won a lot of games with defence. Here Jacques Lemaire, Dryden, and Guy Lapointe concentrate on Toronto's Darryl Sittler. *(Denis Brodeur)*

The Flower in full flight – Guy Lafleur in the late 1970s was the best player in the world. *(Denis Brodeur)*

Serge Savard and Yvan Cournoyer help Guy Lafleur celebrate winning the Conn Smythe Trophy as MVP of the 1977 playoffs, Boston Garden, May 14, 1977. *(Denis Brodeur)*

The 1976-77 Canadiens, the team that won a record sixty games while losing only eight. Back row, l. to r.: Rick Chartraw, Serge Savard, Pete Mahovlich, Pierre Bouchard, Larry Robinson; third row, l. to r.: Mario Tremblay, Doug Risebrough, Yvon Lambert, Guy Lapointe, Bill Nyrop, Murray Wilson; second row, l. to r.: Eddie Palchak, Steve Shutt, Guy Lafleur, Jacques Lemaire, Doug Jarvis, Jim Roberts, Bob Gainey, Réjean Houle, Pierre Meilleur; front row, l. to r.: Ken Dryden, Claude Ruel, Scotty Bowman, Peter Bronfman, Sam Pollock, Yvan Cournoyer, Jacques Courtois, Edward Bronfman, Jean Béliveau, Floyd Curry, Michel Larocque. *(Courtesy Montreal Canadiens)*

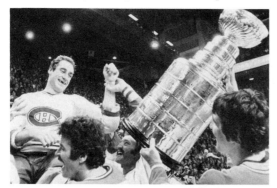

Moments after Canadiens defeated the New York Rangers for their fourth straight Stanley Cup, May 21, 1979, his team-mates hoisted Bob Gainey on their shoulders when he was announced as the playoff MVP. Serge Savard is holding the Cup. *(Denis Brodeur)*

January 12, 1985: Toe Blake and Aurel Joliat drop the ceremonial puck between Gilbert Perreault and Bob Gainey. The Forum saluted the Canadiens' all-time Dream Team as selected by the fans. The team, l. to r.: Jacques Plante, Larry Robinson, Dickie Moore, Jean Béliveau, Maurice Richard, Doug Harvey. *(Denis Brodeur)*

at the time that was a mistake. You go with the guy who is hot and you stick with him until something happens. That's why I went with Dryden. Our other goalers, Vachon and Myre, were inconsistent. Dryden had the hot hand.

In that second game they had us down 5-1 and then Henri Richard scored late in the second period. I didn't say anything special to the guys between periods. I just told them to try and keep the game respectable so we wouldn't be embarrassed going back home into our own building.

When the comeback started in the third period it seemed to me that it just kept building. There was no special feeling on the bench, at least not as far as I could see. It just started to build, the goals went in, and we ended up winning 7-5.

Gerry Cheevers and Eddie Johnston had split the Boston goaltending duties almost right down the middle that season. Cheevers played in forty games, Johnston in thirty-eight, and the Bruins ran away with first place. Boston had the third-best goals-against average in the league, which was impressive for a team that had emphasized offence on its way to a record 399 goals. Tom Johnson's system of alternating goaltenders had worked during the season, so why shouldn't it continue to work in the playoffs?

GERRY CHEEVERS

I played the first game and Eddie Johnston played the second. That was the plan before the series started.

If it's a pre-plan, that's the way it should be. We won the first game 3-1 and I had some luck that night. I remember I was especially lucky a couple of times against Cournoyer.

I know that second game was the turning point of the series. But we had a plan. I have no quarrel with that. The next year, Tom was still coaching and we went right back with the strict alternation. Me and Eddie switched again and we won the Stanley Cup. The way it worked out in '71 could have happened to anyone. It was a shame.

If the Montreal players were reading or listening to playoff predictions, they knew the media didn't give them much of a chance against Bobby and the Bruins. Today those Montrealers have various memories of exactly how they felt heading into the series, but I would imagine most of them felt like Jacques Lemaire, that their chances of winning ranged from slim to none.

JACQUES LEMAIRE

Did I think we could beat Boston? No way. *No way.* I remember before the series, most of us talking in the dressing room about how good they were. Orr, Esposito, they'd had a big year. We were kind of beaten before it started. Then Jean Béliveau got up and said, "We have to play *our* game. Don't worry about their game. Let's just do our job, and we'll see what happens."

The game I remember best is the second game, the 7–5 one. We were down 5–1 when Henri scored late in the second period. It's funny, but that's when we started to think about the score. We were saying "Let's get one more," and when the third period started we did. Then it was 5–3. "One more," and we did, and it was 5–4.

I got the tying goal. Orr had the puck at our blue line and passed it across the ice. I wasn't trying to check him. I just put my stick down and the puck hit it. That gave me a breakaway from our blue line. You don't get a breakaway that long very often and when I was going down the ice I was thinking about the score. We were still saying, "One more," and I got it. I didn't think all that much about what I was going to do. I just shot it and it went in, top corner.

Jean Béliveau. So many of his teammates from that year talk about his leadership in his final weeks as a Montreal Canadiens' player. But Béliveau was a veteran of many Stanley Cup wars, and so was Frank Mahovlich. The Canadiens' older guard went into the series against Boston thinking they had a chance to pull off a major upset.

FRANK MAHOVLICH

When the playoffs started that year I had a feeling that we were as good as anybody. We didn't lose too many games in the last two months of the season with Rogie in the nets. Then Dryden came in toward the end and then he played in the playoffs. I thought we were as good as any other team in the playoffs that year, Chicago, even Boston. So I thought we had a chance to win.

Everybody thought it was an upset because Boston had finished so far ahead. They totally dominated everybody during the season, Espo with his records and all that. But when you dominate during a season there's a chance you might blow it in the playoffs. It's tough to have the right attitude sometimes, and I think that's natural.

When we came from behind in that second game in Boston, what I remember is the way Béliveau played. He ignited things. He was the one who got us going. That was his last year, but that night he was awesome, and we went on from there.

JEAN BÉLIVEAU

I hate to say it, even today, but I always felt they had a stronger team than we had. I remember how well balanced they were. I'm pretty sure I can still give you their lines and their roster. Think of Orr and Green on defence. They had three very good scoring lines with Espo, Bucyk, Cashman, and all those guys. And I don't forget their defensive line, Sanderson, Westfall, and Marcotte.

We had a very good team but they had more depth and balance than we did. But don't forget Dryden in the nets. He kept us in the series. I still can see Espo standing beside our net shaking his head after Dryden made all those tremendous saves, one after the other.

We lost the first game in Boston, 3–1. If we lose the second we go back home down by two. But we had that comeback and won the game 7–5. When I think of it today, I think of what it did to our outlook on the series playing against them. We went back to our home ice tied 1–1, and all the team had a tremendous amount of spirit.

HENRI RICHARD

That Boston series is one of the ones I remember most of all because that was the time I played right wing once in a while. I played on a line with Lemaire because they had a special way they wanted us to check Bobby Orr.

We weren't supposed to let him get too close to us because he is going to go by you if you do, because he was so great. So if it wasn't me it was Lemaire, and we would go to Orr, just about twenty feet away from him. He was the only guy we really focused on because he was the guy who started everything. I guess it worked because he didn't do as much as he usually did, and we won the series.

It wasn't the first time in my career that I play right wing. In my first year Geoffrion got hurt and I played on right wing with Bert Olmstead, and Béliveau, maybe ten games.

Johnny Bucyk holds several Boston Bruin scoring records. A native of Edmonton, Bucyk broke into the NHL with the Detroit Red Wings in the mid-1950s. After two years in Detroit he was traded to Boston, where he played for twenty-one seasons.

JOHNNY BUCYK

I was with Detroit when they played the Canadiens in the finals in 1955 and '56. We won the Stanley Cup in '55 and I even got a ring. Then I went to Boston and played against them in the finals the first two years I was there. After that I played against them many times in the playoffs. The Bruins never beat the Canadiens in the playoffs as long as I was there.

When we were getting set to play them again I don't think I had it in the back of my mind that they always beat us. I never thought that way. I always used to think that it was a new year, a new playoff series. But they still beat us, and usually it was because they had a better team.

The year that Dryden came up, he beat us. That's the year that bothers me because that time we did have a better team. I think back to the second game when we were leading them 5-1 and they ended up beating us 7-5. That turned the whole series around. I guess we thought it was all over and everybody just sat back. They had an explosive team, like Montreal always had. We took them a little lightly and Dryden got hot. He changed it. You get a hot goaltender and anything can happen.

The funny thing is, we won the Stanley Cup in '70 and '72, but I thought we had a better team in '71. That series taught us a lesson and we were better prepared when we won it the next year.

We had a lot of great games against Montreal even when we had bad teams and didn't make the playoffs for eight years. That's what sticks in my mind, the battles we had and the fun we had. It was a lot of fun playing against them. It seems even now, when these two teams play each other, it brings out the best in them. It doesn't matter which building, it's tough to get a ticket.

Ed Westfall was one of the fine Boston defensive forwards Jean Béliveau mentioned. Westfall played eighteen seasons in the NHL, eleven with Boston, seven with the New York Islanders. He was considered one of the premier penalty killers in hockey.

ED WESTFALL

I remember starting in 1961 and it wasn't until the late sixties, '68 and '69, that I lost my fear of playing against the Montreal Canadiens. They were awesome. When I started, Toronto was winning the Stanley Cup, but it seemed Montreal consistently had more power and talent to throw at you.

When I was a Boston Bruin you wanted to play against Montreal because you wanted a yardstick. You wanted to measure yourself against the best, and we always thought Montreal was the best. One year it was Béliveau winning the series in overtime, I'll never forget it.

In 1971 maybe they weren't the best. I keep thinking back to Dryden. He played a big part, and in some ways we beat ourselves. We should have been ahead 2–0. But Montreal has all that history, which somehow seems to work, and they just kept coming at us.

We didn't take hockey seriously enough that year. We won the Stanley Cup in 1970 and it was easy to beat the St. Louis Blues. We just kind of went through the motions and still won. Then Harry Sinden got fired and Tom Johnson didn't have the same kind of approach to coaching. Things weren't as disciplined.

In 1971 it wasn't that we didn't take Montreal seriously. Even today teams should, and do, take the Canadiens seriously. But that year we didn't take ourselves seriously, and that was one of the reasons they beat us.

BOBBY ORR

Yogi [Berra] said, "It's not over 'til it's over." We learned it that year. (laughs) We learned it in the second game.

Let's face it, we had the lead, 5-1. We're playing at home, the Boston Garden. We like to play there, and with the small ice surface we're not letting the Canadiens skate the way they normally do. Yeah, we probably were taking them a bit lightly.

I don't think we were cocky. We just let up. We had a game plan and we let it go, and when we did they didn't stop. We knew there wouldn't be any easy games against the Canadiens. We always knew that. But when we got away from our game plan, that's when they beat us.

I've always thought the defence was the strongest part of the Canadiens through the years. That year they had guys like Laperriere and Harper. They stayed in their own end and they didn't get much offence out of them. But they could handle the puck and they could move it. They were very strong clearing the front of the net, and when they'd get the darn puck you knew it was going to be out of there.

It was a great rivalry then, and it still is. You look at the Boston Bruins. Teams give up on players and they come to play in Boston. They put the sweater on and something happens. It's the same with the Montreal Canadiens. I believe that tradition helps a team win, I really do. Those two teams are the best examples.

In the days of the so-called Original Six the maximum number of playoff rounds per team was two. In 1971 it was three. After their win over Boston the Canadiens played the Minnesota North Stars. In the lore of '71 it's a series that is usually forgotten. The Canadiens won it in six games, but it wasn't easy.

FRANK MAHOVLICH

Everybody talks about our series that year with Boston, and then the one against Chicago. But there was another one, against Minnesota, and let me tell you that was no cakewalk.

We beat them in six games. In the sixth game, in Minnesota, we had them by one goal and there was a face-off in their end with seven seconds to go in the third period. They won the face-off, went down the ice, and they hit the post. With one or two seconds left, they hit the post. The bloody puck went in behind Dryden and came out the other way. There was a big argument. I'm telling you, that was a tough series.

When the Montreal Canadiens won four straight Stanley Cups in the late 1970s one of the team's strong points was the "Big Three" on defence, Serge Savard, Larry Robinson, and Guy Lapointe.

Lapointe was a rookie in 1970–71 and he fitted in easily, right from the start. An excellent skater and puck carrier, Lapointe was effective at both ends of the ice. By the time the season was half over you weren't thinking of him as a first-year player. A product of the Quebec Junior Hockey League, Guy Lapointe played on six Stanley Cup-winning teams in Montreal.

GUY LAPOINTE

I was lucky to play on all those Stanley Cup teams, and I have to say the first one was the best. That was the year we beat Chicago in seven games and I learned right away about the pressure of playing for the Montreal Canadiens.

As a kid I always took the chance to see the Canadiens play. I spent one year in the minors. Then when I joined the big team it was like a dream. I'll never forget my first year. I remember when I was first in the dressing room with John Ferguson, Jean Béliveau, Henri Richard, and guys like that. It took me about a month to realize it was for real.

The playoffs that year were very emotional. That was the best way for a young guy like me to learn about playing in Montreal. There is a special feeling when you put that sweater on and you learn quick that you just don't want to lose. Winning was in our heads all the time. Winning, winning, winning.

At the end of my career, I played for other teams, like the St. Louis Blues. The kids who were there had never won the Cup and they didn't realize what it was like. In Montreal I learned about it right away. Now that I look back, I'm not surprised that we won it so often.

There is an old saying that "Hockey players play hurt." Defence-man Jacques Laperriere was the perfect example during the 1971 Stanley Cup finals, and again in the finals two years later.

JACQUES LAPERRIERE

I broke my wrist in the first game of the finals and we didn't say anything about it. It was painful. They used to freeze it between periods and strap it up. The doctor said there wouldn't be a problem. I didn't mind the pain. I was happy just to play.

But here's the best. Two years later we're in the finals again against Chicago and I got hit by a stick and broke my nose. I went to the hospital and they had to operate. It was broken in seven places, something like that. The next day I showed up at the Forum with a big plaster on my nose and I had two black eyes. Sam Pollock looked at me and said, "Oh, it's not too bad, Jacques. You could play tonight."

I couldn't play in the game that night. Then we had a day off for travel and when we got to Chicago they made me a facemask and I played the next game.

After three years of the old playing the new in the Stanley Cup finals the playoff format changed in 1971. The NHL had expanded again, to Vancouver and Buffalo. There were now two seven-team divisions, East and West. The Chicago Black Hawks finished first in the West with 107 points, ten more than the Canadiens' third-place total in the East. The Hawks eliminated Philadelphia and New York to reach the finals against Montreal.

The final series followed a "home team wins" pattern for the first six games. The Hawks won the fifth game, in Chicago, 2-0. MacNeil had been having problems handling some of his veteran players. John Ferguson threw a tantrum during one of the games in the Minnesota series when he disagreed with MacNeil's coaching. Fergie was in a foul mood for the rest of the playoffs, off the ice as well as on.

In the fifth game of the Chicago series MacNeil had basically benched Henri Richard, using him only sparingly. After the game the normally quiet-spoken Pocket Rocket exploded, saying Al MacNeil was the worst coach he had ever played for.

Richard's outburst caused a storm of controversy in the Montreal media. The French press gave it more space than the story of the hockey game. MacNeil could not speak French. My father couldn't either but managed to dodge the language bullet for the fifteen years he coached the Canadiens. But in 1971 nationalistic fervour was at a far greater pitch in Quebec than it had ever been during the coaching regime of Dick Irvin. Richard's tirade put Al MacNeil on the French-English firing line. But while controversy raged around them, the Canadiens' players, as always, rose above the media linguistic wars. Winning came first.

HENRI RICHARD

I got mad at MacNeil just because he didn't play me. That's the only reason.

He didn't play me in a game in Chicago. After it was over I went into the room and said to myself that I wasn't going to say anything. But I was so bloody mad, so when the first newspaper guy came up to me and asked me how come I didn't play, I was so bloody mad I said right away, "He's the worst coach I ever play for."

I didn't really mean it, but it came out because I was mad. Al was a good guy. But I was just mad, and they made a lot of things about that in all the papers.

Even Guy Lafleur, in his book. He said I said to MacNeil that he shouldn't coach the Canadiens because he couldn't speak French, and all that shit. I never said that in my life.

When the Montreal Canadiens were having a poor season in the late 1940s, irate fans called the Forum saying they would burn down the building if the coach, Dick Irvin, wasn't fired. In 1971 people called the Forum threatening to kill Al MacNeil. When game six began in an emotionally charged Forum on Sunday afternoon, May 16, bodyguards stood alongside the coach of the Montreal Canadiens.

The Black Hawks could have won the Stanley Cup that afternoon, but they didn't. Henri Richard was playing again and the Canadiens won the game 4–3.

Two nights later, in Chicago, the Black Hawks were leading 2–0 midway through the second period. It looked like it was going to be 3–0 when Bobby Hull fired one of his famed slapshots toward an empty Montreal net, but the puck hit the goal post.

A few minutes later the Canadiens made it 2–1 when Jacques Lemaire fooled Tony Esposito with a slapshot from outside the Chicago blue line. Right after that the Canadiens tied the game on a close-in shot by Henri Richard.

The legend of Rocket Richard grew through his flair for the dramatic, his uncanny ability to score memorable goals to create memorable moments in the Stanley Cup playoffs. On a steamy night in Chicago, his younger brother rose to a similar occasion. In the third period of the seventh game of the final series, with the score still tied 2–2, the Pocket Rocket swept around Chicago defenceman Keith Magnuson and scored the Stanley Cup-winning goal, making Al MacNeil the winning coach.

In the traditional post-game ceremony, NHL president Clarence Campbell presented the Stanley Cup to Jean Béliveau. To add to the dramatics of the playoffs of '71, it was Béliveau's last game. Two weeks later the Canadiens' all-time greatest centre announced his retirement. Write a script of all that and they'd call it fiction. But in 1971, it really happened.

JACQUES LEMAIRE

We were going nowhere at that point in the game. I shot the puck from about ten feet past the red line. I shot it because I was tired and wanted to change. At times like that I seldom shot into the corner, usually at the net. I turned to go to the bench and I heard some noise from the crowd. I looked back and the red light was on. I never saw the puck go in.

I always thought Tony Esposito didn't see a lot of shots that came from far out. I never asked him about that one, but I don't think he saw it.

HENRI RICHARD

Those two goals were the best thrills. I always remember that.

It was a hot day and it was hot inside the rink. Must have been eighty, eighty-five degrees. I was sweating like crazy. I was kind of scared because, after all that stuff with Al MacNeil, if I would have made a mistake, give the puck away or something like that to cost a goal or maybe the game, it would have been even worse.

I could have been a bum. I end up a hero.

JEAN BÉLIVEAU

When I was playing that night in Chicago I knew it was my last game. I had informed the organization.

The year before I had wanted to retire. But Sam and members of the Canadiens' management asked me to stay another year. Around 1970 we had quite a few young players on the team. We were in quite a transition period. Sam told me, "Jean, I would like to see you in the room. It's very difficult to go through a long season like we have without having times during the year when it's going to get tough for the young players. It would be nice to have you there."

So I told him, "Okay. One more year, but that's it. That will be the end." I was in my fortieth year when I announced my retirement in June of 1971. Thank God I was lucky enough to come out of it with one more Stanley Cup.

20

Scotty Takes Over

The weeks following the 1971 season were hectic ones. Béliveau retired, the Canadiens drafted Guy Lafleur, and Sam Pollock demoted the coach who had just won him another Stanley Cup.

A major reason the Canadiens defeated Chicago was because Al MacNeil clearly outcoached Billy Reay. MacNeil's work in the playoffs had been exceptional under very difficult circumstances. Even so, Pollock had a problem. If MacNeil remained as coach, Sam knew Montreal's French-language media would give MacNeil absolutely no room for error once the next season began. To keep him as coach would almost have been unfair to MacNeil. Then Sam got lucky. The solution to his problem was handed him on a silver platter by the St. Louis Blues when they fired their coach, Scotty Bowman. Bowman was a Pollock protégé, he was talented, and he was bilingual.

Scotty Bowman had been one of Sam Pollock's disciples from the time he suffered a career-ending head injury while playing for the Montreal Junior Canadiens. After a polite waiting period that allowed Al MacNeil to bask in the glory of his Stanley Cup triumph, Pollock made a change. MacNeil was assigned to coach the Canadiens' farm team in Halifax and Scotty Bowman was hired to coach the Montreal Canadiens.

SCOTTY BOWMAN

After my injury I knew I wasn't going to play anymore. There was a lot of hockey being played in the parks in Montreal and I coached a midget team in Verdun. Mr. Selke asked me if I wanted to get involved and I said I did. The next year I got the chance to coach a Junior B team in Park Extension, and I kinda liked it.

I had a good job because I could get off for about two hours at noon. That was in the early fifties. I would come up to the Forum and I would watch Canadiens practise. Then I'd go back to work. I was lucky that I had a boss who probably didn't know where I was.

That Junior B team was a pretty good one and we got to the finals. Then I had a chance to go to Ottawa under Sam Pollock. That was around 1956, and from that time on I knew that I really wanted to coach.

And coach he did – junior hockey, senior hockey, head coach, assistant coach. Whatever Sam Pollock wanted him to do within the Canadiens' system, Scotty did it.

In 1966 the NHL awarded new franchises to six cities. One was St. Louis, where they named the team the Blues and hired Scotty as the assistant to coach and general manager Lynn Patrick. Early in the Blues' first season Patrick gave up the coaching part of his job and Bowman took over.

So that the new teams wouldn't feel like poor cousins compared to the six established clubs, the Stanley Cup final was between the old and the new for the first three years of expansion. Bowman's Blues made it to the finals each time. They didn't win a game but they made it close against the Canadiens in '68 and '69, and Boston in 1970. That was the year Bobby Orr scored his famous Cup-winning goal in overtime.

The St. Louis team was owned by the Solomon family. The father more or less gave it to his son to run and, as often happens, it wasn't long before the son thought he knew more about hockey than someone like Scotty Bowman.

After the 1971 playoffs Bowman moved from St. Louis back to his native Montreal. During the next eight years, while Solomon the son managed the Blues into near extinction, Scotty Bowman was coaching the Montreal Canadiens to five Stanley Cup championships.

One of the reasons the Canadiens didn't win another Stanley Cup in Scotty Bowman's first season is evident in the 1971–72 team picture. Jean Béliveau is in it, on the extreme right in the front row. But Big Jean is wearing civilian clothes. Béliveau the executive didn't have the same meaning as Béliveau the player. His on-ice leadership was sorely missed.

The picture is also the first team photo that includes Guy Lafleur. The Flower scored twenty-nine times in his rookie season, but he still needed a lot of cultivating before he reached full bloom.

Frank Mahovlich had his best year in Montreal with forty-three goals, and Ken Dryden was rookie of the year. (The Canadiens haven't had one since. Dryden will likely always be the only player to be named the MVP of the playoffs a year before winning the rookie award.)

Not surprisingly, the emotion of the 1971 playoffs didn't carry through the following season. The Canadiens finished third behind Boston and New York, then lost to the Rangers in six games in the first playoff round. The Rangers went on to lose to Boston in the finals. Bobby and the Bruins didn't take any of their opponents lightly that year.

During the 1971–72 season there was another significant off-ice change at the Forum. Just after Christmas, ownership of the Montreal Canadiens passed out of the hands of the Molson family.

In 1957 Senator Donat Raymond sold the team, and the Forum, to Senator Hartland Molson and his brother, Tom. Senator Raymond made the deal partly out of sentiment for the Molson family.

"Senator Raymond had two other offers at that time," Senator Hartland Molson told me. "One was from Quebec City and the other from a group in the United States. But he had always been grateful for the support my father had given him when he was on the Canadiens' board in the 1930s, when others had deserted what looked like a sinking ship. He felt that in selling the team to us he was repaying our family for the help my father had given him through some very trying times."

In the mid-1960s Hartland and Tom sold the same package to

their cousin David Molson and his brothers, Peter and Bill, who said they would make owning and operating the Canadiens their life's work. During their regime, in 1968, the Forum underwent a major renovation. It became one of the best and most colourful buildings of its kind in North America, a far cry from the "dark, ugly cave" Frank Selke, Jr., had first seen in 1946.

On December 30, 1971, the Canadiens and the Forum changed hands again. In a surprise move that displeased Senator Molson, his three cousins sold the hockey team and the Forum to another set of brothers, Peter and Edward Bronfman.

PETER BRONFMAN

The idea of buying the Canadiens first came to me one morning at breakfast when I saw an item in the paper written by Ted Blackman. He wrote that someone might be able to purchase the team if they had enough money, and enough headache pills. What was happening was that the Molson brothers wanted to sell the team to take advantage of a capital gains tax break which was in effect only until the end of the year.

I called a friend of mine, Jacques Courtois, who I knew was plugged in to that sort of thing and asked him to make a few inquiries. Jacques asked around to various groups, but nobody was really interested. We checked with the Royal Bank and they weren't interested but their chairman, Earl McLaughlin, came by one day and helped me go through a list of people and businesses to see who might be a candidate.

We finally found a couple of partners. John Bassett joined us, and so did the Bank of Nova Scotia. But later on both figured there wasn't much use being in on it, so we bought them out.

It was all very fortuitous, really. Before that we had made an offer to buy the Alouette football team for $1 million. We never heard back on that one, thank goodness.

Before the next NHL season a major hockey happening occurred when Team Canada, composed of Canadian NHL players, met the Soviet Union national team in the famed eight-game series of 1972. Six Montreal Canadiens were on the Canada team - Ken Dryden,

255

Serge Savard, Guy Lapointe, Yvan Cournoyer, and the Mahovlich brothers, Frank and Pete.

The series is best remembered because of Paul Henderson's dramatic winning goal in the final moments of the final game, in Moscow. Yvan Cournoyer helped set up the historic series winner.

YVAN COURNOYER

I got a penalty and they scored to make it 5-4. Then I scored and I said, "Well, at least we're not losers. We tied the game and we're going to tie the series."

That was the goal when they didn't turn on the light. I don't know what happened. The goal judge waited a long time and that's when Eagleson started to run on the ice after him. Pete Mahovlich went over the boards and grabbed Eagleson and brought him to the other side.

The last goal. Well, I don't think anybody knows this too much, but if you train a little bit harder, if you stay on the ice after practice, you are able to give a little extra. It comes natural if you love the game and want to give more.

The ice in Russia, it was pretty big. I was playing right wing and in that third period my side was completely opposite our bench. We were changing lines. My left wing went out, and then my centreman went out.

A Russian player had the puck in his zone and I think he thought I was going out, too, but in the middle of the ice I changed my mind. I still had some extra left. I went back into their zone and he threw the puck around the boards because he thought I was going to the bench. He just wanted to clear it out, and that's it, the game is over.

But I came back, intercepted the puck, and I see Paul coming with Phil Esposito . . . they're coming off the bench. I finally give it to Phil in the corner. He missed but he got the puck back. That's when he made another play and Paul got the loose puck and scored.

So you see, in a split second I say to myself I'm going to give a little bit more. There was a minute to go, something like that, and I just changed my mind and it worked. Sometimes it doesn't work but this time it did. The puck was in their zone so I had nothing to lose. I gave it the last effort and that's what happened.

When hockey fans in Canada, and the NHL, *returned to normal after going through the emotional wringer that was the series of '72, the Montreal Canadiens embarked on what would be, up to then, the finest season in the history of the franchise. The Canadiens won fifty-two games, tied sixteen, and lost only ten, finishing thirteen points ahead of the Boston Bruins. The 1973 Habs lost only five playoff games, defeating Buffalo, Philadelphia, and Chicago on their way to the Stanley Cup.*

Bowman had made a few subtle changes to his team's lineup. It needed more speed. He found it in rookies Chuck Lefley and Murray Wilson.

The Canadiens also needed another defenceman after J.C. Tremblay defected to the World Hockey Association. Bob Murdoch became a regular on defence and so did Dale Hoganson, for a while. But Hoganson was never a favourite of Bowman's, and vice versa.

Halfway through the season the Canadiens promoted a twenty-one-year-old defenceman who was in his rookie pro season in Halifax. Twelve years later he would skate onto the Forum ice alongside Jacques Plante, Doug Harvey, Jean Béliveau, Dickie Moore, and Maurice Richard in a ceremony honouring the Montreal Canadiens' all-time Dream Team, as voted by the fans. The kid's name was Larry Robinson.

LARRY ROBINSON

I played my first game for the Montreal Canadiens January 8th, 1973, against the Minnesota North Stars, at the Forum. That's something you don't forget.

I was at the camp that year and I thought I'd done pretty good. I was still there for the home opener, which was against Minnesota, but I didn't play. I sat in the press box and then they sent me down to Halifax the next day. I came back up in January and played regularly for the rest of the year. They gave me number 19 right away. There's a funny coincidence there. Terry Harper had worn it before me and when he left Montreal he went to Los Angeles, just like I did.

Even though I played regularly, when the playoffs started they didn't use me. We played Buffalo in the first round and about six of us didn't play. Floyd Curry ran practices with us and we skated, and skated. He really worked us hard and we stayed in good shape.

We beat Buffalo and then played Philadelphia. I was dressed for the first game and played only one shift. They beat us that night. Rick MacLeish scored in overtime.

I was dressed again for the second game and didn't play that much either, maybe two or three shifts until the third period. Then Jacques Laperriere got hurt and I played the whole third period. That game went into overtime, too, and I scored the winning goal.

Gary Dornhoefer had cleared the puck into our end and I started back up the ice with it. I was going to pass it to Frank but he ran a pick on Dornhoefer and yelled at me, "Go with it!" So I kept going and shot the puck from the left wing. I used to think it was from just over the red line but I've seen replays and it was just over the blue line. I should have realized my shot wasn't that good. (laughs) Doug Favell was in nets, and he just missed the shot. I went crazy. What a feeling that was!

We played Chicago in the final and that was the series they called the "Battle of the Goaltenders." We had Dryden and they had Tony Esposito. They had been the two goalies for Canada against the Russians in the big series.

We went ahead [in games] 3-1 in Chicago when we beat them 3-0. They only had twelve shots on goal. So we went back to Montreal and that's when they had a big party all set up at the Queen Elizabeth Hotel for after the game. They figured we were going to win it, no sweat. And that was the game Chicago won, 8-7. What a night. The first seven shots on goal went in. The shots were 4-3, and the score was 4-3. On their winning goal, I went to hit Ralph Backstrom along the boards and missed him. They went in and scored. I tried to get back and ended up inside the net behind Kenny after the puck went in.

So we had to go back to Chicago and we were down 2-0 in the

first period. But Henri scored a goal for us right at the end of the first period and we won the game. Yvan got the winner. My first Stanley Cup.

In those days you noticed right away that the team was like one big family. Unlike today, when you seem to be playing or travelling every other day, you seemed to have a lot more time off. So you had more time together for parties or whatever. I was just a rookie, but I remember going to parties with Serge, Claude Larose, all the guys. The only one who almost never showed up was Kenny. Everybody else hung around together. I remember Yvan Cournoyer coming to pick me up at the house. He was a big star and I was just a rookie. But it was part of the ritual.

Guy Lapointe was a big help to me then. We hung around a lot together and he was always giving me advice, helping me out. I played mostly with Serge. It worked out we were a pairing for almost seven years. He never changed his game. He was really steady, so I knew I could take chances and he would always be back to cover up. Once I saw him get the puck I knew he'd do that little spin move of his, so I'd just get going and take his pass. I had the speed and I'd just take it up and look for Guy or Yvan. Guys like them helped me get a lot of points over the years.

The big star for the Canadiens in the 1973 playoffs was Yvan Cournoyer. The Roadrunner had kept running following his heroics for Team Canada with a forty-goal season and a scoring record in the playoffs. His performance was a gutsy one because he was playing hurt through the final couple of months.

YVAN COURNOYER

I got hit by Ted Harris, who used to play for us, in a game against Minnesota. I kept playing that night but after the game I had a problem with my stomach for a long time, right to the end. But when you start with a good feeling like in 1972, you want to do it all the way.

In the playoffs that year I had the most goals, fifteen. It was a record in those days. But I had to be frozen in the stomach before every game because the muscles were really hurting.

I scored the winning goal in the last game. It came off the glass, right on my stick. Esposito turned to his right and I put the puck in behind him, top corner.

We only lose ten games that year and we think nobody is going to really do that again. Then a few years later we lose only eight. (laughs)

I flew back to Montreal on the Canadiens' charter immediately following their Stanley Cup win that night in Chicago. My most vivid recollection is what happened right after we landed in Montreal.

The media, as always, sat in the front of the aircraft so we were the first off. We waited on the runway to watch the players deplane. The first one through the door and down the steps was Claude Larose, who was being carried on a stretcher by his buddies. Larose had broken his leg in the Cup-clinching game and should have been in a hospital in Chicago. But there was no way he was going to miss the ride home to Montreal with the Stanley Cup.

CLAUDE LAROSE

In that '73 final our line checked Pit Martin, Dennis Hull, and Jim Pappin. I was checking Dennis Hull and in the last minute of the second period in the last game, in Chicago, he got away from me. He and Pit Martin had a two-on-one break against Serge, who was the only man back. I came back as fast as I could and yelled that I would get Hull, so Serge covered Martin. He passed the puck across to Hull and I just dove at him and intercepted the pass. I kept going head first into the net. The weight of my body hit the goal post. I knew I had hurt my head but I didn't feel anything in my leg.

I got to the dressing room and they put a bunch of stitches in my head. When I got off the table to go back out to play, I couldn't walk. I said, "Hey, there's something wrong with me." So they looked at my leg and it was broken.

They took me to the hospital and I listened to the game on the radio. They told me I would have to be there for a week. But when I knew we had won the Cup, I didn't want to stay in Chicago.

The people at the hospital understood, so they put a cast on my leg and took me to the airport so I could go home on the plane with the team. When we got to Montreal the boys carried me off the plane first, on a stretcher. But then I had to stay in hospital for a week, so I missed all the celebrations, all the parties.

It would be two years before the Canadiens would again enjoy the parties that go with winning the Stanley Cup. In 1974 and 1975 the celebrating would all be done in Philadelphia, where the Flyers, a.k.a. the Broad Street Bullies, combined skilful and rough-and-tumble players into a team that had people thinking the best route to the Stanley Cup was via the penalty box.

In 1974 the Canadiens fell to the New York Rangers in the first round of the playoffs. Montreal had finished the season with ninety-nine points, twenty-one fewer than their awesome season a year before. One major reason was their defensive record – fifty-six more goals against. The reason was simple. Ken Dryden didn't play.

Following the Canadiens' Cup win in 1973 Dryden put his legal training to work and did some investigating into what his fellow goaltenders in the NHL were being paid. What he found out didn't please him.

Dryden was considered the best but his contract wasn't the best. The Canadiens wouldn't change it. Shortly before training camp was to start the Canadiens' Vezina Trophy-winning goalie held a news conference at Montreal's Windsor Hotel. Outfitted in a gaudy black-and-white checkered sportscoat, Dryden talked at great length abut his situation. I was there with a TV news crew. This is part of what he had to say.

KEN DRYDEN

You feel you make a contribution to a team, within a league. You look around the league and you see somebody else that you feel makes no more or no less a contribution and you see where he is at, and it is very difficult to accept. I could name six goaltenders that were higher paid than I was a year ago, and that number would increase next year. That bothers me. Certainly Montreal does very well. They're not impoverished in any way. If other teams can, it seems to me that they should be able to as well.

This is by far the most difficult decision that I have ever made, but it's one I feel I have to make. I think I am doing the right thing, although that doesn't make it any easier at all.

I will not play this year. What I will do is article with a law firm in Toronto.

Wayne Thomas and Bunny Larocque were pressed into the goal-tending breach as Dryden hit the law books in Toronto. The 1973–74 season saw a significant addition and a significant deletion. Long-time defence star Jacques Laperriere retired because of a chronic knee injury. Bob Gainey, the team's first draft pick in 1973, played the first of his sixteen seasons with the Canadiens.

Guy Lafleur continued to be a disappointment, managing a mere twenty-one goals in his third season. Sam Pollock talked with Scotty Bowman and assistant coach Claude Ruel about trading the Flower. They finally made the very wise decision to sign him to a new contract.

Before the next season began Ken Dryden also made a wise decision. He decided to play goal again. So, as the training camp began, there I was again with a camera crew getting these comments about his return to the Canadiens.

KEN DRYDEN

Other people have done it and haven't apparently shown any ill effects. Plante was out for three or four years. My brother didn't play for a year. Sometimes people with injuries are, in effect, out for a whole season.

What is not in your favour is that you have not had the continuous competition. You haven't seen the plays for a whole year, so your anticipation isn't quite what you would like it to be.

It's mental and it's physical, but I think it will be more mental. You have to go through sixty minutes of concentration, which is an effort. You've been concentrating on other things, but now you have to get back into hockey concentration. Beneficially, you are enthusiastic, and because you are not quite sure what shape you're in, you have to work harder at it.

Dryden did work harder at it, but he wasn't quite vintage Kenny during the 1974–75 season. The Canadiens scored eighty-one more goals than the previous season, with a suddenly full-blooming Flower getting fifty-three of their league-leading total of 374. But their goals-against record improved by only fifteen. Montreal, Philadelphia, and Buffalo all finished the season with 113 points. The Sabres eliminated the Canadiens in the Stanley Cup semifinals.

The Canadiens of '74–'75 were an improved team, but one still not quite good enough to win it all. A significant absentee was Frank Mahovlich, who returned to Toronto to play for the Toros in the WHA. Significant additions were centre Doug Risebrough and right-winger Mario Tremblay, two hard-working, aggressive young-sters who would play major roles in the dynasty that would begin the following season.

While Larry Robinson got the chance to play once he joined the Montreal Canadiens, other rookies were spending a lot of time watching games from various press boxes around the NHL. They were called "the Black Aces," and one of them was left-winger Steve Shutt.

The Canadiens picked Shutt as their number-one draft choice in 1972. He had been a star with the Marlboro juniors in his home town, Toronto. The Marlies' line of Shutt, Billy Harris, and Dave Gardner was the highest-scoring line in junior hockey. But while Larry spent a lot of time playing once he joined the Canadiens, Shutt spent a lot of time watching.

STEVE SHUTT

When I first came up, the first two years, I was in the press box. I was watching how to play the game and I learned from that. By the third year I knew how to play. I was never the best defensively, but when it came down to the crunch I played good defensive hockey. I had to or else I wouldn't have played.

In my first year we won the Stanley Cup. In the playoffs that year I was on the ice for one shift, in the series against Philadelphia. I had led the team in points in games against Philly that season. Mind you, we didn't get very many points against them. But I was our leader, and then I just played that one shift against them. That was it for me in the whole playoffs. But I got my name on the Stanley Cup.

When I made the team was in my third year. In my second year I scored fifteen goals and was in and out of the lineup all year. After the season I rented a farm in Bracebridge and I went up there with my dog. I didn't even have a car and I was right in the middle of nowhere. I wasn't married then, so I was all alone. I went there to think. I decided I was either going to make it as a hockey player the next season or I wasn't going to make it at all. I disciplined myself to concentrate on thoughts like that.

When I went to camp the next season I was really helped by the fact that Frank Mahovlich, Réjean Houle, and Marc Tardif had all gone to the WHA. The Canadiens were at a point where they had to play me. But at the same time I was at a point in my life where I was mentally prepared to do the job.

At that time Pete Mahovlich was a star. Guy Lafleur hadn't lived up to expectations, and I hadn't lived up to expectations. They put Flower and me with Pete right from the start that season. Pete took us under his wing and said, "Come on, guys, this is how we're going to play." And he showed us. He really looked after us for a while. You could see Lafleur starting to get confidence, and I started getting my confidence. The line had a lot of success. The reason Scotty finally broke us up was that Pete and Flower both played a style where they had to have the puck a lot.

Pete was always very much underestimated in the opinion of the Canadiens' fans. He was a pretty good hockey player and meant a lot more to the team than people gave him credit for.

Steve Shutt wasn't exaggerating when he said Guy Lafleur had not lived up to expectations. Lafleur had been the oustanding junior player in the country. (When Mario Lemieux was setting all-time junior scoring records in Quebec he was breaking Lafleur's records.) The Canadiens drafted Lafleur in 1971, the day after Jean Béliveau retired. Fans throughout Quebec thought all was right with their hockey world. One French-Canadian superstar had left but there was another all set to take his place. It didn't work out that way.

The young Flower struggled through his first three seasons with goal totals of 29, 28, and 21. Lafleur was a member of, but not a major contributor to, the 1973 Stanley Cup-winning team. The Canadiens even thought of trading him. Fortunately they didn't, and, as the saying goes, the rest is history.

GUY LAFLEUR

The happiest time for me in Montreal was when I first came up with the team. It was tough the first three years because I was not playing that much. But still, I was with a great bunch of guys who won the Stanley Cup. It was great to be on a team where they created a winning feeling. They really influenced me to get the right attitude and to think positive. When it came time to have fun, we had fun. When it was time to play hockey, we played.

I joined the team right after Jean Béliveau retired. It didn't bother me that much except for the pressure on my shoulders. Everybody was thinking I was replacing Jean Béliveau. I was there as myself to play the game and try to do my best. I would have really liked to play with Jean Béliveau. It's too bad he retired that year. He was my idol.

I know there was talk that they thought about trading me after my first three years. I never thought about it. I knew it was going to be tough to make the team because of the reputation of the Montreal Canadiens. Look at Yvan Cournoyer. He only played the power play for a long time when he started.

The most successful NHL executive in recent years has been Glen Sather of the Edmonton Oilers. In his playing days Sather was what is termed in the trade a "journeyman." One of his stops was in Montreal for the 1974-75 season.

GLEN SATHER

I played one year in Montreal, the year Dryden came back after his holdout. Sam Pollock had traded for me and the first day I got to the Forum I saw him on the other side of the rink. I walked across the ice to say hello and he didn't know who I was.

I had the chance to apprentice under a lot of guys because I was traded six times. I had the opportunity to watch good people running their teams and also poorly qualified people who really didn't know what they were doing. I figured out I should take the best from certain organizations and try to apply it myself when I got into management.

I learned about the Montreal Canadiens right away, in the first meeting. They only talked about two things, finishing in first place and winning the Stanley Cup. That's all. Winning.

In Montreal you felt it everywhere, from cab drivers, waitresses. Everywhere you went all they talked about was the Canadiens winning. I could see then there is a lot of pressure on the players who play in Montreal. That's not a bad thing. It's good. Check their record.

Midway through the 1970s the Montreal Canadiens were on the verge of becoming one of hockey's true dynasties, a team that would win the Stanley Cup the next four years. But during the summer of 1975 one of the greatest players in the history of a team of great players, Henri Richard, retired. The little man who was first thought to be too small to play in the NHL appeared in more games, 1,256, and more seasons, twenty, than anyone else in the history of the Montreal Canadiens. Henri Richard is the only man in hockey history to have played on eleven Stanley Cup-winning teams.

Early in his final year Richard suffered a broken leg and played in only sixteen regular-season games, plus six more in the playoffs. Ironically, another great Montreal centreman, Elmer Lach, broke a leg during his final season. Both men had worn the number sixteen, which was eventually retired in their honour.

HENRI RICHARD

I decided I wanted to retire. I could have stayed maybe one more year but I wouldn't have been playing regular. I would have been sitting on the bench. I wanted to play.

I could have stayed for one, maybe two years. My contract said they would pay me the year following when I retired, which they did. So I could have played one more year and then get paid the following year. But I would have been sitting on the bench, and I didn't want that to happen.

Yeah, I won eleven Stanley Cups. Right place, right time.

During the final years of Henri Richard's career the Canadiens frequently travelled on a chartered airplane. Henri always sat in the same seat, halfway down the plane, on the aisle.

The year after Henri retired he was hired by a Montreal radio station to cover the Canadiens during the Stanley Cup playoffs. After a game on the road he flew home on the team's charter flight. When Henri walked onto the plane Pete Mahovlich was sitting in what used to be Henri's seat. Mahovlich immediately got up and sat elsewhere. Henri walked down the aisle and took his accustomed spot. No one even thought twice about a media man sitting in the section reserved for the players. The Pocket Rocket was back where he belonged.

Same place. Different time.

VI

Four in a Row:
The Second Dynasty

Many thought the NHL was at a critical crossroad after the Philadelphia Flyers won their second straight Stanley Cup in 1975. The Flyers were called the "Broad Street Bullies," a phrase that became as widely used as the team's official name. Fans in Philadelphia, and many of the players, revelled in the image, and so did the team's publicity department. (Even today hockey fights are shown on the big TV screens hanging over centre ice at the Spectrum during intermissions of Flyers' home games.)

The Philadelphia team was a strange and successful mix. Alongside tough guys Dave Schultz, Don Saleski, Moose Dupont, and "Hound Dog" Kelly were skilled performers like Rick MacLeish, Bill Barber, and Reg Leach. Orchestrating things from behind the bench was "The Fog," coach Fred Shero. On the ice Flyers' captain Bobby Clarke, a truly great player and competitor, controlled the tempo. Backstopping the team was goaltender Bernie Parent, the playoff MVP in both of his team's Cup-winning years.

But the skilful Philadelphia players got second billing, after

269

the goon squad. A replay of a riot at the Spectrum was fast becoming hockey's main image. Even though the Flyers became the best draw in the league, their style of play upset most of hockey's establishment. Many wanted to prove that the quickest way to the Stanley Cup was not via the penalty box.

The team Sam Pollock was assembling in Montreal through the period of Philadelphia's domination seemed to be taking hockey in that direction, and it eventually worked out that way. But before it did the Canadiens established some very important turf when they successfully challenged the Flyers with a goon squad of their own, in a pre-season exhibition game right in Philadelphia.

Then, midway through the 1975–76 season, another game proved to be very important in the development of the next dynasty at the Forum. It, too, was an exhibition, but it ranks as one of the most famous games in the history of the Montreal Canadiens.

21

A Memorable New Year's Eve
at the Forum

What was the greatest hockey game ever played?

Most of the people who were there will say it was the one played at the Montreal Forum, December 31, 1975. Others, like me, will allow it was likely the greatest one-sided hockey game ever played.

Halfway through the 1975–76 NHL season the Montreal Canadiens had the league's best record. Around that time two teams from the Soviet Union, the Wings and the Red Army, were playing a series of exhibition games against NHL clubs. Red Army, the best Soviet team, played the Canadiens on New Year's Eve. When the game was over the Canadiens had decisively outplayed the Soviets, and had outshot them 38–13. Yet the final score was 3–3.

Best game? Artistically, no, because of its one-sidedness. Emotionally? Probably, yes.

The two hockey systems had met head on in 1972 in the historic eight-game series involving all-star teams. Now we had the real thing, our best "team" against their best "team." For one night, the NHL's regular season seemed to pale in comparison.

The famed New Year's Eve game was the one that put Soviet goaltender Vladislav Tretiak into our Hockey Hall of Fame. Tretiak's record in major international matches after that wasn't Hall of Fame calibre very often. His performance that night was.

We expected the players on the two best teams to rise to the dramatic occasion, and to their credit they did. The Canadiens shut down the powerful Red Army attack with a display of team defence in all parts of the ice the Soviets had rarely encountered. Tretiak was bombarded, and he responded with an amazing performance. Yvan Cournoyer scored one of the Montreal goals after Tretiak had stopped three rapid-fire, point-blank shots while his team was playing two men short.

Inside the Forum, as the saying goes, you could have cut the tension and emotion with a knife. It was a remarkable game of hockey involving several of the world's greatest players. Anyone who saw it hasn't forgotten it.

Why 3–3, when the shots were 38–13? Simply, Tretiak was hot, Dryden was not. No matter. Nothing but happy memories remain.

LARRY ROBINSON

Before the opening face-off, when they were singing the anthems, the feeling that I got just standing there at the blue line was really something.

I knew that millions of people were going to be watching the game. It was frightening, to say the least. It gave you a tingle all over. If there was a cat in the building you thought it was singing the national anthem. It was just a terrific feeling.

YVAN COURNOYER

1972 was still a very strong memory. We had six guys on that team from the Montreal Canadiens. We had it in our minds that we were still the best so we prepared very seriously for the game. I remember stepping on the ice, it was like 1972 coming back to me again.

I think Tretiak was a good goalie. But in that game I scored on a wrist shot, and he missed that one. But for him to be in our Hall of Fame, I don't see him there. If he would have come to the NHL, play a few years and be the best goalie, okay. But for me, I think Kenny was better than him.

When we played them on New Year's Eve we knew a little bit what to expect. In '72 we didn't know what to expect. They told us they had no shot, they could not skate. We didn't know about them. But that's when we found out they were pretty good hockey players.

They do a lot of things well. They got the best wrist shot. I respect them, but I never liked them. I still don't like them.

STEVE SHUTT

It was a very special game for our team because at that time we were leading the NHL. The Red Army team was obviously the best in the Soviet Union. Everybody, not only the players on the teams, but everybody in the whole city knew this was going to be a special game.

At that point in time both of the systems were much different than they are now. It was a case of the Canadian style, a much more rough-and-tumble type of game, versus the Soviet style, which was more of a finesse, passing style of game.

For us, it was like playoff hockey. Our previous league game had been in Washington. They didn't have a good team, so we were thinking more about playing the Red Army, getting geared up for them. And we were geared up. We outshot them by a big margin. In those types of games, when you have possession of the puck and you're not scoring, you say, "Oh, oh. They're going to go down and get one." And that's how it worked in that game.

The funny thing was, they didn't score on the best chance they had. Mikhailov went down on a break and hit the cross bar behind Kenny. We nicknamed him "Jughead" because he looked like the guy in the Archie comics. He thought he'd scored on that one. That was the best chance they had.

The Soviet system dictated the way their players lived. They really didn't have to get in shape to play hockey. Now we see their players coming here to play in the NHL, now they have to get in shape for a long season, not just for special games or tournaments. That's why the older Soviets have had a hard time adjusting. Now the Soviets are going towards a North American style of hockey, not only playing but off the ice, too. That's why the younger players who come here are adjusting much better.

But when we played them that night, the systems were totally different. It was ours against theirs.

The referee for the game was Wally Harris, who officiated NHL games for nineteen years. He, too, found himself caught up in the emotion of the moment.

WALLY HARRIS

When the game started I was aware that this was the first time we had met the Russians on a team-against-team basis, their best against our best.

About two or three minutes into the game I made a call and Yvan Cournoyer got very upset. He skated up to me ranting and raving all over the place. I said, "Take it easy. Settle down. There's pressure on everybody here tonight." Cournoyer said, "I know. But we have to beat these bastards."

What I remember most of all is Tretiak. When you're two or three feet away from a goalie you get a good look at him. That night, I never saw him make the first move. I can't remember a goaltender who could stare down the guys the way he did that night.

It was one of the top games I ever worked.

For the past few years the National Hockey League made it obligatory for all teams to play one game per season against a team from the Soviet Union. The league billed it as a "Super Series," but the games were far from "super" in the minds of fans in most league cities. Unless the games were included in the season ticket package crowds were small and interest next to nil. With several Soviets now in the NHL, the uniqueness is gone. The rivalry at the club level is not even close to what it once was, either for the fans or the players.

SERGE SAVARD

That New Year's Eve game was a hell of a game with a lot of emotion and pressure. For us it was like a Stanley Cup game. There was a lot of pride involved. I know the shots were one-sided, but the emotion was something else.

Today, there's no feeling for the Russian games. This year about six guys went to Pat Burns and said they didn't want to play in the game. There's no feeling anymore about those games. No pride.

22

Those Who Made It Happen

In my first book, Now Back To You, Dick, *I wrote that my choice as the greatest hockey team of all time was the 1976-77-78 version of the Montreal Canadiens. Nothing has happened since to change my mind. Here is a brief overview of that team's record before you read the words of the men who made it all happen.*

The Montreal Canadiens won the Stanley Cup four years in a row, starting in 1976. During that time they played 378 regular season and playoff games. Their record: 277 wins, 56 losses, 45 ties. In the 1976-77 regular season the Canadiens won sixty games and lost only eight, a record that should stay in the book forever. In the first three of their four awesome years the Canadiens played 282 games and were beaten only 36 times.

There were fifteen players whose names were inscribed on the Stanley Cup after each championship season; there were twelve on all five Cup winners in the Canadiens' five in a row of the 1950s. During both dynasties only two regular players had been with other NHL teams prior to winning Cups in Montreal: Bert Olmstead and Marcel Bonin in the fifties; in the seventies Jim Roberts and Pierre Larouche each played on two of the four championship teams.

During the four years Montreal players earned a total of sixteen individual NHL awards and sixteen All-Star selections. Guy Lafleur was the big winner with three scoring championships, two Hart trophies, and one Smythe Trophy. Ken Dryden won the Vezina Trophy four times, by himself in 1976 and with Bunny Larocque the

275

*next three years. Both Dryden and Lafleur were first All-Star team
selections all four years.*

*From 1976 through 1979 the Canadiens played in fifty-nine
playoff games, winning forty-eight. In six of the twelve series they
played they did not lose a game. Only once, against Boston in the
1979 semifinals, were they extended to the full seven-game distance.
Only twice did a series go as long as six games. In the finals, when
they played Philadelphia, Boston twice, and the New York Rangers,
they were beaten only three times in nineteen games.*

*Statistics can be numbing so I'll stop, but I think you get the
message. Simply, the Canadiens outplayed, outclassed, overpow-
ered, and overwhelmed the rest of the National Hockey League.*

*As I listened to the players who made all of this happen, they
were keenest about two topics as they reminisced. One was their
1976 final series sweep of the defending champions from Philadelphia, especially the final game at the Philadelphia Spectrum, when
the Canadiens' speed and skill convincingly conquered the brute
strength and clout of the Broad Street Bullies. The other favourite
topic was their coach, Scotty Bowman.*

SCOTTY BOWMAN

You could see it coming after I was here about two years. Fellows
like Guy Lafleur, Larry Robinson, Steve Shutt, Bob Gainey had
all arrived. And, of course, Ken Dryden who was well established
by that time. They had a good draft in 1974 when they picked
Doug Risebrough and Mario Tremblay, who were young players
who had a good impact on the team.

We knew by the mid-seventies that we had a lot of good,
hungry young players who hadn't reached their peak. The question at that time was how good they might be.

They all seemed to blossom at the same time. Robinson blos-
somed as a great defenceman and he had strong help from Guy
Lapointe and Serge Savard. I don't remember a team since, or
even before my time, that had three defencemen on one team who
all could be all-stars. Many nights I only played them about thirty
or forty minutes a game. (laughs)

The pool of players was very strong. Young players were coming up who had won championships in Nova Scotia under Al MacNeil. Everyone developed at the same time.

Lafleur was a great scorer. Gainey and Doug Jarvis became top defensive players. We had the best defence in the league, and the best goaltender in the league. It was no secret that the team in '76–'77 that lost only eight games just wouldn't lose games. They were out of a few but somehow found a way to come back and win.

JACQUES LEMAIRE

It started in Philly. Maybe I have another point of view than Larry or some of the other guys because I was never a rough player. But even when we would play them in an exhibition game they would try to beat us up, intimidate us. That year we played an exhibition and we brought up some fighters from the minors, Glen Goldup, Rick Chartraw, Sean Shanahan. Doug Risebrough started it, with Bobby Clarke. They didn't beat up on us that night. You check it out. We didn't win a game from them the two years before. After that I don't think we lost to them in the next four years.

That put the guys together. Never will there be a team like we were that year, the way we stuck together. It's tough to play against a team that tries to intimidate you, but we knew we could do it against them, and we did.

That last game in the finals against them, the way we felt before that game, I still feel it. I still get goose bumps all over my body when I think about it. I played a lot more games at the Spectrum, and I coached there, too. I always felt that chill before the game started. I never got over it until maybe this year. I think it's finally wearing off, but it's taken a long time.

GUY LAFLEUR

When I think of the team that won four straight Stanley Cups I think of the togetherness of the team. We were a family. We used to stick more together with the players than with our wives. Our wives used to criticize us. They'd say, "You're always with the players. You go on the road with the guys. Why don't you stay home with your wife instead of going out with the players again?"

It was that kind of chemistry between all the players. We had fun, and we really enjoyed playing hockey, even the guys who didn't play much at that time. We were all in the same boat, going for the Stanley Cup. You say Doug Risebrough said we were "professional." I know exactly why Dougie said that. Everybody took the responsibility for what they were supposed to do.

Scotty was the right coach for that bunch of guys. We needed a guy like him, or like Sam Pollock. When Sam used to come in the room between periods or before a game everybody had their head between their legs and nobody was talking. Scotty had been brought up by Sam so when he was talking too, everybody was listening. If you didn't listen, and if you didn't work, you'd be sent down to the minors.

I had a lot of highs. For me, the tying goal against Boston in 1979 I will always remember. Beating the Flyers for the Cup was something, too. They had a team with a bunch of goons. Stanley Cup parades on Ste. Catherines Street were unbelievable with everybody so happy for you.

There was also Team Canada and the 3–3 tie against the Russians on New Year's Eve. There was a lot of emotion in those games. A lot of fun, too.

Yvan Cournoyer

I'll always remember the time we won in Philadelphia, when we beat them four straight. I never saw a team so high in my life. That was the first time I heard the national anthem sung and no one was standing still. It never happened before in my life, guys skating around tapping each other with their sticks saying, "Let's go. Let's go."

When we won against Philly we had to create an example. You don't have to be big and rough, and fight all the time, to win the Stanley Cup. We had the size and we had the scorers. That's why we beat them. If you don't score, you don't win, no matter how good a fighter you are.

For all those years we were afraid to lose and that's what made us a winner. That's why I think we were the best. I remember the year Boston was supposed to beat us. Maybe they had us beaten before they started. That was another time we were afraid to lose, and that's why we beat them.

I played with four coaches and I won the Stanley Cup with four coaches. Toe Blake was the first and he was like a father to me. He sent me back home to live because I was living in an apartment my first year and he didn't think that was good for me. He was right. Toe was very honest and I really respected him.

Don't tell me Claude Ruel was a good coach. He was a good teacher but he was not a good coach. But we managed to win the Stanley Cup just the same. Then there was Al MacNeil. He was a different kind of a coach. I think he was okay.

In his first two years Scotty Bowman was a great coach and a great guy. But after his second year he thought maybe he was too good for the guys. He used to really give it to us because we were doing advertising. The first thing you know he was doing more advertising than us. You never knew what he was going to do. He would change his mind like he would change his underwear.

My most embarrassing moment in hockey was when Scotty was not using me, was not dressing me for a game. It happened in Boston. He thought he didn't need me. It hurt because I knew I was still good enough to play. I don't know why he was doing that. He said he had to dress his big players. I couldn't watch the game that night. I stayed in the dressing room pounding my fist into my hand and walking all around the room. When we got home I tried to call him but he wouldn't answer his phone.

My best time in my life was when I put on a Montreal Canadiens' sweater for the first time. The worst time was when I retired. Hockey will always stay with me. It took me five years to really accept retirement. Hockey was my game, and I still love it.

In the summer of 1973, after a season in which the Montreal Canadiens lost only ten games and won the Stanley Cup, Sam Pollock's trading machinations had made it possible for the team to draft number eight overall. When the Canadiens selected a forward from Peterborough, Bob Gainey, the reaction in Montreal was "Bob

Who?" A couple of weeks later Gainey was introduced to the Montreal media at a news conference. The kid was either too shy, or too
scared, to say anything so we ended up interviewing his agent.

History has proven Pollock and his scouts knew exactly what
they were doing. Bob Gainey played sixteen seasons for the Montreal Canadiens, retiring in 1989 with the reputation as one of the
greatest players in the history of the franchise. Soviet hockey officials once called him the most complete player in the world. He
easily won the Frank Selke Trophy as the NHL's best defensive forward the first four years it was up for competition.

No Canadiens' player has ever led by example any better than
Bob Gainey. Despite being a defensive specialist Gainey developed
one of the highest profiles on the team, on and off the ice. Along the
way, the shy rookie who didn't say anything at his coming-out party
turned into one of the best interviews in the business. If we wanted
an intelligent and concise version of what had happened in a game,
or why his team was either winning or in a slump, our easiest and
best way out was to ask Bob Gainey.

BOB GAINEY

We were a team that was based on good defence. In '73 when I
joined the Canadiens the team had lost Dryden and our defensive
play was very poor. We finished with quite a few points but we
really were not a strong club and we weren't good in the playoffs.
Dryden came back the following season and they added some
checking players. We checked a lot harder and they built the team
around defence. The offence came naturally.

When the team that won four straight Stanley Cups was put
together, it was a team that was motivated from within. There
were a lot of players who enjoyed being part of the team and they
wanted to grab their own little bit of success. But inside the club
we kept ourselves motivated by attaining team records.

The NHL wasn't that strong through that period and there were
a lot of teams who weren't able to beat us if we played well. We
knew that, so the challenge was more how we would play our own
game rather than how the competition would play against us.
When we would go against the better teams during that period,

like the Bruins, Islanders, Toronto, teams that were good and who could beat us, that's when we really came up to our best.

Scotty was a great coach. He motivated a large group of young players who came in at the same time. There was myself, Jarvis, Tremblay, Risebrough, Nyrop, Lambert, a whole group who eventually became the part that brought the team up. We had veterans like Savard, Cournoyer, and Lapointe who could show us the things we needed to know. But as far as picking up the tempo, Scotty knew how to control the young players and keep them moving in the right direction. He wouldn't allow us to stop. He kept on top of the ones who needed that sort of treatment the most.

There were a lot of people who didn't like Scotty. But when you coach you have to be yourself, and I guess that was Scotty. He had ideas he wanted to put into effect and they weren't always agreeable with the players. So he wasn't well liked by many of them, although I don't know of any coach who is well liked by all of the twenty players he has to work with.

I guess a lot of people feel 1979 was a highlight year for me because I won the Conn Smythe Trophy when we won our fourth straight Cup. Actually, that was a stressful season. Our team had shown some cracks. Sam Pollock had left and we had some problems in management. We had players who were becoming spoiled by all the success. Not a lot, but enough to make it more difficult for us to win. We also had stronger competition. But we managed to win in the end.

You can go back over a lot of moments in the playoffs. To win the championship you have to go through so many competitive and challenging games, and you have to play so many great games. It's hard to pick one or two.

I know one year we had the Islanders down and they beat us in the Forum, 4–3, in overtime and I had missed two breakaways. So we went back to the Island, won 2–1, and I scored both goals. So that was a good year. That was a good one for me.

STEVE SHUTT

The key guy on our team was Scotty. He realized that the only team that could beat our team was ourselves. We had such a good team that petty little grievances could develop that might bring the team down. So what Scotty did, he made himself the focal point. The one thing that we had in common was that everybody hated Scotty.

You could have a bad game on the ice and other guys on the team would be bitching at you. Then the next day you have lunch or a beer and start in on Scotty and the guys who were on your back the night before would agree with you.

You know, Scotty is basically a very shy person. But he figured he had to be the front man if he was going to keep the team together. I think he pulled off a pretty big act throughout the years.

When we were down by a couple of goals, or if the game was very close, he'd be pretty quiet on the bench. But if we were up two or three goals he'd start ranting and raving, and screaming at everybody. So we'd start playing games. When we'd be up a couple of goals the word would start going up and down the bench, "Keep it close." (laughs) And most nights, we were good enough to be able to do it.

Playing on a line with Lafleur? He was strange. I mean, any guy who would be in his hockey uniform, skates tied tight, sweater on, and a stick beside him at four o'clock in the afternoon for an eight o'clock game has to be a little strange. (laughs) On the ice, he played 100 per cent on instinct and emotion. He used to drive Scotty crazy in practice because he could never do a set play. In all the years we had a good power play we'd only practise it once or twice a year because Flower would screw it up.

Playing on a line with him, I had to get inside his head. I knew that whatever he did, it would be an instinct type of play. I had to try to think the way he was thinking.

I've always thought Ken Dryden was an underrated part of that team. One reason was because he had a lot of good defencemen in front of him. Kenny's greatest attribute was that, mentally, he could stay in the game. There were a lot of nights he would have only fifteen or so shots. But one of them would be a breakaway. Mentally, he was so involved in the game, it didn't matter if he had only one shot in the past ten minutes, he was ready. After Kenny left there were a lot of goaltenders who played for us who couldn't do that. Bunny Larocque is a good example. None of them could cope with things the way Kenny did.

The most memorable Cup for me was in 1976 when we beat the Flyers. I think a lot of teams in the league were cheering for us because if we lost, it would have meant three straight for them and a lot of teams would then have started loading up with goons.

Actually, we started to get the upper hand on them when we had a big brawl during an exhibition game before that season. Doug Risebrough started it when he and Bobby Clarke had a bit of a tussle. We were going to play them again back in Montreal and Clarke said, "Wait 'til I get you back in Montreal." Dougie said, "Why wait 'til then?" and he just smacked him. He cut him for about ten stitches over the eye. Then it started. We had a lot of tough guys in our lineup for that game, guys from the farm team, too, like Glen Goldup and Sean Shanahan. And we had Rick Chartraw and Bouchard. Our tough guys took on all of their tough guys and they just pummelled them. I would say that was about the last fight we had in games with the Flyers for about four years.

When it came to the playoffs, I think Scotty won that series. As soon as they put Schultz, Saleski, and Kelly on the ice, Scotty wouldn't counter with our tough guys. Instead, he'd put our line on. One of two things would happen. If they played straight up, we'd score a goal. If they started the goon stuff, who do you think the referees are going to throw off the ice? Fred Shero knew that, so he'd take them off. That was a very big point in that series. Going into the Spectrum and knocking off the Stanley Cup champs, yeah, that was probably one of my biggest thrills.

The Canadiens always treated me well, right to the end. When I had to face the realization that my talents weren't what they used to be, they called me into the office and asked me what I wanted to do. Serge was the general manager by then. I had some choices, to stay and be a part-time player, or help coach their farm team in Sherbrooke, or go somewhere else if they could trade me. I had already talked to L.A. and I thought I'd like to get some American money.

Serge told me I could go there and play as long as I could and, because I had kept things quiet and strictly between me and the team, they'd pick up the balance of my contract when I was through playing. It had three more years to go, and that's what they did. What Lafleur wrote in his book about how I left the Canadiens wasn't exactly right. They treated me very good.

GUY LAPOINTE

We had a team that could play the game both ways, defensively or offensively. Larry, Serge, myself, we could make some rushes. We could play that kind of a game if we wanted.

I remember that year when we set the record, sixty wins, some games we would be behind by one or two goals with four or five minutes to go. Scotty would say to me, Serge, and Larry, "Okay, now you can go." He would keep saying to us, "Go, go, go," and we would start to rush all the time. We didn't have to worry in behind with Kenny in the net. Most times we would end up scoring a few goals and winning the games. We won a lot of games that year in the third period.

They say one big reason we were winners like that was because the defencemen could score or set up so many goals. So like I say, with that team we could play it both ways.

DOUG RISEBROUGH

Why was that team so good for so long? I think about that a lot, especially now that I'm coaching.

There was a real element of pride. We all realized it was something that went with playing for the Montreal Canadiens. And when we would be winning all the time, Scotty never let us think we were as good as we really were.

I remember the pep talk he gave us in Washington. It was the last game of the season and we were going for our sixtieth win. He told us, "You can do something tonight no other team will likely ever do." We went out and did it.

I played most of the time with Mario Tremblay and Yvon Lambert. We stayed together. We were the tempo setters. We could set the pace.

It was a very, very professional team. I always felt everyone on the team appreciated what I did, even the big-name players. And I wasn't a big-name player.

MARIO TREMBLAY

Players always remember how they start in the NHL. For me, it was when Montreal decide to call up two of us from Nova Scotia, Doug Risebrough and myself. I remember that morning, Dougie was doing pushups and situps. It's a good feeling to think about that day, how I started my career in Boston and play my first game against Bobby Orr, Ken Hodge, and all those big names. It was a big thrill.

Scotty Bowman was ready to do anything, to anyone, to make the team win. As far as myself with him, I had quite a problem with him right up to my third year. I thought after a while that maybe you have to have somebody on your back, but sometimes get off.

I asked him once, "How come you don't play me?" And he said, "I don't like your face." From that time I knew why I had problems with him.

After the third year I start to play regular with Dougie and Yvon Lambert. We were playing very, very well. Then it was the time that Scotty start giving a hard time to Yvan Cournoyer. But I have to give him respect because he was a winner.

You ask me about great players I saw and one comes to mind right away. Guy Lafleur. I watched Flower for ten years and to me he was unbelievable. He could do everything on the ice. He had a great shot and he was a great skater. I know that he put a lot of money into our pockets. So did Ken Dryden, Pete Mahovlich, and other good players.

If I look across the ice I have to say Bobby Orr, although when I played against him he wasn't at his best because of his knees. A guy like Bryan Trottier for four or five years was a tremendous hockey player. I think also of Michael Bossy. Bobby Clarke, in his prime, could really play the game. For a guy like me, it was a real challenge to play hockey against them.

When we won the Stanley Cup in Philly it was my first and I

cried like a baby. That was when they had Kate Smith singing "God Bless America." After the season I went with some friends to a fishing camp for a week. Every night we'd have a few beers and I would start singing, "God Bless America," and everybody would laugh at me. I sang that song every night for a week.

SERGE SAVARD

We had a good club with a lot of balance. When you look back at the lineup, we had a lot of guys who could score more than forty goals.

As far as a leader for us, on the ice, there's no doubt that Guy Lafleur was our best player, game in and game out. He was a great leader for our club, although maybe not off the ice. But he was a leader in his own way. He minded his own business, and for six or seven years he was the number-one player in the league.

When we won our last Cup, in '79, the final was really the semifinal, when we played Boston. After that we played Rangers and it would have taken a plane crash for us not to beat them. That's when I scored a goal in overtime on John Davidson. Before that, on the same shift, Larry had scored but the puck went right through the net and we kept on playing. Before the whistle went again, I scored.

I should not have scored on that play, a backhand shot from fairly far out. A few years ago they had the All-Star game in Hartford and they were showing Stanley Cup highlights on a TV screen in the lobby at the hotel. I was standing beside J.D. and suddenly they show my goal. He started to yell and complain about it and we had a good laugh.

PIERRE BOUCHARD

Scotty was on my case a lot. The guys used to say he was always picking on me but it didn't bother me. At the end of my career in Montreal I wasn't even listening to him.

One time I had an injured arm. They gave me a shot and I had a bad reaction. My arm was swollen and I couldn't use it at all. We were playing a Saturday night game when I was hurt and there was a big snowstorm. I started to drive to the Forum but got stalled by the storm in Varennes, a little town not far from my home. I called the Forum and told them I wouldn't be able to get there and went back home. I wasn't playing anyway. The guys told me that Scotty came into the room and made a big deal out of it, saying I was taking the night off and was having a nice party, with wine and spaghetti, in Varennes.

One day in practice Steve Shutt was passing the puck across the ice to Flower and the puck hit Scotty right on the ankle. He was really hurt but tried not to show it. He said to Shutt, "That didn't hurt. I thought you had a good shot." Shutty said, "That was just a pass. Wait 'til I hit you with a real shot."

But you have to give Scotty credit for knowing what was going on. One time a few of the boys spent a long night in my restaurant – lots to eat and especially lots to drink. The next morning at practice we had to gather in a circle around Scotty, as usual, for our instructions. He could smell the breath of the guys who had been drinking at my place the night before and he started to yell at them. He picked them out, every one of them.

KEN DRYDEN

I was the goaltender for the Montreal Canadiens, playing in the Montreal Forum, which creates a problem because often there is very little role for you. A goalie plays a position where he feels he is a critical part of a win. Playing with that Canadiens team I didn't feel that all the time. In almost every game, especially at the Forum, our team controlled the game. Most of the action was at the other end. Most of the shots were at the other end. It then became the goalie's role not necessarily to win the game, but to not lose the game.

That was a burden I didn't feel all that much the first couple of years, but one I felt as the team got better. I was never completely comfortable with it. It's the same burden that Plante felt, that Worsley felt, that Durnan felt, and one which I'm sure any subsequent goalie will also feel.

Defencemen? In the period of about, say, '72, '73, '74, Guy Lapointe, except for Orr, was the best. He was a very important player on the Canadiens then and continued to be through the four-straight Stanley Cup era. He had such remarkable spirit. He was a fine, fine offensive player with a good shot. He was important on the power play and the kind of player who could change the tempo of a game. Guy had the sense of outrage when things were going wrong. You could see it building in him, and in the dressing room between periods. On the ice he would take hold of a game and change it around. Except for Orr, I don't think there was anyone else who could do it at that time.

Scotty had a wonderful ability to handle the team during a game. It was hard for me to really know any of that because I was on the ice most of the time. The real tip-off to me, beyond the fact that the right people seemed to be on the ice for each situation, was at the end of important games. Players who really didn't want to say a lot of nice things about Scotty at other times, when we'd be in a playoff series against the Bruins and Don Cherry, or the Flyers and Fred Shero, or the Leafs and Roger Neilson, they'd be shaking their heads in the dressing room saying how you just couldn't believe how he had control of the game. They'd be talking about how he would have Shero doing exactly what he wanted him to do, and Neilson, and Cherry. And those were players who were often unsympathetic to Scotty. They just couldn't believe how he could do that during a game.

When you are a hockey player and you look ahead to a season, a lot depends on the team you're on. You gear yourself emotionally to what can be reasonably expected of you. You want to win the Stanley Cup, but somewhere along the line you get the message that the chances are very slight.

When you were playing on the Montreal Canadiens during the 1970s, we knew we had as good a chance to win the Stanley Cup as anyone else. We knew it from the first day of training camp. We knew that in order to feel good about a season, when it was over, we had to win the Stanley Cup. If we lost out in the finals, that wasn't good enough. We couldn't rationalize away being a finalist.

We had to win.

LARRY ROBINSON

The Stanley Cup I remember the best was when we beat Philadelphia in '76. I have never, ever, seen a team so involved emotionally as we were for that one – you know, the Broad Street Bullies and all that. We had a feeling amongst ourselves that the whole league wanted us to win, just because of what they stood for. They tried to intimidate the whole league.

There was a lot going on. They brought in Kate Smith to sing "God Bless America." They tried to introduce their team with spotlights, and we were skating all over the ice not worrying about the introductions and ignoring the whole thing.

Before the last game in Philly every guy was dressed and walking around the room twenty-five minutes before we were supposed to go out for the warmup. The only guy who was sitting down was Kenny.

Talking about Kenny, he was taken for granted a lot during the last few years. But you look back at some of the saves he made in key games, he was incredible. He would keep us in games, early, when we weren't even coming close. We won so many games in the third period it was ridiculous.

Scotty was the right coach for that team, or maybe I should say for that era. I don't know if the coaching techniques from then would totally work now. Mike Keenan tries it. His idol was Scotty Bowman. All his mannerisms behind the bench, eating ice, the arrogance, it's just like Scotty used to do. I'm not sure it works anymore.

Scotty knew when to let up on the guys, when to play certain players, and how to prepare them. Players like Chartraw and Bouchard, our tough guys, when he didn't need them you always heard about the run-ins he'd have with them. They were often his whipping boys.

Scotty always kept you off balance. I remember many a time we'd come off a game when we'd won by four or five goals and maybe they'd only had twelve or fifteen shots on goal. I'd think we'd played a terrific game. The next day he'd blast the living heck out of us. Then we'd play a horrible game, and he'd have a big smile on his face and maybe we'd practise for about a half-hour and that would be it. You could never figure him out. He kept you off guard all the time.

If I had to pick one player I played against in those days who I'd want on my team I'd say Gilbert Perreault. I know he was never on a winner, but he was exciting. Our team? Of course, Guy Lafleur.

I played with Flower when he was at his peak in Montreal. Then I come to L.A. and play with Gretzky. Wayne is the all-time great player. But even when Flower was playing with Quebec at the end, he could still pull people out of their seats. He just had that aura about him that he brought the whole game to life when he had the puck.

When I played with Guy, all you had to do was pass the puck anywhere near him and he'd pick it up, just so long as he could touch it. Put it on the left side, right side, off his skates, he could handle it every way you could think of.

I remember the playoff series against Boston when he shot the puck at Milbury. Before the next game, which was in Boston, the papers there were full of headlines about how the Bruins were going to get him and kill him. We won the game 3–1, and Flower scored two goals.

Lafleur had something that Gretzky might have lacked a bit through the years. He could get away from checkers, like that series against Boston, when they put Don Marcotte on him. He was one of the best defensive forwards in the game. Sometimes they can neutralize Wayne, like Tikkanen has done.

You could not neutralize Lafleur. Somehow he had the strength to get away from tough checking. That's the one ability I think he had over Wayne, plus he was a faster skater. Wayne is more of a magician, the way he handles the puck and looks at the ice. If you are building a team, you want Wayne. But Guy could bring you out of your seat. When it came to that, he's the best I've ever seen.

Brian Engblom was a defenceman who played for the Canadiens from 1977 to 1982. He was one of only a few players who joined what was basically the set lineup of the Stanley Cup championship team of the late seventies.

Don Cherry was an Engblom fan. "They talked about the big three in Montreal in those days but some nights Engblom was as good as any of them," Grapes told me. "There were games against us when it seemed he blocked half the shots we took."

Engblom was a second All-Star team selection in 1982. Before the next season he was traded to the Washington Capitals. A native of Winnipeg, he was inducted into the Manitoba Sports Hall of Fame in 1990.

BRIAN ENGBLOM

My first game was a playoff game in St. Louis. No exhibition games, no nothing. That was my first. I was scared that night, and I played scared the whole time I was in Montreal. If you made a mistake, especially early on as a rookie, you knew you weren't going to see the ice much for the rest of that game and maybe a few after as well.

They taught you through a series of "don'ts." Don't do this, don't do that. Get it up to Lafleur, Shutt, Lemaire, the boys up front. Let them do what they're supposed to do. It was a little bit restrictive but you really couldn't argue with the logic.

I was in and out of the lineup my first full year. I played about half the games, if that many, and it was very frustrating. A lot of guys I played junior with were already regulars with other teams and were making a lot of money. But there were so many great players in Montreal, what could I do? Do you take a chance and ask to be traded? I saw a lot of guys do that along the way and it didn't work out for some of them. So I decided to stay quiet, learn as much as I could, and see what happened.

With the Canadiens, they fit their players into a role, more so than any other team, and that's what made them so great. They had certain pieces of the puzzle and you either fit into one of those pieces, or they dealt you off. If you refused to fit, and they wanted you, they trimmed off the edges a bit to make you fit. I knew what my strength was, blocking shots.

For a new player, there was acceptance, and there was not. Everybody went through the same thing. I remember talking to Steve Shutt in a bar one night during my second year. I said to him, "You were a real asshole to me in my first year." He started to laugh and said, "Good." I said, "What do you mean, good?"

He said, "Well, it was like that for me, so why the hell shouldn't it have been like that for you?"

Shutt was one of the toughest on rookies. He just didn't pay much attention. But at least he came right out and said it when I asked him. Then you had a straightforward guy like Larry. He accepted you as soon as you walked in the door. It took longer with other guys, like Serge. You never really knew Serge, at least I never did. But I could accept that. He just wasn't the kind of guy you got to know real well.

Dryden never seemed to spend a lot of time with anybody in particular, and I don't mean that in a detrimental way. Every once in a while he'd ask you about this or that when he was in one of his inquisitive moods. But I can tell you, he wasn't the same behind the mask as he was in civvies.

Kenny would yell and scream at you a lot of times, especially in pressure-filled games when he was under the gun. One time he was yelling about something and I yelled back at him. He was always yelling, "Do this, do that," so I said, "Shut up and leave me alone." You have to do things with your own timing after a while. At first I felt I had to do just what he told me. But finally I answered back. It wasn't a major thing. He still went on, but I think it was kind of a compromise.

Everybody had a run-in with Scotty. We used to hear how he would be on Lafleur when he first came up, telling him that Dionne was better. So the guys used to rationalize by saying that if he could do it to Flower, he could do it to anybody.

Scotty coached the team along the lines of the movie *The Dirty Dozen*, like Lee Marvin on a suicide mission. Marvin took all those guys out of jail and promised them they wouldn't have to go back if they survived. And what he did was treat them all so bad, they all hated him. His men had a common bond. He became the enemy. I always wondered if Scotty did it on purpose or if it just happened that way.

I think in the end he stepped over the line too many times with too many people. It went farther than just trying to get the best out of certain players. That's what a lot of the players objected to. His last year wasn't a very happy one for him. When I went to other teams, Washington and L.A., and told them Scotty stories, the players had no idea what I was talking about. They'd never been through anything like that. But they'd never won anything either.

I think now I can understand what he was doing, and you sure can't argue with the results. But when I think of playing for Scotty Bowman, I still see Lee Marvin in *The Dirty Dozen*.

Following the game that clinched the Stanley Cup in Philadelphia in 1976, the one that most of the four-in-a-row gang talk about as being the best one, I was in the dressing room doing interviews for CFCF Radio. I still have the tape, and here are two items that are on it from that night.

SCOTTY BOWMAN

On the matchups it's pretty hard to keep one player away from another unless you don't play him. We didn't particularly want to play Lafleur against Schultz because, who knows, they may get into something and we lose our top scorer to the penalty box. But you have to do it sometimes.

We had to get our power play going. Getting an early goal on the four-minute penalty to Schultz was a big factor. That's how you're going to stop the rough stuff. You're not going to stop it by crying to the referee. If they get a penalty, you gotta score.

SAM POLLOCK

I think that Scotty did an excellent job, you have to say all year, but in the playoffs particularly here in Philadelphia. I thought Thursday night here, the third game, was an absolute masterpiece. I thought he controlled the game completely.

Tonight, it was much the same thing. It was tremendously more difficult because the Flyers were going with four lines, and they had the last line change. I think Scotty did a remarkable job of having the right players on the ice at the right time.

Early in Scotty Bowman's tenure in Montreal he was on the phone with Roger Neilson, who was then coaching the OHL junior team in

Peterborough. Roger told Scotty that he had "the best face-off man in hockey" on his team. Scotty thought Roger meant in junior hockey. "No," insisted Neilson, "in all of hockey." Roger was talking about Doug Jarvis.

A couple of years later, Jarvis was Scotty's best face-off man in Montreal. Starting with his rookie season, 1975–76, Doug Jarvis played on four Stanley Cup winners in four years. He quickly became the Canadiens' number-one defensive centreman and, along with Bob Gainey, a member of its top penalty-killing unit. During that time Jarvis never missed a game. He later played for Washington and Hartford and eventually became hockey's all-time ironman, playing 962 consecutive games. A devout Christian, Jarvis nevertheless quietly fitted in with a Montreal team that had its share of fun-loving, party-going characters.

DOUG JARVIS

I felt very good about things right from the beginning. There was quite a variety of personalities on that team and I always felt that made for a very good atmosphere and helped make us a good team. I was the only rookie to make it at the start of my first year and they accepted me pretty well. The older players made me feel quite at home. There was a line put together with Bob Gainey, Jimmy Roberts, and myself. Jimmy shared a lot of his insight into the game with me, and as a line we developed a pretty good bond.

The Canadiens got me in a trade with Toronto, who had originally drafted me. I can remember that summer, Sam Pollock called me in because there was talk that I was going to go to Houston. They had my WHA rights. But I felt I couldn't turn down the chance to try out with the Montreal Canadiens. It would be something I'd likely regret the rest of my life. Sam told me it looked as though there would be a couple of spots open, so I went to camp determined to put my best game on the ice and see what happened from there.

Through the first four years, when we won the four Cups, our defensive system never really changed. Scotty used to emphasize that. Right from the start he said the main thing the team was concerned with was keeping the puck out of our net. The other end will take care of itself.

I remember a team meeting about halfway through my first year. Scotty asked me how many goals I had and I sheepishly answered, "Three." It wasn't the kind of a total that would normally keep anyone playing for the Montreal Canadiens. He said, "That isn't what concerns me the most. What I'm concerned about is that you're doing your job defensively." That was a big boost for me, confidence-wise.

Looking back, two moments come to mind as the best. The first was my first game in the NHL. Standing there for the anthem before the game, I guess I had feelings about all the years when I was growing up and going through minor hockey in Peterborough. At that moment I had at least got myself to my first game in the NHL. Then the year culminated with the Stanley Cup, and that's something very special at the end of a first season.

After we had won four straight and then had lost the next year, in 1980, it felt very strange. It seemed to me that it was natural to play this game until the end of May, and at the end you won, and then you went home for the summer. It had never been any other way for me. It was still April, and we weren't playing anymore. It just didn't feel right.

I went into the Canadiens' dressing room after their 1980 playoff elimination by the Minnesota North Stars. Larry Robinson, Steve Shutt, Guy Lapointe, Bob Gainey, and the others were sombre and grim-faced as they struggled through interviews with the media. As the now former champions tried to explain why their Stanley Cup dynasty had come to an end we, sympathetically, avoided interviewing one member of the team who was sitting in his place in the dressing room, crying. It was Doug Jarvis.

23

Those Who Saw Them

In 1977 the Canadiens won the Stanley Cup when they defeated the Boston Bruins in four straight games. Jacques Lemaire scored the Cup-winning goal, in overtime, at the Boston Garden. The following year the teams met again in the final and Montreal again clinched the Cup in Boston. That series lasted six games, so the Bruins were gaining ground.

In 1979 there was a Montreal-Boston semifinal. As Serge Savard said, the final series that year was really the semifinal. The Bruins seemed set finally to overtake and pass the Canadiens when they were leading game seven with a couple of minutes to play in the third period. But Guy Lafleur tied the game when he scored his most famous goal, on a power play, after the Bruins had been penalized for having too many men on the ice. Later, in overtime, Yvon Lambert's goal won the series for Montreal.

It had been three straight years of total playoff frustration for the Bruins and their coach, a chap named Don Cherry. Some recollections from "the Coach's Corner," therefore, help us to know how others saw this Montreal dynasty.

DON CHERRY

There was a lot happening in those three years we played them in the playoffs. For example, Mike Milbury hated Guy Lafleur, and

Lafleur hated Milbury. I don't know why, but that's the way it was. Milbury would climb all over Lafleur, really rough him up, and nobody would ever come to his rescue. You know, Bossy had Gillies looking after him. Gretzky always had Semenko. But nobody ever seemed to want to help out Lafleur.

Anyway, near the end of one playoff game Lafleur shot the puck at Milbury's face. Our bench was going crazy. We were going back to Boston and Milbury and Cashman and all the guys were saying how they were going to kill Lafleur when we got back to Boston. One reporter asked Lafleur what he thought of it. Lafleur's answer was, "I know Don Cherry as a coach. He won't let it happen." I never forgot that. As it turned out they didn't do anything to him in the game. Maybe they should have. They beat us and Lafleur scored two goals.

At one time the Montreal Canadiens had a habit of everybody jumping on the ice to congratulate the guy who scored after they scored a goal. My brother saw it on TV when they were playing Toronto in the playoffs one year before they played us. He thought it was a ploy of Scotty Bowman to intimidate the other club.

So now we have to play them and my brother has an idea for me. He figured that if they scored the first goal, I should get all my guys to jump on the ice and go down to our goalie and pat him on the back. Sure enough, they score the first goal in the first game, and Scotty has them all jump on the ice. So now I send everybody out, even the back-up goalie. There were forty guys on the ice. Cheevers was our goalie. He didn't know about it and he's wondering what the hell was going on. I remember the referee was Dave Newell. You should have seen the look on his face with forty guys on the ice milling around. He said to me, "You can't do that." I said, "Show me in the rule book where it says I can't. If they can go on, we can go on." The league came to us after that and made us stop it.

Scotty and I used to get into it pretty good. When we were in the finals one year, the referees used to go for a skate in the morning. Scotty would stand beside the boards and yell at them. He'd say, "You won't call anything against Boston. You don't have the guts to call anything against Boston." He'd keep it up for their whole morning skate.

That was around the time he had a videotape made of all our penalties, or what he said should have been our penalties, and showed it to the reporters. I have to admit he was always one up on me in things like that. I would say things about what Scotty was doing, going after the referees and all that, and it got to a point where the media were going nuts.

So John Zeigler called us in. I'll bet it's the only time two coaches got a lecture from the president of the NHL right before a game in the Stanley Cup finals. He said, "This has got to stop. For the good of hockey you guys have to stop."

As he's talking I'm lookin' at Scotty, and he's wearing a blue suit with brown wallabees on his feet. I'm all dressed up perfectly, as always, so I [later] said, "Surely any son of a bitch who wears brown shoes with a blue suit isn't going to beat me out of the Stanley Cup."

That made the papers, but it was the only thing I got out of that night. They beat us, again.

In conducting interviews for this book I drew a blank in one area. I couldn't find anyone who dislikes the Montreal Canadiens organization. I didn't hear it from opposing players and I couldn't find even one disgruntled ex-employee. (There are a few out there, I'm sure, but obviously I don't have their phone numbers.)

All great teams are accused of being favoured by the referees. Over the years players and coaches have claimed the referees especially favour the home team in Montreal because the NHL head office is there. This was especially true during the presidency of Clarence Campbell, who was constantly writing notes as he watched games at the Forum. The visitors were sure the referees thought Campbell was monitoring their work, hence a perceived edge to the home team.

But today things like refereeing are mentioned only in passing. To a much greater degree the word "respect" kept cropping up in the conversations. In fact, a few of their opponents still wonder if they, and their teammates, suffered from having a bit too much respect for the Montreal team.

GERRY CHEEVERS

They were a great team. I think our problem was that we respected them rather than hated them. As we went along we developed hate for a lot of teams, but for some reason we respected the Montreal Canadiens. I think we thought it was all right if they beat us, which obviously is wrong.

I don't think we had the killer instinct. Maybe they were better although I always thought there were a couple of series when we were as good as they were, maybe even better, I don't know.

I won a lot and hopefully was a good team player. But somewhere along the way you still have to go goaltender versus goaltender. My Achilles' heel in all my hockey career is that I never beat Ken Dryden. That remains with me to this day. I had success against Parent, Esposito, Giacomin, the so-called big goalies of that time. They're all in the Hall of Fame. I had decent success, but I never beat Dryden and that bothers me more than anything. I think of him and how, if everything broke down, which didn't happen too often with them, he was always there. You have to have a guy like that if you're going to win.

The Forum was what I would call a fast rink. Everything was faster. I used to hate going there and watching the Canadiens' morning skate the day of the game. Those guys were drilling the puck off the glass on every shot. Steve Shutt now tells me they always did it on purpose when they'd see the visiting goalie watching them. We used to think we got screwed by the refs in Montreal. I don't know how much the rules were geared for that rink at that time, but that's not an excuse.

From the first time I saw Guy Lafleur he was special. I always gauged guys on their ability to give and take a pass. I know he struggled in his first few years and I'm sure the pressure in Montreal was unbelievable. But whenever we played them, he never missed on a passing play. They tell me that was the first sign of greatness in Orr. Same thing, the passing. Good players never miss passes.

With Lafleur, I think of him as class incorporated, that's all. I had a chance to play with him in 1976 on Team Canada. He was very quiet, a real treat. He was something else, and I really respected him.

When the Canadiens defeated the Philadelphia Flyers to win the Stanley Cup in 1976 Bill Barber was the Flyers' best left-winger. Barber played twelve years in the NHL, all with the Flyers. He is Philadelphia's all-time leading goal scorer with 420 and was elected to the Hockey Hall of Fame in 1990.

BILL BARBER

That was the series everybody was looking forward to. We had won the previous two years, but we had never played Montreal in the playoffs. People talked about that, so they were waiting for that series.

If you look at the personnel we had in 1976 you'll see we had as good a team, if not a better one, when you compare it to the teams we had when we won our two Stanley Cups. But the one ingredient missing was goaltending. Bernie Parent was hurt and couldn't play. I'm not faulting Wayne Stephenson, but he wasn't Bernie Parent. I'm not saying that we would have won. What I'm saying is that it wouldn't have been as short a series as it was.

If you looked at the series closely, there was at least one bad goal scored against us in every game. Every game. You can't win that way. What did we lose by? They beat us by one goal in the first three games and by two in the last one.

Montreal always had tough teams. They were tough physically and they were willing to take the bangs to win games. They never had the write-ups we had. We were tattooed as the Broad Street Bullies, and it went on from there. Even before they started winning those Cups, I remember playing against Henri Richard. You could hit him all night, but he'd be back out for the next shift every time. That told me something about the Montreal Canadiens early in my career. As far as I could see, they never changed.

When he was leading the Philadelphia Flyers to two straight Stanley Cups in the mid-1970s Bobby Clarke represented the true meaning of the word "competitor." It's impossible to make a hockey player more intense than Clarke was when he was battling his way toward the Hockey Hall of Fame.

When I interviewed him Clarke had become the general manager of the Minnesota North Stars. I asked him why the Canadiens were able to defeat the Flyers in the 1976 finals. As he began answering, Bobby's jaw tightened, his eyes squinted, and again I was interviewing Bobby Clarke, captain of the Philadelphia Flyers. For a few moments it seemed he was back at the Spectrum wearing his familiar jersey number 16, desperately trying to stop the Montreal Canadiens from taking the Cup away from his team. When our conversation was over I was glad to know that Bobby Clarke will always be Bobby Clarke, and that deep down he still is not completely convinced the best team won that year.

BOBBY CLARKE

They were better than we were. They had better talent all the way through their lineup, and they were young. They had great speed.

But what everybody forgets is that Montreal also had the toughest team in the league, too. While they didn't do any of the goony stuff that the Flyers had a reputation of doing, and did do, Montreal always had as many, or more, tough guys than any team in the league.

I mean, they had Lupien, Chartraw, Bouchard, those kind of guys. I've talked to Serge Savard about it. Serge always says, "Oh yeah, but you had Schultz and guys like that."

But what's the difference? Serge refuses to admit that Montreal would have that type of player for that purpose. But they did have. I think when they had so many it probably meant there would be less of it, less of the rough stuff, because both teams had it. But they had a bunch of tough guys.

And Bowman. Bowman wouldn't use them until the right time, until they played teams like us. That's what they were there for. Montreal never had the reputation for that and that was the difference.

But they were just a great, great hockey team and really just getting started as a great team in that era. That was when Gainey, Risebrough, Jarvis, guys like that were just getting started.

We played them that year without Bernie Parent and Rick MacLeish. In hindsight, maybe if we had had them we might have beaten them. We would have been a better hockey club. We had Wayne Stephenson in goal. He was competent, but not in Bernie Parent's class. But I don't know. They were just better, that's all.

Bryan Trottier's name was frequently mentioned by the Canadiens of the seventies when they talked about good players on opposing teams. Trottier was then the top centreman on a New York Islander team that was gradually learning what it took to win the Stanley Cup, which they eventually did four straight times starting in 1980.

BRYAN TROTTIER

When I think of the Canadiens back then, two names stand out, Dryden and Robinson.

When you look at the amount of net Dryden covered, it was like you saw no net. All you saw were his goalie pads, his big glove, and that mask of his that was almost scary in itself. You'd ask yourself, "Where's the mesh?" He played the angles so well. I used to think the only way I could score was to put it through him, and I very seldom did. His presence was very intimidating.

Larry Robinson was so big, so mobile, and especially so strong. I can remember when I was first up, I was young and feeling my oats, figuring nobody could get the best of me in the corner. I was digging for the puck in the corner against Robinson and all of a sudden I could feel myself lifting off the ice. There's this big, gentle man behind me, lifting me off the ice. My feet are dangling up in the air. I've got no leverage and I'm feeling like a puppet.

So I just relaxed, and waited for him to let me down so I could skate away again. His attitude was like, "Well, there you go, young fellow. Away you go now, go catch up to the play." He was overly polite about it, and that drove me crazy. I mean, here was a guy you couldn't get mad at. He was just massive, and strong. You couldn't get around him.

John Davidson was a goaltender in the NHL during the Canadiens' reign in the late 1970s. J.D. broke in with the St. Louis Blues in 1973.

After two seasons in St. Louis he played for the New York Rangers until injuries ended his career in 1983.

In 1979 Davidson starred in the playoffs when the Rangers upset the New York Islanders, who had finished first overall. He was in the nets for the Rangers when the Canadiens defeated them in the finals to win their fourth straight Stanley Cup.

JOHN DAVIDSON

In my first game at the Forum we lost 3-2. I remember stopping Henri Richard on a breakaway. It was the thrill of my life.

There was something special about coming into the Forum, something special about Montreal's hockey team. The way they looked in their uniforms made them look larger than life. We'd come to the Forum to practise the day of a game and Claude Ruel would be on the ice with about fifty pucks around him, yelling at the players, drilling passes at them like slapshots. Jacques Lemaire would be shooting rockets from the red line. It was intimidating. You'd see their speed and how their players were doing everything just a little bit better than anyone else in the league - not necessarily as individuals, but as a team. You were already a goal or two down before the game even started.

One play I'll never forget was in the finals in '79. We were playing at the Garden and the puck was in the corner to my left. Bob Gainey came into the corner and knocked Dave Maloney off his skates, knocked him flat. Gainey got the puck, skated around to the front of the net, and scored. That was such a dominant play you could see the Rangers sag. That was the series as far as I was concerned. Gainey won the Conn Smythe Trophy that year.

Jacques Lemaire may have been the only guy I ever played against whose shot could scare you. It was such a heavy shot and he could blow it by me from anywhere. In the final game in '79 he scored from outside the blue line. My knee popped on the way down and the puck blew right past me.

Scotty's team had a lot of flair and a lot of tenacious players like Risebrough and Tremblay. The Big Three on defence could all shoot the puck a little better than any defencemen in the league. Robinson, Lapointe, Savard, you'd see them in practice or warming up before a game and their sticks seemed longer, their arms seemed longer. There was just something about them. No other team had three defencemen like that. Serge scored on me in overtime in '79. It should never have gone in, a backhand. Every time he sees me he asks me, "Remember that goal?"

In one of our playoff games against them Lafleur had thirteen shots. Eight or nine of them were going for the top corner, glove side. It got to the point I'd see him coming and say, "Here we go again." I think we played them in fear - fear of being totally embarrassed.

Ken Dryden was the best in the business at being in games when he might get only eighteen or twenty shots and seven or eight would be classic scoring opportunities, and he'd always be there. He could keep his mind focused even though he wasn't getting a lot of work.

Ken played the game under such control. It was like someone pushed a button and an arm came out. Then someone pushed another button and a leg came out. Everything he did was done for a purpose. They played the game at such a speed that Dryden had to rely on instinct to keep himself under control and never get caught. Everything he did was concise and for a reason. He was magnificent.

Harry Neale coached the Vancouver Canucks during the late 1970s. Harry is now a respected and popular analyst and colour commentator on Hockey Night in Canada. *His brief remarks, and those following, from sports writer Red Fisher, summarize the awesome control goalie Ken Dryden had in a game and on a game. And in this era, it should be noted, hockey had become a faster game than in earlier times.*

HARRY NEALE

Dryden is the only goalie I have ever known who, when he was at the top of his game, gave you the feeling you would not score a legitimate goal on him. If you were going to score it would have to be on a tip-in, or a deflection, or during a goal-mouth scramble. I felt that way coaching against him, and I know the players on the ice felt that way, too.

RED FISHER

Dryden was a vastly underrated goaltender. Plante was under-rated at times, too, but I don't think nearly as much as Dryden was. Plante had a great team in front of him. They both did. But Dryden was a great goaltender and deserves to be in the Hockey Hall of Fame.

Ken Dryden was different from any hockey player I have ever covered, ever met, and perhaps ever talked to. There aren't too many graduate lawyers playing the game. He has written best-selling books. When I think of all of the players I've met through all of the years I've been around, yes, he was different. Very.

Bernie Federko was a solid centreman for the St. Louis Blues for fourteen seasons. He is the all-time St. Louis team leader in games, goals, and assists. His sweater number 14 was retired by the Blues in 1991.

Federko joined the St. Louis team late in the 1976–77 season, just in time for his first appearance in the Stanley Cup playoffs against a Montreal team that had won a record sixty games during the regular season.

BERNIE FEDERKO

We finished first in our division and had a bye into the second round. Emile Francis was our coach and he worked us hard for three days. Then on the fourth day he had us meet in the TV room to go over the tape of one of our games against the Canadiens. When the tape started Gus Kyle, one of the announcers, came on and said, "If the Blues play well tonight against Montreal they might lose by only five or six goals." Francis jumped up and said, "We're not watching this thing!" and that was the end of that.

We had a game plan for the series. The centres would stay in the centre-ice area at all times unless we had a good scoring chance. The wingers were to be the forecheckers, and all that. Emile wanted us to play for 1-0 games. My line started the first game and in the first shift Bob Gasoff slashed somebody, a real two-hander. He got a penalty and thirty seconds later the Canadiens scored. Our 1-0 game plan went right out the window.

We never thought we'd win. In the last game of the regular season against them we had beaten them 7-2, in St. Louis. Now we're in Montreal to start the playoffs and the atmosphere in our dressing room was unreal. Brian Sutter and I had never played in the Forum so we were scared. But the older guys were laughing, wondering if we would even get a shot on goal, stuff like that. They knew the Canadiens would be pissed off because of the 7-2 game, and they were.

They beat us four straight and we only scored four goals in the four games. It was a joke.

When the New York Islanders were developing into the team that would succeed the Canadiens as hockey's best and win the Stanley Cup four straight times starting in 1980, Chico Resch was one of their goaltenders. NHL media types loved the loquacious Chico. He was one of those unique athletes whose answers were usually better than the reporter's questions.

CHICO RESCH

The one thing I remember most about playing the Canadiens was that it was like when you are a kid, thirteen or fourteen years old, and you think you're getting pretty strong. You'd start to wrestle with an adult and they'd grab you so you couldn't move. You couldn't understand it, but it proved you weren't as strong as you thought you were. I can remember saying, "That's the way it is playing against the Canadiens." Once you thought you were ready to beat them, they put their mind to it and beat you instead.

We thought we were coming around at the same time they were winning everything. We played them twice in the semis and in one game it was 0-0 and Jimmy Roberts had the puck. I was saying to myself that he wasn't the kind of a player who would make the difference, what with all the firepower they had. Then he makes a great move and beats me with a shot upstairs, under the crossbar.

Another time it was Gainey who beat us. We had them down 1-0 and then he got two goals. On one he came out of the corner and tried to pass the puck and it hit one of our defencemen on the knee and went right through my legs.

Then there was Murray Wilson when he beat me to the puck. It was coming around the net and I took two strides after it and there he was. He had to be offside because I can't believe he could get there that fast. But he did, and our two sticks chinked together and the puck went up in the air and into the net. That gave them a 2-1 win. So with them, they had so many good players it wasn't always just the big guys who were beating you.

They had the three great defencemen and late in games, when it was close, they would be on the ice all the time. I remember thinking, "Come on, Scotty, you chicken. Why don't you put somebody else on, your fourth or fifth defenceman?" With those three guys out there we really didn't have a chance.

Steve Shutt would get the luckiest goals, tipping pucks out of the air and things like that. He'd be giggling after he scored because he knew some of them were so flukey. I can remember Shutt and Pete Mahovlich kibitzing a lot on the ice about their goals.

Jacques Lemaire was the one with the heavy shot but it could be wild, too. I think he shot wild at times just to scare us. I would yell at him, "Keep the puck down!" Lafleur was the guy you feared the most when it came to beating you, but Lemaire's shot could hurt you.

I lost my share of games to them, but I will say this, there was the feeling that "you didn't mind losing to the Canadiens." It was gut-wrenching in one way, but they always won classy and I guess that was part of their mystique. I think some of that is gone now. But to those of us who grew up in the sixties, the Canadiens were like the New York Yankees.

It was an honour to lose to Montreal, if that's the right word. When we'd lose to Philly or the Rangers we'd get mad and say, "How could we lose to those guys?" But when you talked to the older players on our team they all said how great it was when

Montreal beat the Flyers for their first Cup. They did that with class, too, and set the trend for how the game should be played for a long time after that.

As powerful as the Montreal Canadiens were during the late 1970s, they could have been even more so had a couple of scenarios worked out differently.

The New York Islanders followed the Canadiens' four Stanley Cup wins with four straight of their own, starting in 1980. Two of their outstanding players were defenceman Denis Potvin and right-winger Mike Bossy. Both were French Canadians. Potvin played junior hockey with Ottawa in the OHA. Bossy played with Laval in the Quebec Junior League. Both became superstars with the Island-ers. Both could have become Canadiens, as Jimmy Devellano and Scotty Bowman explain.

Devellano is now the senior vice-president of the Detroit Red Wings. In the 1970s he was in charge of scouting for the New York Islanders.

JIMMY DEVALLANO

In our first year in New York, 1972–73, we finished dead last, which gave us the first pick in the draft after the season. Denis Potvin had been a star for the Ottawa 67's for a few years and he was the obvious choice.

Sam Pollock wanted Potvin so he offered us a package of players in return for our first pick. The players the Canadiens were offering were about numbers fifteen, sixteen, and seventeen on their NHL roster.

Our GM, Bill Torrey, was under pressure in New York to make a deal like that. He was new down there and they were calling him "Bow Tie Bill." Sam was putting pressure on him, too. Bill gave the offer a lot of thought. I spent a lot of time scouting the Canadiens' farm team, the Voyageurs.

The players offered by Sam Pollock would have made the Islanders a better team right away. We would have been more competitive with the other new team in the league, Atlanta. But

Bill decided to keep our draft pick and we got Potvin. The year after that we drafted Bryan Trottier. Things worked out okay.

SCOTTY BOWMAN

My phone rang at midnight one night and it was Claude Ruel. He was all excited and said, "Scotty, I've just seen a junior player who lift me out of my seat. First one since Guy Lafleur. Michael Bossy. We gotta get him."

I had never seen Bossy play but I did later on and liked him right away. He was eligible for the draft that year, 1977, so Claude and I started to promote him to Sam. But our scouts didn't like him.

In those days Sherbrooke had a junior team that was full of goons. Games there had fights all the time. When we'd talk about Bossy, Ron Caron and the scouts would say, "Wait 'til you see him play in Sherbrooke." They questioned Bossy's courage.

Sam went with the scouts. At the draft Bossy was still available when it was our turn. Sam picked Mark Napier.

VII

Does the Tradition Continue?

Anyone writing the story of the National Hockey League in the 1980s would have to deal, as I have in this book, with the word "dynasty." But he or she would not be including the Montreal Canadiens in that category. They would be writing instead about the New York Islanders and the Edmonton Oilers. The Islanders won the Stanley Cup four years in a row, starting in 1980. The Oilers won four times in five years, starting in 1984. In 1986 the Canadiens managed to sneak in a twenty-third for the franchise to prevent Edmonton from equalling their five-in-a-row record.

The decade of the eighties was, of course, the Wayne Gretzky era. Needless to say, space does not permit a detailed account of the greatness of the Great One in this book. But the game had never seen a one-man domination to match his – and will never see it again. Many of the former NHLers I interviewed mentioned Gretzky as a player they admire, one they are sure would have been a superstar in any era. Maurice Richard told me Wayne would have won the scoring championship in his day, too, although he wouldn't have managed as many points.

When Rocket told me that, Gordie Howe was sitting with us during a TV interview. Gordie, who was almost always winning scoring championships in Rocket's era, was non-committal on that one. Call it pride. But as the 1980s came to a close, Gretzky replaced Howe as hockey's all-time leading point scorer.

Mario Lemieux had to wait until 1991 to win his first Stanley Cup, but he, too, was a product of the eighties. So were Steve Yzerman, Patrick Roy, Paul Coffey, Raymond Bourque, Denis Savard, and Mark Messier, all skilful, entertaining players who gave TV commentators much to talk about and fans much to enjoy. And difficult as it was for their diehard supporters to come to grips with, hockey went through a decade with the Montreal Canadiens winning only one Stanley Cup.

24

Six Coaches, One Cup

*The Montreal Canadiens played the Minnesota North Stars in the
second round of the 1980 Stanley Cup playoffs. The Canadiens led
the series 3–2 when the teams played game six on the North Stars'
home ice. Montreal totally dominated the first period, firing fourteen shots at Minnesota goalie Gilles Meloche, but the score at the
end of the period was 0–0.*

I was hosting the Hockey Night in Canada *telecast of the game
and Steve Shutt was the guest in the first intermission. As techni-
cians were hooking up his microphone during the commercial
break, Shutt quietly said to me, "I think we just blew it." He was
right.*

*The Canadiens lost that game 5–2. Two nights later the defending
champions were eliminated from the playoffs when the North Stars
defeated them 3–2 in Montreal. There would not be another five-in-
a-row dynasty at the Forum.*

*The story line of the series was a familiar one at playoff time.
The favoured Canadiens had been victimized by a hot goaltender.
In this case it was Gilles Meloche, whose work in the series was
outstanding.*

GILLES MELOCHE

The big thing for me that year was the fact that it was the first
time I had been in the playoffs and I had been in the NHL for about

313

ten years. I'd been playing for teams like Oakland and Cleveland. Then in my first year in Minnesota we didn't make the playoffs.

Being French Canadian and playing against Montreal in a series like that was quite something. I guess it was special that the Canadiens were going for their fifth straight Stanley Cup, but I can't remember thinking about that too much. Just being in the playoffs was the big thrill for me.

April 27, 1980, is the official date the Montreal Canadiens' last dynasty came to an end. In reality the team's last great era began unravelling in the few weeks following their 1979 Stanley Cup victory.

When Ken Dryden pulled off his goaltending equipment moments after the Canadiens had won their fourth straight Cup he was doing so for the last time. Dryden retired and has never worn goalie equipment since, even in old-timers' games.

Scotty Bowman, upset that he had been passed over for the managing director's job when Sam Pollock retired, spent a disquieting last season in Montreal working for Pollock's successor, Irving Grundman. During the 1980 NHL meetings in June, Bowman left the Canadiens to assume a Pollock-like job with the Buffalo Sabres.

The third major change within the ranks of what had been hockey's greatest team came when Jacques Lemaire retired.

JACQUES LEMAIRE

I still wanted to play. But I never took any chances in my life. I was always very conservative and never did anything crazy. Almost every season there would be talk of trading me. I don't know how many times I was traded to Detroit in the papers. At the time we got Frank Mahovlich from them, I found out later that Detroit tried to get me in the deal.

One thing I always wanted was the Conn Smythe Trophy. The best players get to the Stanley Cup finals. That's when it's the best against the best, and I got there eight times. I don't think I ever should have won it, but I know my name was mentioned. I was close, and I was happy about that.

I grew up a lot in my last four years as a player. I had an offer from Europe. It came at the right time. I told myself that I was getting older, so why not take advantage of something that would help me enjoy life, take the kids overseas and go skiing with them. My wife had always been very close to her family, not the kind of a life she had to lead when I was a hockey player. Now we could be together a lot more, so I went overseas to Sierre, in Switzerland.

When I made my decision I felt I had done the right thing. I had no regrets. I played twelve years and we won the Stanley Cup eight times. I know I contributed to all that. I'll never forget it.

SCOTTY BOWMAN

I was concerned that we were missing the leader in Sam Pollock. And I was concerned for myself as a coach. I knew the other teams were getting better.

Then again, I guess I was ready for a challenge. I probably would have stayed if they had offered me the job. But it might not have worked out well for myself. So I don't look back on that.

This is a book about the Montreal Canadiens' greatest eras. That phrase applies to the Canadiens' story for four decades, beginning in the 1940s. But the usage has to stop with the advent of the 1980s.

True, the Canadiens were a good team on a fairly consistent basis during the eighties and certainly they still are one of the most popular. For further proof, ask NHL box-office managers (and ticket scalpers, too) in places like Winnipeg, Vancouver, and Toronto. A game in the atmosphere of the Montreal Forum was still a special event, especially when one of the NHL's new teams, the Quebec Nordiques, came to town. An instant Canadiens-Nordiques rivalry produced an emotional atmosphere on the ice and an even more emotional, circus-like atmosphere in the French-language media. But winning the Stanley Cup is always the measure of a hockey dynasty, and in the eighties the Montreal Canadiens won it just once. It was the first decade since the 1920s in which the team failed to win the Stanley Cup at least twice.

For years the Montreal Canadiens had profited from consistency in the coaching position: Irvin for fifteen years, Blake for thirteen,

Bowman for eight. In the ten seasons after Scotty Bowman left, the Canadiens employed six different coaches. Bowman's successor, Bernie Geoffrion, quit before Christmas of his first season. The faithful Claude Ruel replaced Geoffrion, signalling a strangely busy time for the man who painted the name sign on the door of the coach's office at the Forum. Ruel was succeeded by Bob Berry, who was replaced by Jacques Lemaire, who gave way to Jean Perron, who was succeeded by Pat Burns. This was not the Canadiens' traditional style, and it showed, especially at playoff time.

At the 1980 NHL meetings the Canadiens had the first draft pick, a carryover from Sam Pollock's machinations in the hockey flesh market. The club felt they needed a big, strong centreman so they selected Doug Wickenheiser from the Regina Pats. Their choice was between Wickenheiser or Denis Savard, a flashy, high-scoring junior sensation who had played his home games right in the Montreal Forum. But Savard was considered too small to cure what ailed the team. Savard was drafted by the Chicago Black Hawks. In ten years in Chicago Savard amassed over 1,000 scoring points and was among the top-ten NHL scorers five times. The unfortunate Wickenheiser lasted in Montreal less than four seasons.

Could the Canadiens have built another dynasty around Denis Savard? Could Guy Lafleur's career have lasted longer in Montreal playing with Savard? These are pertinent questions when the Canadiens' story of the 1980s is examined.

STEVE SHUTT

The eighties didn't represent a great era, that's for sure, and there were some good reasons. The most obvious thing at first was when Dryden and Lemaire retired. And don't forget Cournoyer. We played almost the whole of that season without Yvan because of his bad back and that was a big reason we weren't as good the fourth year we won the Cup as we had been the first three. And then he retired, too.

When we started the next season without Scotty Bowman it didn't take long for the inmates to start running the asylum. Geoffrion took over and that was about ten or twelve years too late because they had told him he might be coach after he retired.

Geoffrion did a terrible job. Even with the talent we had we needed a coach who could keep bringing us down to earth, especially in Montreal where everyone was such a big hero. And with Sam Pollock gone you could sense things were shaky up top, at the management level.

You could see it coming. There was an accumulation of bad draft picks, and I don't mean it started with Doug Wickenheiser. He would have been the first pick of almost every other team. He was rated number one by Central Scouting. But before that they had drafted players like Robin Sadler and Cam Connor, and they didn't draft Mike Bossy. It was an accumulation. We were on the downside, guys like me and Flower and Serge, and they didn't draft a group of young players who were able to come in and take over the leadership of the team.

It was tough for Wickenheiser, a kid from the West, to come into Montreal and try to be a star. Put him in a place like St. Louis or Minnesota where he could have developed more slowly at that age and it would have been a different story for him. Denis Savard wouldn't have been as big a star in Montreal as he was in Chicago. There he was able to freewheel and play an offensive type of game. In Montreal the centres always have to play a two-way game with a lot of emphasis on defence. It wouldn't have fitted his style.

They didn't give Sam's job to Scotty because he would have wanted to break up the team. He would have traded guys like me and Guy Lapointe and a few others. In retrospect that was probably what should have happened. But Molson's had just taken over the team and they needed it as a marketing tool. They didn't want to be accused of breaking up a Stanley Cup winner. You can't really blame them because something like that is such a touchy situation in Montreal.

Steve Shutt was traded to the Los Angeles Kings early in the 1984–85 season. A few weeks later Guy Lafleur, by then a very unhappy camper under the coaching of his one-time centreman Jacques Lemaire, announced his retirement – the first one, that is. The Canadiens finished that season with seventy-five points, their lowest total in thirty-two years.

Lafleur's retirement was the biggest Canadiens' story to that point in the 1980s. It was still a big story in 1991 on the occasion of his second retirement. The Flower continued to amaze. Four years after he had supposedly left the game he was back, playing for the New York Rangers. Between times he had tried to work in the Canadiens' front office but was unable to find happiness there, as had been the case with Maurice Richard years earlier. He had also been elected to the Hockey Hall of Fame and had convinced himself he could still play in the NHL. In 1988 the Rangers gave him a chance to come back. He played one season in New York, then two more with the Quebec Nordiques before retiring again, at the age of thirty-nine.

Lafleur's final few weeks as a Nordique featured a series of sincere pre-game farewells around the NHL. As luck would have it, the Nordiques and the Canadiens played back-to-back games on the final weekend of the season. On Saturday night, in Montreal, he received a terrific send-off from the Canadiens and their fans. Joining him on the ice were stars from the past, including the Rocket, Jean Béliveau, Yvan Cournoyer, and Dickie Moore. Then, true to his flare for the dramatic, Guy Lafleur scored what would be the final goal of his career in the second period. The ovation was deafening as the chant of "Guy, Guy" reverberated through the Montreal Forum for the last time.

The following night a long and expansive farewell took place at the Colisée in Quebec City, one that lacked the emotion there had been at the Forum the night before. During his remarks Lafleur spoke briefly in English, and his words helped me better understand how Guy had been able to maintain his level of excellence game after game, season after season, during the period of five or six years when he was the best player in the world. Addressing the young players on both teams, he told them, "Play every game as if it was your last one." So that was it.

Leading up to his retirement the media kept referring to the unhappy and controversial times in Lafleur's life, especially the alcohol-related car accident that almost cost him his life. It seems the press is never going to let that one fade away. They also kept bringing up old and new stories about the ill-will often expressed by Guy and his wife toward the Canadiens' organization. At the con-

clusion of the Forum's salute Lafleur walked down the aisle behind the players' benches to shake hands with Canadiens' president Ronald Corey. Whether that gesture signalled a change in the relationship remains to be seen. Certainly the Flower's memories of his last days with the Canadiens are not happy ones.

GUY LAFLEUR

My low point in Montreal was the end of my career there. I was always dreaming about having a nice retirement and working for the organization, but it didn't happen. Maybe I was too young to retire then. Maybe I should have kept going, or maybe I should have told what my feelings really were at that time.

I understand now what really happened and that's why today I'm ready for retirement. What happened with the Canadiens, I don't regret it. I feel sorry sometimes it happened that way, but that's the way I am.

By then another of Flower and Shutty's ex-mates, Serge Savard, was the general manager at the Forum. In 1986, when the Canadiens won their lone Stanley Cup in the eighties, only Bob Gainey, Larry Robinson, and Mario Tremblay remained from the glory days of the late seventies. Joining them were the likes of Mats Naslund, Bobby Smith, Ryan Walter, Rick Green, Guy Carbonneau, Brian Skrudland, Mike McPhee, and Chris Chelios.

The Canadiens' Cup win in 1986 had overtones of the 1971 championship. It was unexpected, their coach Jean Perron was a rookie, and the individual hero was a rookie goaltender, Patrick Roy. Like Ken Dryden, 1971's rookie surprise, Roy was the MVP of the playoffs. Roy's feat of stopping thirteen shots in the first nine minutes of a winning overtime game against the New York Rangers is still the most remembered of his career. It was a big first step toward the $1 million contract he signed in 1990.

The Canadiens defeated the Calgary Flames in the 1986 final. The Flames had been aided and abetted by the famous Steve Smith-Grant Fuhr goofy goal that helped them eliminate the Edmonton Oilers. The Oilers were hockey's best team that year, as they were the previous two when they won their first two Cups, and the next two when they won two more. But once in a while there are funny bounces and strange results in the Stanley Cup playoffs. For further proof, check what happened in 1991.

The best Montreal team of the 1980s might have been the one that reached the finals in 1989. That season the Canadiens finished with 115 points, two back of the overall leaders from Calgary. The two teams met again in the finals but this time the Flames won, in six games, clinching the series in Montreal. It was the first time Canadiens' fans had to watch the visiting team carry the Stanley Cup off the ice in triumph, at the Forum. Perhaps it was a fitting way to end a decade that doesn't fit into our great-era category.

25

Today's Team

The word "tradition" has appeared fairly often on the preceding pages and you hear it when people talk about the Montreal Canadiens. But do those of us in the old-timer category overdo it? Does what happened in the past really matter to hockey players today, as compared to those who played in the years principally covered in this book, the years before the million-dollar contracts?

If you want a link with the winning tradition of the Canadiens all you have to do is walk down the corridor of the office area of the Montreal Forum. Seated behind desks in various offices are Serge Savard, who played on eight Stanley-Cup winning teams, Jacques Lemaire, who also played on eight, and Floyd Curry, who was on four. And you'll see Jean Béliveau, a ten-time Stanley Cup winner who is still one of the most respected figures in all of hockey.

Overseeing the operation today is Ronald Corey, who assumed the presidency of the Canadiens in November of 1982. Almost from the beginning one of his priorities was restoring respect for the rich history that is part of the hockey team's story. Shortly before Corey took over I had an experience that proved to me tradition was being forgotten at the Forum. I received a phone call from a Forum employee asking if I would like to have a portrait photo of my father that had been hanging in the Forum for several years. When I said I would the caller replied, "Good. I found it, and a lot of other old pictures, in the garbage this morning."

There is now an Old-Timers' room at the Forum, which was set up by Corey and is sponsored by Molson's Brewery, who purchased the hockey team from the Bronfmans in 1978. Réjean Houle, a former player, is in charge of running the room. Houle says, "When Mr. Corey set up the Old-Timers' room, it was the best thing he could have done for the players from the past. Ken Reardon, Elmer Lach, Dickie Moore, Marcel Bonin, Henri Richard and Maurice, Bob Fillion, Yvan Cournoyer, all the boys show up sometimes and they love it. It means a lot to them to know the Canadiens have not forgotten them and what they did."

Ron Corey is a fan as well as the president of the team and obviously has a deep appreciation of what has gone on before. "If I could meet Senator Donat Raymond today I would be very nervous," Corey told me. "I am president, and he was president. For me that would be just like a player of today meeting Jean Béliveau. I hope the players appreciate it when the veterans come around. They have to have a sense of what hockey is all about, where it has been. Any player who is in the game strictly for the money isn't going to go very far."

Want more tradition? How about the Canadiens' dressing room? There, plaques line the walls that contain the rosters of every Canadiens' team dating back to the first Stanley Cup-winning team in 1916. A picture of every former Canadiens' player now in the Hockey Hall of Fame is on another wall under the words from the poem "Flanders Field": "To you from failing hands, we throw the torch, be yours to hold it high."

Then there's the Forum itself. I often meet fans from out of town who appear more excited about seeing the building than the hockey game. There will be genuine sadness when the old Forum gives way to the new Forum in a few years.

So now, does all this mean anything to the players of today? Are they interested in the rich history of the Montreal Canadiens? Are they inspired by the stories and memories of all those Stanley Cups won by many of the finest players in the history of their sport? Here are some answers from people involved in the Montreal Canadiens' organization, 1990–91 edition.

PATRICK ROY

It meant more to me when I was drafted than it did afterwards. I was never a Montreal fan. When I was a kid I hoped every team would win except Montreal. But I was happy when they drafted me because I didn't want to go somewhere far away.

When I first came up Larry Robinson and Bob Gainey were with the team and helped me understand the Canadiens. They had played on a lot of Stanley Cup teams and they did things that helped you learn how to win.

Rogie Vachon was one of my heroes but that was when he was with L.A., not Montreal. I remember watching Ken Dryden in one series against Buffalo when his brother was goalie for the Sabres. Gilbert Perreault was awesome but Dryden stopped him.

Bill Durnan won six Vezinas with Montreal and George Hainsworth had twenty-two shutouts in one year. But I never heard of them until I started playing for the Montreal Canadiens.

Eddy Palchak has been the Montreal Canadiens' equipment manager for twenty-five years. His name is on the Stanley Cup nine times.

EDDY PALCHAK

The past still means something to the players, but not as much as it did ten years ago. I personally think that today the big thing is money.

Ten years ago kids, especially those from the province of Quebec, wanted to be drafted by Montreal. They wanted to wear the "C-H." I went to all the drafts at the Forum and I saw kids who would cry because they weren't picked by the Canadiens. Now when we draft some of them they are disappointed. They were hoping to get with a team that would pay them in American money.

I've been in every dressing room in the league. Ours is the best one for history and tradition. It's very impressive to a player when he comes in here for the first time, a guy like Russ Courtnall, for example. He didn't know anything about it until he got here. Now I don't think he would be happy to leave.

RUSS COURTNALL

When I was traded from Toronto to Montreal I wasn't thinking about any kind of tradition. It didn't mean anything to me at the time. I wasn't a Montreal fan when I was growing up. But when I got there it was really exciting, right away. I walked into the dressing room and I went, "Wow!" It really took me by surprise, all the plaques of all the teams, the pictures of the players in the Hall of Fame. I said, "So this is what it's all about."

I hadn't read too much about the Canadiens or followed them. But when I got there it all came rushing back, in little bits and pieces, things I'd heard about. I had played in Toronto where there was nothing done about the past. Then I came to Montreal and it was out of this world. Almost right away I started meeting players from out of the past.

It all made me realize what a great organization it was, and had been for years. It really gave me a good sense and feeling of the team and how proud they were.

RYAN WALTER

There is no doubt that when I came here from Washington there was a sense of awe about being in Montreal, in the dressing room, and playing for the Canadiens. The first thing I felt was pressure. In Washington there was never the kind of pressure to always be there, to not only be in the playoffs but to win the Stanley Cup, to always be there. I don't know if it's part of the tradition that drives you, if it comes from the fans, or if it's from the media, or if it's a combination of the three. But it's there.

It makes Montreal a tough place to play hockey, but it also makes it a good place to play hockey. The best example I can give you goes back to the first year I was with the Canadiens. We lost to Buffalo in the playoffs when they beat us three straight. I remember walking down the mall in a shopping centre and the first four or five people I met all asked the same thing. "What happened? How come you guys lost?" My wife and I got so upset we got in our camper and drove to San Diego. I wanted to get away. So in that sense Montreal is a very tough place to play because the fans expect so much.

Another example I can give you is Toe Blake. After we would win a game in the playoffs, or even an early series, he'd come in the dressing room and he'd talk to a lot of the guys. He'd say the same thing to everybody, "You haven't won anything yet. You haven't won anything yet." At first you'd think he was just an old guy hanging around, but then you would realize what he was saying was what the Montreal Canadiens are all about. That was the tradition of the Canadiens speaking. You can't be content just to win a game, or a series. There's more to it than that.

A lot of teams are happy to make the playoffs or even just win a series in the playoffs. I remember the team dinner we had after losing to Calgary in the finals in '89. It was like we were in a morgue because everyone felt so bad. We'd gone as far as a team could go, to the finals. But that wasn't good enough. We didn't win.

I learned more about hockey and more about myself after coming to Montreal than at any other time in my life. Here, they put you into a certain hockey mould, you learn to fit that mould so you are a better team player, and you win. That's what I've liked about Montreal.

The Canadiens have won twenty-three Stanley Cups. I won one. But I think about being part of a franchise that has won twenty-three Stanley Cups. On a road trip this year I wore my Stanley Cup ring and I passed it around to some of the young guys. I wanted them to feel it, to try and realize what it means to win one. I guess you could say I was trying to get them to appreciate what this team is all about.

GUY CARBONNEAU

I don't think it is as great for kids now because by the time they get here they have seen so much hockey on TV. They're not as easily impressed anymore. When I was a kid you didn't get all that much on TV and where I lived, in northern Quebec, the only team you saw was the Montreal Canadiens.

In those days you either loved them or hated them. They usually were winning, so it was like watching boxing. You start out wanting one guy to win but by the time it was over you were feeling sorry for the other guy. That's the way it used to be for me watching the Canadiens.

Does the tradition still count? I would say yes. At least for me it counts, especially when I see some of the old-timers around the Forum and in our dressing room. You know what they did in their day, how many Stanley Cups they won. Sometimes you stop and think about that and hope that you can do the same thing.

But hockey is more of a business now than it was for them. Today agents are telling kids about signing for a million dollars and about all the money they'll have in the bank when they retire. They don't think about things like tradition and that's too bad.

DENIS SAVARD

The first thing I noticed when I was traded to the Canadiens was the leadership shown by the players who had been here a few years. It's something that obviously has been passed down from older players from the past to the younger players who are here today. That's what I noticed right away, the leadership and winning attitude from players like Carbonneau, Skrudland, McPhee.

I've always been a Canadiens' fan. When I was growing up the Montreal Canadiens were my team. Even though I was in Chicago for ten years, I always watched the papers to see how they were doing - all the time for those ten years.

When I was a young kid watching the Canadiens Guy Lafleur was a great player and I guess you could say he was my hero. The Canadiens have always had a team where kids could pick out a lot of heroes and I thought of that when I walked into their dressing room for the first time. It was a great feeling, being part of that family with all the great tradition from all of the years that had gone on before. I was so happy to think that now I was a part of it.

CLAUDE MOUTON

I have been the public relations director and the PA announcer for the Canadiens for the past seventeen years and I would say the team means as much to the people of Quebec now as it did when I started.

You can't judge only by the people you meet at the Forum and I do travel a lot, especially in the summer when we have our ball team. We've been travelling around the province playing ball games for fourteen years and at every little town the people look at these guys like they are twenty feet tall. The players feel it. They know they are appreciated and, to those people, very important.

As far as the actual tradition of the team goes, the young players are always impressed right away. But some of them lose it fast, as soon as they start making the big bucks, and that's the sad part of it.

I'll never forget the day we traded Pete Mahovlich to Pittsburgh for Pierre Larouche. Larouche was known as an easy-going guy who always wanted to have fun. We had an assistant trainer named Pierre Meilleur. He had Larouche's sweater for him to put on for his first practice with the team. Larouche was talking to someone so instead of waiting, Pierre dropped the sweater on the floor right beside him. Larouche said to him, "I don't know your name, kid. But never drop that sweater on the floor again. I've been waiting all my life to wear one." The way he said it, just like that, I know he meant it.

But today, it doesn't mean what it used to mean. Definitely not. They care too much about money today rather than tradition, or the team. Not all of them, mind you, but the majority.

BRIAN SKRUDLAND

When I was growing up in Saskatchewan, hockey was always the big interest in my life. On Saturday nights my dad would be home, off the road, and we'd sit down with steak and pizza and watch the hockey games. Saturday night it was always hockey, hockey, hockey.

We always got either Toronto or Montreal on TV and Montreal was my favourite. I can remember Bob Gainey in his rookie year, Mario Tremblay, Larry. They were always my favourites and when I got the opportunity to play with them it was like a dream come true.

The past has to mean something, whether it's the Stanley Cup banners hanging over the ice or the pictures and names on the walls in the dressing room. Today we look around and see so many big names from the past who are still at the Forum – Serge Savard, Jacques Lemaire, Jacques Laperriere. You go upstairs and see Jean Béliveau and Floyd Curry. I looked around one night during a game and Dickie Moore was sitting in the front row, right behind me. The list goes on and on.

The idea of winning is drilled into you from the time you come to Montreal. These people are around you and the stories they have to tell prove that everything you've heard about hockey in Montreal is true.

Another interesting way the young kids appreciate this sort of thing is from the ex-players who are now broadcasters. They get here and suddenly they're being interviewed by Mario Tremblay or Pierre Bouchard. It seems that every which way you turn you're meeting and seeing players who were part of the winning tradition in the past. You just can't avoid it.

When I came here my agent said to me, "You might not get a chance to make the team and play for it. But if you do, you'll never have a better chance to win a Stanley Cup."

Was he ever right on that one. We won it the first year I was here.

Players on the Montreal Canadiens are expected to live up to the tradition of those who went before them, and so are the coaches. There are enough pictures of previous Stanley Cup teams hanging in the Forum, plus the banners above the ice, to remind the coach of the team that the Irvins, Blakes, and Bowmans did a fair amount of winning in their day.

The current coach at the Forum is Pat Burns, who reached the Stanley Cup finals as a rookie in 1988-89. The 1991-92 season is his fourth, which makes Burns the longest-serving Canadiens coach since Scotty Bowman left in 1979.

PAT BURNS

I don't really know what it is. But there's something there. There's definitely a mystique. The Montreal Canadiens never stay in trouble very long. They always find a way to get out of it. Other teams get into trouble and it stays with them for a long time. It just never seems to happen that way with the Canadiens.

The first time I walked into the dressing room as the coach I was shaking. I mean really shaking. I used to watch them play at the Forum sitting in the cheap seats. Now here I was, coaching the team.

Larry Robinson and Bob Gainey represented a lot of the tradition when I got there. Larry would sit in my office and talk about what had gone on in the past. He'd say, "Scotty did it this way. Scotty did it that way." He wasn't trying to tell me what to do. He was just saying that things should continue for the Canadiens the way they always did, and he was right.

Bob Gainey would tell me how certain things were going to work out, and they usually did. Again, a case of everything continuing the way it had always been. It happens that way with this team.

The first time I walked out and went behind the bench at the Forum as the coach was in an exhibition game. I couldn't believe my feelings. I looked up at all those Stanley Cup flags, and I looked around the building, and I said to myself, "This is it."

EPILOGUE

A couple of hockey seasons ago the Montreal Canadiens practised at the Pacific Coliseum in Vancouver the day before they played a game against the Canucks. I was there with the rest of the team's travelling media entourage, along with a large crowd of Vancouver sports reporters. An official of the Canucks was amazed at the turnout. He pointed out a couple of writers and broadcasters who seldom attended games, let alone a practice. So I spoke to them and asked why they were there. Their answers were all the same, "Because they're the Canadiens."

I pointed out that this was a Montreal team lacking in star quality when compared to teams from the past. I kidded them that Béliveau, Harvey, and Cournoyer didn't play for the team anymore. But the names didn't matter. The sweater did.

The next night the Canadiens won the game easily and the chant of "Go Habs Go" steadily grew in volume as they piled up the score. I felt sorry for the Vancouver players having to hear that in their home building. I guess if I had asked fans why they were cheering for the visiting team the answer would again have been, "Because they're the Canadiens."

With the exception of Calgary, where the image of Montreal's 1986 Stanley Cup win over the Flames is still vivid, the Vancouver story is repeated in every Canadian city in the NHL. When the Montreal team plays in Edmonton, Winnipeg, or Toronto, it's amazing how many fans are there wearing red, white, and blue sweaters. If the Canadiens are beating the Maple Leafs in Toronto they feel as if they are playing a home game. Even in Quebec City, where the rivalry is greatest, there is a definite noise factor when the Canadiens score, but it's the same at the Forum when the Nordiques score.

When Larry Robinson and Bob Gainey left the Canadiens after the 1989 playoffs it meant that for the first time in forty-five years there would not be a player on the team who had played on more than one Stanley Cup-winning team. For years the Canadiens had successfully exploited continuity with great championship teams from the past. Now that continuity was gone from the team's dressing room.

When the Canadiens were eliminated by the Boston Bruins from the 1991 playoffs, a Montreal team that once represented dynasties had managed just one Stanley Cup victory in twelve years. They had won the Cup eight times in the twelve years before that. Only two players of recent vintage, Patrick Roy and the now traded Chris Chelios, have consistently been All-Star material. Yet the mystique of the Montreal Canadiens lives on.

In the prime of its Wayne Gretzky era, the Edmonton Oilers, one of the greatest teams in hockey history, never seemed to generate whatever emotion beats in a hockey fan's heart the way the Canadiens did when they were winning championships, and still do when they're not. People much closer to the scene than I am, like Pat Burns, struggle when they try to explain the Canadiens' continuing popularity. They fall back on the word "mystique," which is defined in my dictionary as "an aura of mystical power surrounding a particular occupation or pursuit."

How much longer will it last? Will we still talk of an illustrious tradition if the Montreal Canadiens settle into the middle of the pack and go another twelve seasons with perhaps just one Stanley Cup victory? Will fans in cities other than Montreal still chant "Go Habs Go" with the same fervour? I think not. Time will march along and memories will dim, even of the Rocket, Big Jean, and Doug, and of dynasties that won the Stanley Cup four and five times in a row. For a meaningful tradition to continue there will have to be more than one championship in the next twelve years at the Forum.

The game has changed more off the ice than on it. John

Ferguson mentioned how in his day they played for "the sweater" much more than players do now. Modern-day attitudes are distressing to players from Fergie's era and before. Yet, were they playing in today's game, who among them could say they wouldn't be caught up in the burgeoning financial and legal elements of the sport, with their agents bartering for free agency and big bucks. And why not?

Not every hockey fan is a Montreal Canadiens' fan, but the majority of them respect what the franchise has accomplished throughout its long history. During the years we have covered here, the Canadiens compiled an overall championship record that will likely never be matched. Reminiscences of those years by the men who are the real authors of this book help us realize where the game has come from, how important it was to them, and how much they respect it.

I have enjoyed many wonderful experiences through my life-long association with hockey. Sharing and recording the memories of these men has been one of the best.

ACKNOWLEDGEMENTS

There are many people I wish to thank for their help in putting this book together, principally the over one hundred men who shared their memories with me. Ken Reardon and Jean Béliveau were asked to put in some extra ice time and I thank them for their patience and co-operation.

As he did in the preparation of my first book, Michael Barnett of IMG put the project together and was a constant source of encouragement.

Mac McDiarmid, one of the great hockey collectors, kindly provided several photographs. Denis Brodeur in Montreal and Phil Pritchard at the Hockey Hall of Fame in Toronto were also very generous in supplying photographs. Carole Robertson transcribed many of the interviews from tape to paper.

Books written by two friends, Claude Mouton's *The Montreal Canadiens* and Brian McFarlane's *One Hundred Years of Hockey*, were a great help when it came to names, dates, and final scores. Anyone who writes a book of this nature must refer to the late Charles Coleman's three-volume *Trail of the Stanley Cup*, which I did very frequently.

It was a pleasure to again collaborate with McClelland & Stewart and I thank them for assigning me a very talented editor, Richard Tallman.

And finally, thanks to the three most important people in my life, Wilma, Nancy Anne, and Doug, who were cheering for me all the way, from the drop of the puck to the final siren.

APPENDIX

Selected Team and Individual Statistics, 1917-18–1990-91

Year-by-Year Record

Season	Won	Lost	Tied	Points	Playoff Results
1917-18	13	9	0	26	Lost NHL final
1918-19	10	8	0	20	Cup final, no decision
1919-20	13	11	0	26	Out of playoffs
1920-21	13	11	0	26	Out of playoffs
1921-22	12	11	1	25	Out of playoffs
1922-23	13	9	2	28	Lost NHL playoffs
1923-24	13	11	0	26	Won Stanley Cup
1924-25	17	11	2	36	Lost Cup playoffs
1925-26	11	24	1	23	Out of playoffs
1926-27	28	14	2	58	Lost final
1927-28	26	11	7	59	Lost semifinal
1928-29	22	7	15	59	Lost semifinal
1929-30	21	14	9	51	Won Stanley Cup
1930-31	26	10	8	60	Won Stanley Cup
1931-32	25	16	7	57	Lost semifinal
1932-33	18	25	5	41	Lost quarterfinal
1933-34	22	20	6	50	Lost quarterfinal
1934-35	19	23	6	44	Lost quarterfinal
1935-36	11	26	11	33	Out of playoffs
1936-37	24	18	6	54	Lost semifinal
1937-38	18	17	13	49	Lost quarterfinal
1938-39	15	24	9	39	Lost quarterfinal
1939-40	10	33	5	25	Out of playoffs
1940-41	16	26	6	38	Lost quarterfinal
1941-42	18	27	3	39	Lost quarterfinal
1942-43	19	19	12	50	Lost semifinal
1943-44	38	5	7	83	Won Stanley Cup
1944-45	38	8	4	80	Lost semifinal
1945-46	28	17	5	61	Won Stanley Cup
1946-47	34	16	10	78	Lost final

1947-48	20	29	11	51	Out of playoffs
1948-49	28	23	9	65	Lost semifinal
1949-50	29	22	19	77	Lost semifinal
1950-51	25	30	15	65	Lost final
1951-52	34	26	10	78	Lost final
1952-53	28	23	19	75	Won Stanley Cup
1953-54	35	24	11	81	Lost final
1954-55	41	18	11	93	Lost final
1955-56	45	15	10	100	Won Stanley Cup
1956-57	35	23	12	82	Won Stanley Cup
1957-58	43	17	10	96	Won Stanley Cup
1958-59	39	18	13	91	Won Stanley Cup
1959-60	40	18	12	92	Won Stanley Cup
1960-61	41	19	10	92	Lost semifinal
1961-62	42	14	14	98	Lost semifinal
1962-63	28	19	23	79	Lost semifinal
1963-64	36	21	13	85	Lost semifinal
1964-65	36	23	11	83	Won Stanley Cup
1965-66	41	21	8	90	Won Stanley Cup
1966-67	32	25	13	77	Lost final
1967-68	42	22	10	94	Won Stanley Cup
1968-69	46	19	11	103	Won Stanley Cup
1969-70	38	22	16	92	Out of playoffs
1970-71	42	23	13	97	Won Stanley Cup
1971-72	46	16	16	108	Lost quarterfinal
1972-73	52	10	16	120	Won Stanley Cup
1973-74	45	24	9	99	Lost quarterfinal
1974-75	47	14	19	113	Lost semifinal
1975-76	58	11	11	127	Won Stanley Cup
1976-77	60	8	12	132	Won Stanley Cup
1977-78	59	10	11	129	Won Stanley Cup
1978-79	52	17	11	115	Won Stanley Cup
1979-80	47	20	13	107	Lost quarterfinal
1980-81	45	22	13	103	Lost prelim. round
1981-82	46	17	17	109	Lost div. semifinal
1982-83	42	24	14	98	Lost div. semifinal
1983-84	35	40	5	75	Lost conf. final
1984-85	41	27	12	94	Lost div. final
1985-86	40	33	7	87	Won Stanley Cup
1986-87	41	29	10	92	Lost conf. final
1987-88	45	22	13	103	Lost div. final
1988-89	53	18	9	115	Lost final
1989-90	41	28	11	93	Lost div. final
1990-91	39	30	11	89	Lost div. final

Coaches

1917-18–1920-21	George Kennedy
1921-22–1924-25	Léo Dandurand
1925-26–1931-32	Cecil Hart
1932-33–1933-34	Newsy Lalonde
1934-35	Newsy Lalonde, Léo Dandurand
1935-36	Sylvio Mantha
1936-37–1937-38	Cecil Hart
1938-39	Cecil Hart, Jules Dugal
1939	Babe Siebert*
1939-40	Pit Lépine
1940-41–1954-55	Dick Irvin
1955-56–1967-68	Hector "Toe" Blake
1968-69–1969-70	Claude Ruel
1970-71	Claude Ruel, Al MacNeil
1971-72–1978-79	Scotty Bowman
1979-80	Bernie Geoffrion, Claude Ruel
1980-81	Claude Ruel
1981-82–1983-84	Bob Berry
1983-84–1984-85	Jacques Lemaire
1985-86–1987-88	Jean Perron
1988-89–	Pat Burns

*Named coach during the summer but died before season began.

Team Captains

1917-21	Newsy Lalonde
1921-25	Sprague Cleghorn
1925-26	Bill Coutu
1926-32	Sylvio Mantha
1932-33	George Hainsworth
1933-36	Sylvio Mantha
1936-39	Babe Siebert
1939-40	Walter Buswell
1940-48	Hector "Toe" Blake
1948	Bill Durnan
1948-56	Emile Bouchard
1956-60	Maurice Richard
1960-61	Doug Harvey
1961-71	Jean Béliveau
1971-75	Henri Richard
1975-79	Yvan Cournoyer
1979-81	Serge Savard
1981-89	Bob Gainey

1989-90	Guy Carbonneau, Chris Chelios
1990-	Guy Carbonneau

Career Points

Guy Lafleur	1,246
Jean Béliveau	1,219
Henri Richard	1,046
Maurice Richard	965
Larry Robinson	883

Career Goals

Maurice Richard	544
Guy Lafleur	518
Jean Béliveau	507
Yvan Cournoyer	428
Steve Shutt	408

Career Games

Henri Richard	1,256
Larry Robinson	1,202
Bob Gainey	1,160
Jean Béliveau	1,125
Claude Provost	1,005

Regular Season 100-Point Scorers
136 – Guy Lafleur, 1976-77
132 – Guy Lafleur, 1977-78
129 – Guy Lafleur, 1978-79
125 – Guy Lafleur, 1975-76
125 – Guy Lafleur, 1979-80
119 – Guy Lafleur, 1974-75
117 – Pete Mahovlich, 1974-75
110 – Mats Naslund, 1985-86
105 – Pete Mahovlich, 1975-76
105 – Steve Shutt, 1976-77

Regular Season 50-Goal Scorers
60 – Steve Shutt, 1976-77
60 – Guy Lafleur, 1977-78
56 – Guy Lafleur, 1975-76
53 – Guy Lafleur, 1974-75
52 – Guy Lafleur, 1978-79
51 – Stéphane Richer, 1989-90

50 – Maurice Richard, 1944-45
50 – Bernard Geoffrion, 1960-61
50 – Guy Lafleur, 1979-80
50 – Pierre Larouche, 1979-80
50 – Stéphane Richer, 1987-88

INDEX